I0881405

During the American Revolution, British light infantry and grenadier battalions figured prominently in almost every battle and campaign. They are routinely mentioned in campaign studies, usually with no context to explain what these battalions were. In an army that employed regiments as the primary deployable assets, the most active battlefield elements were temporary battalions created after the war began and disbanded when it ended. This work is the first operational study of these battalions during the entire war, looking at their creation, evolution and employment from the first day of hostilities through their disbandment at the end of the conflict. It examines how and why these battalions were created, how they were maintained at optimal strength over eight years of war, how they were deployed tactically and managed administratively. Most importantly, it looks at the individual officers and soldiers who served in them. Using first-hand accounts and other primary sources, *These Distinguished Corps* describes life in the grenadiers and light infantry on a personal level, from Canada to the Caribbean and from barracks to battlefield.

Don N. Hagist is managing editor of *Journal of the American Revolution* (http://allthings-liberty.com), and studies the lives and service of individual British soldiers in the 1770s and 1780s, relying almost exclusively on primary sources. His books include *Noble Volunteers: the British Soldiers who Fought the American Revolution* (2020) and *British Soldiers, American War: Voices of the American Revolution* (2012), and he has published numerous journal articles. He is an engineer for a major medical device manufacturer, and lives in Providence, Rhode Island.

These Distinguished Corps

British Grenadier and Light Infantry Battalions in the American Revolution

Don N. Hagist

Helion & Company

Helion & Company Limited
Unit 8 Amherst Business Centre
Budbrooke Road
Warwick
CV34 5WE
England
Tel. 01926 499619
Email: info@helion.co.uk
Website: www.helion.co.uk
Twitter: @helionbooks
Visit our blog at http://blog.helion.co.uk/

Published by Helion & Company 2021
Designed and typeset by Mach 3 Solutions Ltd (www.mach3solutions.co.uk)
Cover designed by Paul Hewitt, Battlefield Design (www.battlefield-design.co.uk)

Cover: 'A View of the Attack against Fort Washington and Rebel Redoubts near New York.' (New York Public Library) and image of a light infantry officer. (Yale Center for British Art) Composite image by Matthew Kandarian

ISBN 978-1-914059-84-1

British Library Cataloguing-in-Publication Data.
A catalogue record for this book is available from the British Library.

Contents

List of Plates

Introduction

It was dark, the middle of the night, chilly, early spring, and William Yeacott stood on a remote road by a marsh. The 28-year-old carpenter from County Durham in northeast England was waiting for food that he did not need. He was wet up to his knees. It was not a good way to begin a 40-mile walk. It was not a good way to begin a war.

Yeacott was a soldier in the light infantry company of the 38th Regiment of Foot, on an expedition from Boston, Massachusetts on 19 April 1775 that marked the opening shots of the war that led to American independence from Great Britain. He was with about 700 other troops, all grenadiers and light infantry, the elite 20 percent of each British infantry regiment. It was the first time that these grenadier and light infantry companies had worked together since arriving in America the previous year. They would continue to work together for the next eight years of war.

Grenadier and light infantry battalions figured in almost every major engagement of the 1775–1783 war in America. In most campaigns, they were at the forefront of every march, among the first to engage and the last to disengage, the most mobile and farthest-ranging of the infantry. As such, they are included in nearly every campaign and battle study, but only in consideration of an individual campaign or battle. But these organizations, although temporary, had longer lifespans than the campaigns in which they participated; some soldiers, like William Yeacott, spent the entire war in one.

This book follows the flank battalions through the war, from their first formation in 1775 through to disbandment in 1783. The emphasis is on how these composite battalions operated, and the experiences of the officers and soldiers who served in them. They were only part of each campaign; readers are advised to refer to other works for broader views of the campaigns and battles described here. Also, this is not a comprehensive study of activities of British grenadier and light infantry companies, many of which fought in other places but not as part of flank battalions.

The lowest rank in the army in the 1770s and 1780s was called 'private soldier.' The word 'private' was not used as a title like sergeant and corporal; we find, for example, 'Serjeant Barker,' 'Corporal McLeod,' but 'Thomas Knight, private soldier'; nowhere do we find 'Private Knight.' This book uses the same convention: names of private soldiers are not preceded by titles. Infantry regiments were called regiments of foot, to distinguish them from cavalry (regiments of horse) and artillery (regiments of artillery); because this book deals solely with infantry, 'of foot' is usually omitted.

Most quotations in this book are from handwritten manuscripts that are replete with abbreviations, superscripts, spurious capitalization, and irregular dots, dashes, and scrawls for punctuation. For readability, abbreviations are spelled out, punctuation is modernized, and capitalization is not always consistent with the original, without using square brackets or other indications. This is done because the focus is on understanding the information rather than replicating the handwritten material.

1

‘First upon all attacks’ and ‘skirmishing through woods’: Grenadier and Light Infantry Companies

At the onset of war in America, British infantry regiments were organized into 10 equally-sized companies, among which were something old and something new: the two flank companies. Old, in terms of heritage in the army, was the grenadier company; grenadiers had been part of the established regimental organization since the creation of a standing army in the 1600s. Their original function, as the name indicates, was to throw hand grenades. As such, tall men were selected for the role, perhaps because they were likely to be able to throw a small iron bomb the farthest. Grenades had fallen into disuse by the middle of the eighteenth century, in the army at least, but the roll of grenadiers had evolved into an elite force of ‘the tallest and briskest men, consequently the first upon all attacks.’[1] The clothing of grenadier companies is discussed in Appendix I and II.

Maintaining this elite company at full strength meant periodically transferring out men who were no longer fit for active service, and bringing in suitable men from other companies. A 1768 military textbook recommended because ‘the Grenadier Company is to be constantly kept compleat, from the best and tallest Men in the Regiment, whenever the Captain of it wants a Man to compleat, or improve it,’ he could choose a man from another company, and upon agreeing with that company’s commander, take in the new man in trade for ‘the worst looking Man of the Grenadiers.’ The author cautioned that ‘Recruits are improper for the Grenadiers, as that Company should always appear at Exercise, as compleat as possible, and have such Men only in it, as are perfect masters of their business,’ adding:

> It is a mistaken notion, that size alone is a qualification for Grenadier, if a full face, broad shoulders, and well proportioned legs do not accompany it, his figure does no great credit to the judgement of whoever chose him, as experience proves that Grenadier Company, which covers most ground when under Arms, to be much superior in point of Marching, and every sort of fatigue, to one, which only boasts of Size.[2]

1 George Smith, *An Universal Military Dictionary* (London: Millan, 1779), pp.177–178.
2 Bennett Cuthbertson, *A System for the Compleat Interior Management and Œconomy of a Battalion of Infantry* (Dublin: Boulter Grierson, 1768), pp.15–17.

Reports on inspections of regiments in Britain and Ireland in the early 1770s show that these recommendations were largely followed: grenadiers were in general taller than men in other companies, averaging about five feet 10 inches tall with some exceeding six feet, compared to an average of about five feet eight inches for the regiment in general. Most regiments had men in other companies tall enough to be grenadiers, indicating that regiments were following the guidance that height was not the only consideration for service in this elite company.[3]

* * *

Grenadier companies included a drummer and two fifers, who might be teenage children of soldiers in the regiment, or career soldiers.[4] The fifers were the only two fifers on the regimental establishment – that is, only two were allowed by the government for each regiment – and as such were only nominally part of the company; as will be seen, when grenadier companies were detached and formed into battalions, the fifers sometimes stayed with the regiment.[5] The tables of men's height in inspection returns often include two men in the grenadier company who were significantly shorter than the others, presumably drummers or fifers, but this does not mean that they were young.[6] Fifer Charles Gardiner, a Limerick native in the 38th Regiment, began service at the age of 10 and was 25 years old when the regiment arrived in Boston in 1774. Late in 1775 he left the grenadier company to serve

Grenadier of the 69th Regiment of Foot wearing the uniform prescribed in 1768, sketched by Philip James de Loutherbourg in England, 1778. He has a bearskin cap, a brass match case on his chest, and wings on the shoulders of his coat. The knee-length gaiters prescribed in 1768 were not used in America, where calf-length spatterdashes or trousers that buttoned around the ankles were preferred. (Anne S.K. Brown Military Collection)

3 The National Archives (TNA): WO 27/32 and WO 27/35: inspection returns for various regiments.

4 For details on the careers of drummers and fifers, see Don N. Hagist, *Noble Volunteers: The British Soldiers who fought the American Revolution* (Yardley, PA: Westholme, 2020), pp.47–50.

5 TNA: WO 12: muster rolls for various regiments.

6 TNA: WO 27/32 and WO 27/35: inspection returns for various regiments.

as a drummer in a battalion company, and remained in that capacity until the end of his career 12 years later.[7] He was replaced in the grenadier company by 17-year-old Dubliner Alexander Carleton, who had been in the regiment for two years and continued as a fifer for the rest of the war.[8]

Drums were useful for training, providing signals for every marching movement a soldier learned and sounding cadence for marching and handling firearms in unison. With fifes, drums added to the pageantry of regiments marching through towns and performing at field reviews. In garrisons and camps, drums and fifes sounded tunes for all sorts of activities from reveille (the wakeup call) to taptoo (for lights out at day's end), signalling meal times, assemblies, summoning non-commissioned officers, and a host of other things. But on the battlefield, 'the noise of the artillery and musketry generally renders it impossible to use any signals by the drum,' according to a popular military writer; soldiers were taught to take orders directly from their officers rather than from the drum because 'it can answer no purpose to have Soldiers trained to what can never be attempted on real service.'[9] In February 1776 General William Howe ordered regiments in Boston 'not to use the drum or fife for marching or signals when in the field.'[10] The exceptions were a few commands to direct the overall movements of a battalion – advance, retreat, commence firing, cease firing, and so forth. Appendix VIII describes manoeuvres used by grenadier

This grenadier of the 6th Regiment, sketched by Philip James de Loutherbourg in England, 1778, wears spatterdashes. (Anne S.K. Brown Military Collection)

7 TNA: WO 116/9: 'Examinations of Invalid Soldiers,' 18 June 1787, Pension Admission Book; WO 12: muster rolls, 38th Regiment.

8 TNA: WO 121/33/218: discharge of Alexander Carleton; WO 12: muster rolls, 38th Regiment.

9 Cuthbertson, *System*, p.169.

10 General orders, 6 February 1776, B. F. Stevens (ed.), *General Sir William Howe's Orderly Book* (Port Washington, NY: Kennikat Press, 1980), p.209.

battalions in New York in 1780, including the simple set of drum commands. With only a few drummers required for signalling on campaign, grenadier company drummers might carry axes, officers' baggage, assist the wounded on the battlefield, or even serve in the ranks as private soldiers.[11]

* * *

New in the regimental organization was the light infantry company, added in 1771, increasing the size of each infantry regiment from nine to 10 companies.[12] The change made official a practice that had already begun. During the Seven Years War in Germany and the concurrent French and Indian War in America in the 1750s and early 1760s, fast-moving troops with minimal baggage had proven invaluable, leading to the establishment of light infantry companies and then entire regiments that were disbanded at the conclusion of the conflict. Some regiments had continued to maintain light companies even though they were not part of the established regimental organization; a popular military writer in the 1760s even included a chapter, 'Of a Light Company, with a scheme for training one in Time of Peace, though not allowed on the Establishment' in his book on regimental management.[13] When these new companies were created, there was no change in the overall number of private soldiers in a regiment; instead, the nominal number of men in each company changed such that each company was a bit smaller.[14] Regiments transferred men from their existing companies – except for the grenadiers – to create a new company. Similar to the grenadiers, only men whose 'activity and particular talents for that duty' were selected – those with an aptitude for 'leaping, running, climbing precipices, swimming, skirmishing through woods, loading and firing in different attitudes at marks, and marching with remarkable rapidity.'[15] Inspection returns from England and Ireland in the early 1770s show that light infantry men were, on average, a bit shorter, averaging about five feet six and a half inches and seldom exceeding five feet eight inches tall; rarely did a man have less than a year or two of service before entering the light infantry.[16]

Muster rolls show that, before embarkation for service in America, some men were transferred out of flank companies and others transferred in; as will be discussed in later chapters, wartime prompted an increase in size of these companies, resulting in new men being added quickly, and attrition led to annual, sometimes more frequent, replenishment of the flank companies.[17] Muster rolls show men's names, and allow determination of how long each man served, from which it can be readily confirmed that, usually, only men with at least a year or two in the army were put into flank companies. There is no comprehensive data showing how tall men were in grenadier and light infantry companies while on service in

11 For details activities of drummers and fifers on campaign, see Hagist, *Noble Volunteers*, pp.209–213.
12 J. A. Houlding, *Fit for Service: The Training of the British Army 1715–1795* (Oxford: Clarendon Press, 1981), p.129, n60.
13 Cuthbertson, *System*, pp.189–192.
14 TNA: WO 12: muster rolls for various regiments.
15 Cuthbertson, *System*, pp.190–191.
16 TNA: WO 27/32 and WO 27/35: inspection returns for various regiments.
17 TNA: WO 12: muster rolls for various regiments.

America. Common sense suggests that, of all the requirements for serving in these companies, height was the least important, and anecdotal evidence confirms that, during the war, there were some short grenadiers and tall light infantrymen, compared to peacetime. In the 22nd Regiment of Foot, for example, Israel Schroder and Andreas Strüwig, both five feet 11 inches tall, were transferred into the light infantry during the war.[18] William Doulton was a private soldier in the 22nd's light infantry company when it was inspected in 1774, at which time it included no men over five feet eight inches; in July 1775 he was transferred to the grenadier company, which when inspected had no men under five feet nine-and-a-half inches. His height is not known, but it is clear that he was shorter than any grenadiers in the company the year before he joined it.[19] In regiments that served in the American Revolution there were many transfers like these, indicating that neat peacetime sizing was secondary to wartime needs of fitness and experience.

During the Seven Years War and the French and Indian War, the value of grenadiers as troops 'first upon all attacks' and light infantry 'skirmishing through woods' was enhanced by deploying them not as individual companies in support of their regiments, but by massing those companies into regiment-sized battalions;[20] grenadier companies were detached from their regiments and operated together, while light infantry organizations were created for the war.[21] During the peaceful years of the late 1760s and early 1770s this practice fell aside as regiments for the most part were scattered about Great Britain and British colonies, often alone and seldom more than two in any one place. The conflicts that occurred during those years, such as Pontiac's Rebellion and the Carib War, did not involve large enough concentrations of regiments to warrant special grenadier and light infantry formations. The concept, though, remained firmly in the minds of military thinkers, particularly when permanent light infantry companies were established. In 1772 the Lord Lieutenant of Ireland, Lieutenant General George Townsend, wrote a document called 'Rules and Orders for the Discipline of the Light Infantry Companies in His Majesty's Army in Ireland.' The first known detailed discussion of the expectations for these companies, it included the assumption that companies from different regiments would operate together, such as 'When a Corps of Light Infantry is composed of Companies from different Regiments they must do Duty by Companies with their own officers.'[22]

The grenadiers traditionally formed for parade on the right flank of the regiment; the new light infantry company formed on the left flank. From this positioning came the term flank companies. The remaining eight companies of an infantry regiment were all the same and

18 TNA: WO 12: muster rolls, 22nd Regiment. The height of these two men is given in TNA: WO 43/405: 'Liste Des Recrués Anglois embarqués á Stade pour Spithead en Irlande ce 14me de Mai 1776', the discharge of another man agrees with his height recorded on this list, confirming that the measurement scale is the same. TNA: WO 121/61/14: discharge of Peter Federheim.

19 TNA: WO 27/32: inspection return, 22nd Regiment; WO 12: muster rolls, 22nd Regiment.

20 Quotes from Smith, *An Universal Military Dictionary*, pp.177–178 and Cuthbertson, *System*, p.191.

21 J.F.C. Fuller, *British Light Infantry in the Eighteenth Century* (London: Hutchinson & Co., 1925), pp.76–110.

22 George Townsend, 'Rules and Orders for the Discipline of the Light Infantry Companies in His Majesty's Army in Ireland,' 15 May 1772, in R. H. R. Smythies, *Historical Records of the 40th (2nd Somersetshire) Regiment, Now 1st Battalion The Prince of Wales Volunteers (South Lancashire Regiment) From its Formation in 1717 to 1893* (Devonport: A. W. Swiss, 1894), pp.549–552.

were called battalion companies. This leads to nomenclature that can be confusing – the word battalion describes the composite organization of grenadier companies and of light infantry companies, hence the term flank battalions, composed of flank companies. But battalion also describes the eight companies of a regiment when the flank companies were detached, because it is no longer a complete regiment. Throughout this book the term 'regiment' is usually used for the eight battalion companies without their flank companies, even though it is not quite accurate, to avoid confusion.

* * *

In the years immediately following the establishment of light infantry companies, the formations and tactics used by grenadiers and light infantry began to blend. At annual reviews, regiments in Great Britain performed a standard set of formation manoeuvres – taking the regiment from line into column and back into line, advancing and retiring by companies, firing by platoons, companies, and divisions (pairs of companies), and so forth.[23] But regiments could show off other manoeuvres, sometimes engaging an imaginary foe. Descriptions of these field days reveal grenadiers and light infantry being used in complementary ways, as skirmishers deployed rapidly to provide covering fire while battalion companies changed formations. The report on the 17th Regiment of Foot's review in 1771 included passages like, 'Upon the Grenadiers being ordered to cover the flanks of the battalion, the Light Company divided into two Platoons, took post upon the flanks of the Regiment in a single rank, facing outwards … and in that position began an irregular fire.'[24]

The same year, the 35th Regiment staged a mock attack during which, after a charge by the battalion, the 'Light Infantry dash'd forward from both flanks, upon the broken Enemy to keep up the Route, till the Battalion was restored to order'; during an advance, the 'Light Infantry covered both flanks, Marching by files two deep,' and while the battalion retreated, 'Light Infantry formed on the flanks in an Indian file, covering the extent of the Battalion and protected it by their firing to the Flanks.' During another manoeuvre, 'Light Infantry skirmished in front, supported by the Grenadiers, who fired in one body & charged.' When the battalion changed fronts, 'Light Infantry run to that front & skirmish'd.' Demonstrating how to seize a bridge, the 35th's 'Light Infantry run to the banks on both sides of the Bridge, and fired upon the opposite shore, to make way for the Grenadiers who secured the Bridge'; after the battalion crossed, 'the Light Infantry run over the Bridge and took post in the rear of both flanks in a rank entire.'[25]

Onlookers at a 1772 review of the 17th Regiment of Foot in Edinburgh enjoyed 'the new and irregular method of firing' used by the regiment's light infantry company.[26] The 33rd Regiment went so far as to have the entire regiment perform 'all their new manoeuvres

23 Anon., *The Manual Exercise, As ordered by his Majesty, In 1764. Together with Plans and Explanations Of the Method generally Practis'd At Review and Field-Days, &c.* (London: Adjutant-General's Office, 1764)

24 TNA: WO 27/21: review of the 17th Regiment, 1771.

25 TNA: WO 27/21: review of the 35th Regiment, 1771.

26 *Caledonian Mercury*, 11 May 1772.

as light Infantry' developed by the commander, Colonel Charles Cornwallis.[27] In a mock engagement during their 1772 review, the 33rd's light infantry company took post in a village while 'the grenadiers concealed in a wood, at a small distance,' and 'the Battalion descended in a line, two deep, from very strong ground.' Later on in the mock fight, the battalion lined 'a strong hedge ... where they kept up a brisk & irregular fire. On the Retreat beating, the men ran back independently to the brow of the hill, where they instantly formed.'[28]

Lord Townsend's 1772 'Rules and Orders' for light infantry companies in Ireland emphasized that 'the Service upon which they are likely to be Employed, is very different from that of heavy Troops.' Townsend explained that because light infantry were expected 'always to Engage in open Order and the Attack may frequently become personal between Man and Man, It is therefore necessary to be particular in selecting Men for this Service not only of Activity and Bodyly Strength but also of some Experience and approved Spirit.' He made it clear that 'the Light Infantry Companies are to be instructed in the manual and every other Evolution which the Battalion may be ordered to perform,' including close-order marching with the firelock on the shoulder; because the light infantry was composed of men already trained in the battalion, they had already mastered these fundamentals. The standard formation for battalion companies was in three ranks (rows of men), with the men just four inches apart, the second and third ranks each one pace behind the rank ahead of it.[29] Some regiments demonstrated manoeuvres in two ranks, particularly for the flank companies. Townsend's 'Rules and Orders' codified this, directing that 'The Light Infantry Companies are always to be drawn up two Deep with a space of Two Feet between the Files.' For 'Marching in a Wood upon any Service of a Secret Nature,' they were to carry their firelocks diagonally at their side in their right hand, a position called 'trail arms'.[30] Townsend stressed the importance of files – the man in the front rank and the man in the rear rank directly behind him – working together:

> It is to be particularly observed that each file has an entire dependence upon itself and that the Firelocks of the front and rear Men, are never to be unloaded at the same time, When the front Rank Man Fires, the Rear Rank Man is to make Ready and step up briskly before his Comrade, but is by no means to discharge his Firelock untill the other has loaded, and then he is to step briskly before the Rear Rank Man, and this method to be followed untill a signal shall be given for ceasing to Fire. This Mutual Defence and Confidence is one of the most Essential Principles of Light Infantry.[31]

Rather than wheeling to face a line to the right or left, the light infantry changed fronts quickly by having the file on one flank face the new direction, and the other files run to their place in the line; 'when a few files are formed the Commanding Officer is to order an

27 *General Evening Post* (London), 27 June 1771.
28 TNA: WO 27/24: inspection return, 33rd Regiment.
29 Anon. *The Manual Exercise, As ordered by his Majesty, In 1764*, pp.15–16.
30 The name for this position is given in Anon., *The Volunteers Companion* (Dublin: W. Coles, 1784), p.11.
31 Townsend, 'Rules and Orders', p.549

Irregular Fire to begin, and to Continue untill the signal shall be given for Ceasing.' Fighting in woods, which had proven essential during the French and Indian War, was emphasized:

> The Men when in a Wood are to be taught to Cover themselves with Trees by placing the Right Foot about six inches behind the left, and presenting to the Right of the Tree, and after Firing to step back two paces, and give Room to the Rear Rank man to come up to the same Tree and to fire alternately, according to the directions before mentioned.[32]

Woods were not the only possible cover; 'The Light Infantry must also be taught to take Advantage of large stones, broken Inclosures, old Houses, or any strong feature which presents itself upon the face of a Country. But they must take particular Care not to run in Crowds to these objects.' Most importantly, 'The success of any Engagement in a Wood or Strong Country depends upon the Coolness and presence of Mind of the Commanding Officer, and the Silence and Obedience of the Men fully as much as upon their Bravery.'[33]

Townsend discussed having battalions of light infantry 'march through a Wood or inclosed Country that can admit of it' by having each company form a single or double file and then advance 'in parallel Lines.' Such a formation required 'flanking parties to March in front and the Files to move at the distance of ten yards from each other'; when an enemy was discovered, the front and flanking parties were 'not to run into the Main Body, but to take posts immediately and begin an attack.' Where battalion companies used drums for sounding basic commands like Advance and Retreat, light infantry officers were advised to 'fix upon signals for extending their Front to the Right or to the Left, or to both Flanks, or to Close to the Centre, to retire, or to advance, and these signals must be made by a loud whistle, a posting horn, or some other instrument capable of conveying a sufficient sound to be heard at a considerable Distance.' It was essential that 'the Men to be silent and attentive without which it is scarce possible that any action in a wood can be successful.'[34]

Again, showing the importance of individual responsibility, Townsend advised that 'The Arms of every Soldier should be always be kept in good Order, But the Light Infantry Man, in particular, must not neglect his Arms,' or ammunition. In addition, 'Each man must have a sufficient Number of Cartridges made up, But as it may be necessary to have recourse to the Horn, The Men are to be taught to load from it,' referring to powder horns used only by the light infantry. Marksmanship was part of the routine training of British soldiers, but Townsend went farther, advising that instead of relying on ammunition produced in bulk for the regiment, 'The Light Infantry are to be taught to fire at Marks, and each Soldier is to find out the proper Measure of Powder for his own Firelock and to make up his Cartridges accordingly' (but there is no evidence that this was practiced on service in America). Further, each man was not to 'throw away his Fire, as his Existence may depend upon a Single Shot's taking place.'[35]

32 Townsend, 'Rules and Orders', p.549.
33 Townsend, 'Rules and Orders', p.550.
34 Townsend, 'Rules and Orders', p.549.
35 Townsend, 'Rules and Orders', p.551. For training in marksmanship, see Hagist, *Noble Volunteers*, pp.66–68.

Flank companies had the same overall composition as battalion companies; in the early 1770s, an infantry company consisted of three officers, two sergeants, three corporals, a drummer, and 36 private soldiers (some sources indicate 38 private soldiers; the War Office provided funding for two non-existent 'contingent men' in each company to allow for various expenses, but this was strictly a financial mechanism).[36] Battalion companies were commanded by a captain or more senior officer, with a lieutenant and an ensign as 'subalterns' (subordinates). Because ensigns were the lowest-ranking and least experienced officers, they, like inexperienced soldiers, had no place in flank companies; instead, each flank company was led by a captain and two lieutenants.

Sketch by Philip James de Loutherbourg of light infantrymen in England, 1778, showing different styles of caps – a brimless cap with chains around the crown, and a visored cap with a comb similar to cavalry helmets. (Anne S.K. Brown Military Collection)

Townsend recommended that 'the stoutest of the Drummers' be taught to use a posting horn or whistle to sound signals; his context implies that he referred to one drummer in a light infantry battalion, but inspection returns and other records indicate that many light infantry drummers were equipped with horns in the early 1770s; the 43rd Regiment, for example purchased 'a Trumpet & Music for the Light

36 TNA: WO 379/1: army establishments.

Infantry Company' in 1772, and the 20th Regiment had a 'German post horn' at their 1774 inspection.[37] Appendix IX describes a set of signals which may be representative of the types of signalling done by horn or trumpet – simple sounds for major movements like advancing and halting.

Appendix I and III present some known details of different regiments' light infantry companies that served in the American Revolution.

* * *

By 1774 the light infantry were an integral part of each regiment and of the army as a whole. When several regiments garrisoned the same location, their flank companies operated together during part of the annual review. In Dublin, the 22nd, 42nd, 54th, 55th, 62nd and 63rd Regiments performed a mock attack; their 'Light Infantry were detached to skirmish in the front. On their recoiling the Grenadiers were push'd forward to support them, and firing by companys sustained the attack till the Line came up.' Later on in the sham fight, 'The Grenadiers & Light Infantry advanced into the wood & kept up a constant fire there.'[38]

In August and September 1774, Major General William Howe brought together light infantry companies from seven regiments at Sarum, just north of Salisbury, and conducted exercises with them as a battalion using a standardized set of manoeuvres. They performed movements in two ranks, consistent with Townsend's recommendations, and learned to extend that interval to four feet, and to 10 feet. They practiced rapidly forming lines from columns and vice versa, and also forming a new line facing in any direction. Supposedly these companies would return to their regiments and teach the open-order manoeuvres to the other companies, leading to a standardized light infantry discipline throughout the entire army.[39] The manoeuvres taught by Howe at Sarum, and a variation published in 1778, appear in Appendix V and VI.

At the same time that Major General Howe was teaching seven companies in England, Lieutenant General Thomas Gage was training seven regiments in Boston. In response to American colonial resistance to British taxation, Parliament had dissolved the Massachusetts colonial government, imposed a series of punitive measures, and sent troops to Boston to maintain order. The 23rd, 47th and 59th Regiments arrived from other posts in America, while the 4th, 5th, 38th and 43rd sailed from Great Britain and arrived in Boston early in the summer. They encamped on Boston Common and trained for a war they hoped would not come. The 64th Regiment garrisoned a fortification in Boston Harbour. The 10th and 52nd Regiments arrived from Canada before the end of the year, as did a few companies each of the 18th and 65th Regiments from other American posts. Two battalions of Marines from

37 Townsend, 'Rules and Orders', p.549; Lloyds Bank Archives (LBA): A563/115: agent's ledgers, 43rd Regiment; Hew Strachan, *British Military Uniforms 1768–1796* (London: Arms and Armour Press, 1975), p.213, and other examples pp.204–205.

38 TNA: WO/32/32: review of the 22nd Regiment, 14 May 1774.

39 NAM: 6807-157-6: 'Discipline established by Major General Howe for Light Infantry in Battalion'; Houlding, *Fit for Service*, pp.336–337.

British ports also landed in Boston, resulting in an army of about 4,500 infantry when 1774 turned to 1775.[40]

Training consisted of frequent marches of several miles into the countryside laden with arms and knapsacks, and regular firing at marks (target practice) individually, by companies and by regiment. A visitor to the city in March 1775 watched some regiments 'at Exercise' and 'was so well entertained that I spent all the forenoon looking at them.' He wrote,

> Some of the Regiments were extremely expert at their Exercise, & the manouvres & manner of fighting of the light infantry was exceedingly curious. Every regiment here has a company of light infantry, young active fellows; & they are trained in the regular manner, & likewise in a peculiar discipline of irregular & Bush fighting; they run out in parties on the wings of the regiment where they keep up a constant & irregular fire; they secure their retreat; & defend their front while they are forming; in one part of their Exercise they ly on their backs & charge their pieces & fire lying on their bellies. They have powder horns & no cartouch boxes.[41]

Although there were plenty of officers in this little army who had served in the French and Indian War – Gage himself had commanded a regiment of light infantry – there were no measures taken to form the flank companies into battalions. Training was undertaken by individual regiments, their eight battalion companies and two flank companies acting together. Sometimes brigades consisting of several regiments trained together, but with the flank companies still attached to the regiments. As such, by early April each company of grenadiers and light infantry was certainly trained to a high standard, capable of marching long distances at a rapid pace, skilled at individual marksmanship.[42] But in terms of coordination, they had practiced only with their own regiments. Their first experience working together as flank battalions was not a training exercise but an operational mission of utmost importance.

40 For details on this military buildup, see Hagist, *Noble Volunteers*, chapters 1 and 4.

41 Philip Padelford (ed.), *Colonial Panorama, 1775: Dr. Robert Honyman's Journal for March and April* (San Marino, CA: Huntington Library, 1939), pp.43–44.

42 Hagist, *Noble Volunteers*, chapter 4.

2

'Our men must be drilled': Flank Battalions in Boston, 1775–1776

In spite of Lieutenant General Gage's extensive experience with light infantry in America, and the months of training for his 'little army,' as one of his subordinates called it,[1] the first order for the grenadiers and light infantry to be separated from their regiments came on 15 April 1775. 'As the Grenadiers and light Infantry will be ordered out, to learn grenadier exersise,' the orders read, 'and some new Evolutions for the light Infantry, they are to be off all duty till further orders.'[2] On the 16th, orders were given for each regiment's major and adjutant – the two officers typically tasked with teaching new procedures – 'to instruct the Grenadiers of their own Corps in the grenadier exersise to morrow at the most convenient place, near their own barracks,' while 'the light companies will be instructed in the new Manoevers by Lieutenant Mackenzie, Adjutant of the 23rd Regiment who will fix a time of assembling with the respective Captains, tomorrow morning at guard mounting.'[3]

These orders appear to have been only a ruse, to detach the flank companies without indicating that an expedition was afoot. The 'grenadier exercise' was a set of movements that involved slinging the musket, then lighting the fuse on a grenade and throwing it, a procedure included in some military manuals and sometimes demonstrated at reviews but not known to have been used on service in the 1770s.[4] Grenades had no practical application in the operations anticipated in Massachusetts in early 1775 – confiscating military stores, arresting rebel leaders, and keeping the peace. The 'new maneuvers' for the light infantry might have been quite useful, but there is no evidence that any were practiced on 17 or 18 April. Lieutenant Frederick Mackenzie of the 23rd Regiment kept a verbose diary during this period but, other than recording verbatim the 16 April order that he himself was to instruct the new manoeuvres, he made no mention of them. No training occurred, but the flank company soldiers were well-rested and prepared for a major operation.

1 Charles Knowles Bolton (ed.), *Letters of Hugh Earl Percy from Boston and New York 1774–1776* (Boston: Charles E. Goodspeed, 1902), p.34.
2 TNA: WO 36/1: general orders, 15 April 1775; Frederick Mackenzie, *The Diary of Frederick Mackenzie* (Cambridge, MA: Harvard University Press, 1930), p.16.
3 TNA: WO 36/1: general orders, 16 April 1775; Mackenzie, *Diary*, p.17.
4 See, for example, Smith, *An Universal Military Dictionary*, pp.164–165.

At 8:00 p.m. on 18 April, regimental commanders were directed to send their flank companies to be at a beach at 10:00 p.m. – 'a soldier's hour to be in bed,' lamented one light infantryman[5] – where they would receive further orders. They took their arms and 36 rounds of ammunition. Knapsacks were left behind, a distinct difference from the marches in previous months that were for training and fitness, but each man took a day's worth of biscuit and precooked beef in his haversack.

Commanding the expedition was Lieutenant Colonel Francis Smith of the 10th Regiment of Foot, chosen out of respect for his seniority – he was the oldest lieutenant colonel in the garrison, in terms of commission date – rather than respect for the nature of the mission at hand. On an assignment that required rapid movement even if the day remained peaceful and everything went to plan, Smith, called 'a heavy man' and 'a very fat man' by officers in the garrison, could be an impediment regardless of his tactical acumen. Moreover, although he was an experienced officer, he had arrived in Boston only the previous November after spending seven years in Canada commanding a regiment spread out across frontier outposts, far from the advances in tactical doctrine being made in Great Britain and with no opportunity to lead composite organizations like the one he was now tasked with. At 52 years old Smith was a generally seasoned, capable officer, but it is not clear that he was the best choice for this expedition.

Second in command, also chosen based on seniority rather than propriety, was Major John Pitcairn of the Marines. Being the garrison's senior major entitled him to the role and, a year older than Smith, he had considerable experience including service in Canada during the French and Indian War. The Marines, however, were a branch of the Royal Navy, and seldom worked in close conjunction with the army. Pitcairn arrived in Boston in late 1774 at the head of a 600-man detachment of Marines sent from Great Britain to reinforce the Boston garrison. The Marines operated on shore just like the army's infantry regiments, and Pitcairn was part of the duty rotation among army officers of similar rank, but there is no evidence that he had experience with a composite force of flank companies.

The nominal strength of a company included 36 private soldiers, but not every man marched out on the expedition. Exact numbers are known for only one regiment, the 23rd, which sent out 29 grenadier and 35 light infantry 'rank and file', that is, corporals and privates.[6] Each company on the expedition had at least one of its officers, and some probably had all three. A few were certainly absent, like Captain Nesbit Balfour of the 4th's light infantry who was commanding a detachment at Marshfield, Massachusetts, and Lieutenant James Hamilton of the 10th's light infantry who reported himself sick. Balancing this out, several officers who were not from flank companies went on the expedition, which may have contributed to the confusion as events unfolded. Ensign Henry De Berniere, a battalion company officer from the 10th Regiment, went along as a guide since he had scouted the region the previous month.[7] Lieutenant William Sutherland of the 38th, a battalion

5 Margaret W. Willard, *Letters on the American Revolution, 1774–1776* (Boston and New York: Houghton Mifflin Company, 1925), p.187.

6 Mackenzie, *Diary*, p.23.

7 Henry De Berniere, 'Transactions of the British troops previous to, and at the Battle of Lexington,' in Anon. (ed.), *General Gage's Instructions ... with a curious Narrative of Occurrences* (Boston: J. Gill, 1779), p.17.

company officer, 'learned there was a large detachment going from this garrison on which I immediately resolved to go with them,' followed some of the flank company soldiers to the embarkation place, and 'joined Major Pitcairn.'[8] Ensign Jeremy Lister of the 10th Regiment chanced to learn of the expedition because he lodged in a house with an officer of his regiment's grenadier company, Lieutenant James Pettigrew. Lister went with Pettigrew to the embarkation place, where he learned that Lieutenant Hamilton would not be attending. Lister volunteered to take Hamilton's place and served with the light infantry on the expedition, drawing on his four years with the regiment, albeit as a battalion officer.[9]

This grenadier, sketched by Philip James de Loutherbourg in England, 1778, wears the uniform prescribed in 1768, with wings on the shoulders of his coat and a sword – but he wears a cocked hat instead of the formal bearskin cap. (Anne S.K. Brown Military Collection)

From the beach in Boston, boats provided by warships ferried the troops over a half-mile stretch of the Charles River to a landing place northwest of the city, an operation that took two hours. Getting from the landing place to a main road required marching through marshes and wading across two thigh-deep inlets between midnight and 2:00 a.m. on 19 April, a miserable beginning for a day-long march. Once on a road, they awaited delivery of provisions prepared by the navy, even though they had brought food with them from Boston, a mix-up that consumed another hour. To make up time, the light infantry marched off at a fast pace under Major Pitcairn's command, while the grenadiers led by Lieutenant Colonel Smith trailed behind. [10]

8 William L. Clements Library, University of Michigan, Ann Arbor (WLC): Thomas Gage Papers: American Series Vol. 128, William Sutherland to Stephen Kemble, 27 April 1775.

9 Jeremy Lister, *Concord Fight* (Cambridge, MA: Harvard University Press, 1931), pp.21–23.

10 John Barker, *The British in Boston, being the Diary of Lieutenant John Barker of the King's Own Regiment* (Cambridge, MA: Harvard University Press, 1924), pp.31–32; Mackenzie, *Diary*, p.24.

A detailed discussion of the ensuing events is outside the scope of this study; here, the focus is on tactics and procedures used on this first operation by flank battalions in the rebellious American colonies. The many accounts of that day offer only clues to how the battalions formed and fought. Captain William Souter, commanding the light infantry of the Marines, wrote that the companies marched by platoons, a platoon being half a company. In the standard formation of three ranks,[11] a full-strength platoon was seven men wide (six private men and one corporal); with numbers a bit below full strength, five or six man fronts were more likely. Much later in the day, Ensign De Berniere mentioned attempting to form disorganized troops into two ranks for a defensive posture, a formation which, if divided into platoons, resulted in seven to 10 man fronts, perhaps still narrow enough to fit on the region's roads.[12]

* * *

Before arriving at the town of Lexington, the British column learned through various sources that militia were forming in town to oppose them. Lieutenant Colonel Smith and Major Pitcairn both reported soon after the event that, when it became apparent that the countryside was alarmed, six light infantry companies were sent ahead to secure bridges beyond Concord.[13] Pitcairn halted these companies short of Lexington 'in order to make a disposition, by advancing men in front & on the flanks to prevent a surprise.'[14] Lieutenant Sutherland, not a flank company officer, 'went with the front party which consisted of a serjeant & 6 or 8 men,' but apparently did not attempt to command them. Ensign Lister recalled that 'the five front Companies was ordered to load,' but he may have recalled the number incorrectly.[15]

No participant recorded which six companies went into Lexington to face the militia there, but some accounts identify individual companies. The typical order of battle for a flank battalion was to have the senior company – the one from the oldest regiment, based on the date of its founding – on the right, the next senior on the left, the third most senior back on the right, and so forth. If this formation was followed exactly, with the Marines taking their place of precedence between the 47th and 52nd Regiments, the battalion should have formed this way:

5th, 23rd, 43rd, Marines, 59th, 52nd, 47th, 38th, 10th, 4th[16]

11 The three-rank formation was specified in *The Manual Exercise, As ordered by his Majesty, In 1764*, and its use was ordered in Boston on 14 August 1774, 'unless ordered to the contrary.' TNA: WO 36/1: general orders, 14 August 1774.

12 De Berniere, 'Transactions,' p.19.

13 Francis Smith to Thomas Gage, 22 April 1775, and John Pitcairn to Gage, in Vincent J.R. Kehoe, *The British Story of the Battle of Lexington and Concord on the Nineteenth of April, 1775* (Los Angeles: Hale & Co., 2000), pp.37, 42

14 WLC: Thomas Gage Papers: Sutherland to Kemble, 27 April 1775.

15 Lister, *Concord Fight*, p.23.

16 The Marines, established permanently in 1755, were between the 49th and 50th Regiments in order of precedence based on the date each corps was created. Houlding, *Fit for Service*, p.380.

To form a column of march, this line moved off from the right with the 4th Regiment's company first, followed by the 10th, the 38th, and so on. Perhaps the first six companies in the column – the 4th, 10th, 38th, 47th, 52nd and 59th – went ahead, or maybe it was the first six by seniority, the 4th, 5th, 10th, 23rd, 38th and 43rd. When the six companies arrived at Lexington the companies from the 4th and 10th Regiments formed a line to the right to oppose militia formed there, consistent with their being in the front of the column and on the right when formed in a line. Captain Souter of the Marines wrote that his company was third in the column, which does not fit in with other assumptions about the six companies, but he also wrote that his company was 'behind' when the firing occurred.[17] Perhaps his company was not among the six sent out ahead but instead was near the front of the remainder of the column.

After the fray at Lexington, on the march to Concord, 'the Country People had occupied a hill which commanded the road,' wrote Lieutenant John Barker of the 4th Regiment's light infantry company; 'the light infantry were order'd away to the right and ascended the height in one line,' which compelled their opponents to retreat.[18] In Concord, the grenadier companies did the heavy work of destroying military stores, while the light infantry covered two bridges beyond the town. Several accounts confirm that the companies of the 4th, 10th, and 43rd went to the North Bridge,[19] and those of the 38th and 52nd continued past it to search for hidden cannon.[20] When a much larger militia force advanced upon the three companies at the bridge, Captain Walter Sloane Laurie of the 43rd, the senior officer present, ordered a withdrawal across the bridge. Lieutenant Sutherland, eight days after the event, wrote that Laurie 'immediately desired the men to form & extend their front & keep up their fire,'[21] but apparently there wasn't time. Lieutenant Barker of the 4th recorded in his diary that they 'were obliged to form the best way they cou'd,' and that 'the three companies got one behind the other so that only the front one cou'd fire.' Ensign Lister of the 10th recalled that this formation was deliberate: 'our Companies was drawn up in order to fire Street fireing,'[22] a drill-book procedure where the foremost rank fired and quickly moved to the rear, allowing the next rank to fire and retire, and so on.[23] But the opposition was too numerous, and in spite of Captain Laurie 'exhorting his men to Rally & fire,'[24] 'the weight of their fire was such that we was oblig'd to give way then run with the greatest precipitance.'[25] That three officers on the scene recalled the tactics so differently underscores the confusion caused by attempting coordinated manoeuvres with companies that had not practiced together.

17 Kehoe, *The British Story*, p.43.

18 Barker, *The British in Boston*, p.32

19 Ensign Lister wrote that the 23rd Regiment's company was among those at the North Bridge, but this is contradicted by Lieutenant Sutherland; the published edition of Lister's account has other transcription errors, for example, on page 19, '28th' should be '38th.' Lister, *Concord Fight*, p.19, 25; WLC: Thomas Gage Papers: Sutherland to Kemble, 27 April 1775.

20 J.L. Bell, *The Road to Concord: How Four Stolen Cannon Ignited the Revolutionary War* (Yardley, PA: Westholme, 2016), p.161.

21 WLC: Thomas Gage Papers: Sutherland to Kemble, 27 April 1775.

22 Lister, *Concord Fight*, p.27

23 Smith, *An Universal Military Dictionary*, p.91.

24 WLC: Thomas Gage Papers: Sutherland to Kemble, 27 April 1775.

25 Lister, *Concord Fight*, p.27

These are the last specific accounts of how the flank companies formed and fought on this first day of war. After reassembling the entire force in Concord, the expedition set out on the road back to Lexington, harassed all along the way by sniping militia. Ensign De Berniere recalled leaving Concord 'in the same order of march, only our flankers were more numerous and further from the main body.' The light infantry took to the fields and hills on the flanks and the grenadiers engaged from the road, driving off party after party of militia that melted into the countryside, only to reassemble or be replaced further down the road. 'We at first kept our order and returned their fire as hot as we received it,' wrote De Berniere, 'but when we arrived within a mile of Lexington, our ammunition began to fail, and the light companies were so fatigued with flanking they were scarce able to act, and a great number of wounded scarce able to get forward, made a great confusion.' He continued, 'we began to run rather than retreat in order—the whole behaved with amazing bravery, but little order; we attempted to stop the men and form them two deep, but to no purpose, the confusion increased rather than lessened.'[26] Exhausted of both stamina and ammunition, they were greeted just in time by a four-regiment relief force that formed a flank and rear guard, taking over the fight so the whole could retreat to the safety of Bunker Hill peninsula adjacent to Boston. By midnight, the last of the troops had been ferried back into the city.[27]

Lieutenant General Gage reported one officer killed, 13 wounded and one missing; the missing officer was Lieutenant Edward Hull of the 43rd's light infantry, who was captured and later died. Seven other light infantry officers were wounded, almost all of whom recovered and continued to serve in the war; no grenadier officers were among the casualties.[28] For the soldiers, the report listed casualties by regiment but did not distinguish by company, making it impossible to differentiate losses of grenadiers and light infantry; also, the 4th, 23rd, 47th and Marines were part of the relief column that also took casualties, making it impossible to distinguish flank company casualties for those four regiments. Muster rolls, which survive for all but the 5th Regiment and Marines, denote the men killed in each company, but do not denote wounded.[29] Looking at the casualties that can be determined, it is clear that the light infantry lost about twice the number killed as the grenadiers, and that the companies of the 5th and 10th Regiments suffered significantly more wounded than most others. A few soldiers' wounds were recorded on their discharges years later. A sergeant in the 59th Regiment's grenadier company, James Rennison, born in 1744, had joined the army in 1760 after working as a weaver; at Bunker Hill he was wounded in the thigh. John Smith, a native of St. Andrews, Norfolk who had been a dyer before joining the army, was 44 years old and had been in the army for 21 years when he marched out with the 4th Regiment's light infantry company; he had been wounded in the leg during the taking of Martinique in 1762, and on 19 April he was wounded 'through his thigh.' Grenadier Matthew Haymer of the 23rd Regiment, a 29-year-old from Burnley, Lancashire, received two wounds, one in his right thigh and one in his left foot.[30]

26 De Berniere, 'Transactions,' p.19.

27 Mackenzie, *Diary*, p.23.

28 Anon., *The Remembrancer, or impartial repository of public events* (London: J. Almon, 1775), Vol.1, p.41.

29 TNA: WO 12: muster rolls for the various regiments.

30 TNA: WO 121/3/157, WO 121/5/226 and WO 121/8/92: Discharges of James Rennison, John Smith, and Matthew Haymer respectively.

Table 1.1: Soldiers Killed and Wounded on 19 April 1775, from Lieutenant General Gage's report and muster rolls

Regiment	Grenadiers killed	LI killed	Total killed in flank companies	Total wounded in flank companies
4th	1	4	Unknown	Unknown
5th	Unknown	Unknown	5	15
10th	0	1	1	13
18th (grenadiers only)	1	-	1	4
23rd	1	1	2	Unknown
38th	1	2	3	5
43rd	0	3	3	5
47th	0	0	0	Unknown
Marines	Unknown	Unknown	Unknown	Unknown
52nd	2	1	2	2
59th	Unknown	Unknown	3	3

Notes: Gages report lists total killed and wounded from each regiment, but not by company. Muster rolls denote killed but not wounded. No muster rolls are available for the 5th Regiment and Marines.
A drummer of the 38th Regiment was killed, who was not in a flank company.
A private soldier of the 43rd Regiment was killed, who was not in a flank company.
The 59th Regiment's muster rolls record no men killed, but Gage's report lists three.

Within days, Gage stated in orders that 'the men in the late affair, though they behaved with much courage and spirit, shewed great inattention and neglect to the commands of their Officers, which if they had observed fewer of them would have been hurt.' Indeed, from the moment the light infantry were fired upon at Lexington in the early morning hours, 'the men were so wild they cou'd hear no orders,'[31] finally forming only when a drummer beat the signal, 'to arms'.[32] Major Pitcairn stated his regret of 'the too great warmth of the soldiers in not attending to their officers & keeping their ranks' in Lexington,[33] but on the return march there was no maintaining discipline. Lieutenant Frederick Mackenzie of the 23rd, who was part of the relief force and not among those who went to Concord, wrote that the flank company troops had fired 'with too much eagerness, so that at first most it was thrown away for want of that coolness and Steadiness which distinguishes troops who have been inured to service.'[34] When fired upon from houses, the soldiers broke ranks, went inside, and put to the bayonet anyone they found inside – but also took the opportunity to plunder. Matthew Hayes, a 30-year-old grenadier sergeant in the 52nd Regiment, was caught inside a house by rebels who disarmed him and compelled him to surrender. They found him in possession of a pair of silver shoe buckles belonging to a local resident.[35] In becoming one

31 Barker, *The British in Boston*, p.32
32 WLC: Thomas Gage Papers: Sutherland to Kemble, 27 April 1775.
33 WLC: Thomas Gage Papers: Sutherland to Kemble, 27 April 1775.
34 Mackenzie, *Diary*, p.26
35 William Gordon, 'Letter written by an American Clergyman,' *Journal of American History*, Vol. 4 No. 1 (1910), p.70.

of the war's first prisoners, Hayes proved Gage's point that better discipline would have reduced casualties. Altogether, 24 men were reported missing, many of whom later turned up as prisoners of war.[36]

There were probably several reasons for the disorderly conduct of flank company soldiers, chosen specifically for their experience and good discipline. 'The contempt in which they held the Rebels, and perhaps their opinion that they would be sufficiently intimidated by a brisk fire, occasioned this improper conduct,' opined Lieutenant Mackenzie.[37] Animosity towards American colonists both for their rebellion and for their belligerent treatment of soldiers in the Boston garrison since the previous summer, challenges of companies operating together in battalions for the first time, confusion when officers fell as casualties, and the inevitable chaos when tense peace suddenly turns into war, all certainly contributed to the disorder of the day. One of these factors was correctible, and would never again be allowed to occur during this war. But not immediately.

* * *

On 20 April the grenadiers and light infantry were ordered 'to do duty with their Corps till further orders.'[38] Each regiment now set about recovering from the day's losses. Most flank companies had suffered losses, but none were devastated by casualties. Some regiments transferred men from their battalions into their flank companies before the end of April to restore them to strength. The 10th Regiment moved three men into the grenadier company and three more into the light infantry, but transferred only two light infantrymen to the battalion, probably because of wounds. The 43rd light infantry suffered four killed and one missing, and one was transferred out of the light infantry; six men from the battalion replaced them. Their grenadiers had just one man missing and one transferred to the battalion, but brought five men from the battalion to bring the company to full strength. The 4th, 23rd and 47th Regiments, on the other hand, did not replace their flank company casualties, even though the 4th lost two grenadiers and four lights killed, the 23rd one grenadier and two lights killed. The 47th transferred two grenadiers and three lights into their battalion without replacing them.[39]

Some days passed before it was obvious that an all-out war had begun. Instead of returning to their homes with shock and revulsion at the violence and bloodshed, militia from all over the New England colonies flocked to the towns surrounding Boston. The British garrison was under siege. Eight more regiments were already on the way from Great Britain, but events around Boston were unfolding too fast. In the course of May, the city was fully sealed off from the countryside, both armies multiplying their fortifications and calculating their next moves.

At the end of May, the flank companies were again detached from their regiments and formed together, this time to embody them as battalions for the long term rather than for a single expedition. Regiments on Boston Common reduced the size of their encampments, filling in the room formerly occupied by their flank companies, to make room for

36 Anon., *The Remembrancer*, Vol.1, p.41.
37 Mackenzie, *Diary*, p.26
38 TNA: WO 36/1: general orders, 20 April 1775.
39 TNA: WO 12: muster rolls of the various regiments.

encampments of the two newly-formed flank battalions.[40] On Monday, 5 June at 9:00 a.m. the flank battalions set up their new camps.[41] Lieutenant Colonel James Abercrombie, a 43-year-old Scottish officer who had served in America during the French and Indian War, took command of the grenadier battalion.[42] He had arrived in America on 23 April to serve on Gage's staff; his regiment, the 22nd Regiment, was still on its way to America.[43] His appointment to the grenadiers, in the words of Lieutenant General Gage, was 'more to his wishes, and in a way more adapted to his genius.' Abercrombie had misgivings, not about his new post but about the nature of the war, which at this early stage still appeared to be a local insurgency. 'If the War was with Spain or France,' he wrote on 5 June, 'I should have been proud of the Command, but I do not like such fine fellows should be Shott at by such Rascals, were they not to be made great use off possibly I should not have had the Command.' Abercrombie also doubted the choice of command for the light infantry battalion, Lieutenant Colonel George Clarke: 'Lt Col Clark of the 43d has asked for the Light Infantry and I believe will get them, but I am afraid his Constitution will not permit to bear the fatigue of the Campaign.'[44]

To each battalion was also appointed a major, an adjutant, a quartermaster, and a surgeon's mate, giving them staffs similar to established regiments. With the exception of the adjutants, these posts were filled by officers from battalion companies of various regiments, leaving those corps below their full complements.[45]

On 3 June, just before the flank battalions were embodied, Gage ordered that 'The troops will draw up two deep on their Regimental parades as well as on the General parade. The Light Infantry companies when by themselves to be accustomed to draw up in open order.'[46] This formation of two ranks, rather than three, increased the frontage of each company and each battalion, allowing more ground to be covered (laterally) with the limited numbers of troops available. For now, the battalion troops and grenadiers continued to form in close order, with barely any space between the men, while light infantry's 'open order' of about 18 inches between men was better suited for running, surmounting obstacles, and skirmishing.

On 7 June Gage directed that 'The Light Companies to have no men sent to them, but such as are capable of the service; the Commanding Officer of that Corps, to represent such as are not,' and on the 12th, 'As there are several men of the light Infantry and Grenadiers, who are unfit for service, they are immediately to be sent to their Regiments, and others to be sent in lieu of them.' On the 15th Gage directed regiments to complete their flank company complement of officers, which was particularly necessary for companies that had lost officers on 19 April.[47] More regiments were arriving from Great Britain to bolster Gage's army, bringing the opportunity to expand his tiny peninsular enclave. The first target was a loaf-shaped

40 TNA: WO 36/1: general orders for 31 May 1775.
41 TNA: WO 36/1: general orders for 4 June 1775, directing that the companies encamp 'tomorrow'.
42 TNA: WO 36/1: general orders for 4 June 1775.
43 James Abercrombie to Cadwallader Colden, 2 May 1775, *Proceedings of the Massachusetts Historical Society* second series Vol. XI (Boston: published by the Society, 1897), p.305.
44 National Records of Scotland (NRS): GD3/5/1101: Papers of the Montgomerie Family, Earls of Eglinton, Abercrombie to the Earl of Eglinton, 5 June 1775.
45 TNA: WO 36/1: general orders, 6 June 1775.
46 TNA: WO 36/1: general orders, 3 June 1775.
47 TNA: WO 36/1: general orders, 7, 12 and 15 June 1775.

peninsula that protruded from the mainland north of Boston to within a half mile of the city's north end. The peninsula had a peak on the north end called Bunker Hill that overlooked a neck of land connecting it to the mainland; at the opposite end, facing Boston, was a lesser eminence known as Breed's Hill, and on the western waterside was the town of Charlestown. Fortifying Bunker Hill would bring Charlestown within British lines, provide a layer of protection for Boston, and afford another avenue to the mainland for further operations. Gage planned to occupy the hill on 17 June. His opponents were one step ahead of him.

* * *

The breaking daylight on 17 June revealed a freshly-made rebel redoubt on Breed's Hill, teeming with soldiers and activity. Although well-positioned, it was not yet strong enough to be impenetrable. A wide, deep ditch provided earth to form a rampart behind it, a four-sided redoubt that was a formidable obstacle but far from a refined military fortification. A system of rail fencing extended from the left side of the redoubt down to the shore, feeble but nonetheless providing some defensive shelter. As the morning progressed, it became clear to Gage and his subordinates that that swift action was necessary. Besides the threat the redoubt posed to Boston, the fortifications were an aggressive display of American initiative requiring a decisive response. There was little doubt that the position could be taken; in spite of the events of 19 April, British officers were keenly aware that their opponents were haphazardly brought together, poorly supplied and just learning how to establish their own organization. Gage charged Major General William Howe with quickly planning and executing an attack on the position.

Howe saw the best approach as getting behind the fortifications to compromise their strength and prevent reinforcement. The peninsula should have been easy to isolate and then reduce either by siege or by storm depending on the defenders' fortitude. The problem was how to get men behind the fort. At a council of war, senior British officers discussed options of which two came to the forefront. The most tactically effective approach was to land men behind the redoubt to secure the neck. The logistical drawback was that this required a lengthy trip in rowboats from Boston. After a first wave of troops landed, they would have to stand their ground with no support or avenue of retreat, waiting for boats to return with a second wave. The alternative was to ferry troops the shortest distance from Boston, putting the assault force in front of the American fortifications but out of musket range and allowing quick reinforcement.

It was clear that landing troops at the closest point to Boston was the safest plan. From there, there was no intention of making a frontal assault on a fortified position. Instead, the grenadiers would advance towards the American works while the light infantry rapidly made their way around the flank, to the right of the grenadiers. The grenadiers would not assault the works immediately, but occupy the defenders while the light infantry invested their rear, attacking only when the enemy was thrown into confusion. It was a sound plan based on good military principles.[48]

48 Harold Murdock, *Bunker Hill Notes and Queries* (Boston: Houghton Mifflin Company, 1927), pp.22–25. Although deficient in many points of detail, this is one of the first histories to accurately present the British strategy based on primary sources.

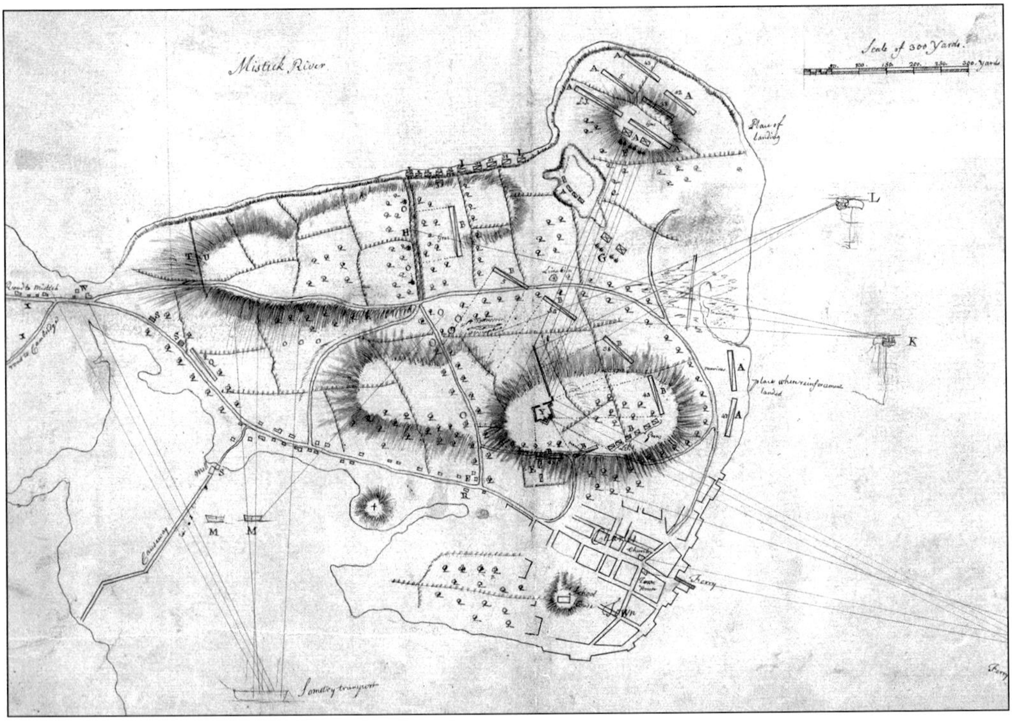

Map of the battle of Bunker Hill. The light infantry advanced along the beach at the upper centre, then reformed on a rise in the right centre and fired on the advancing grenadiers, here shown just below the beach in the centre. (Library of Congress)

With the plan in place, the embarkation orders given at 10:00 a.m. on 17 June were characteristic of almost every tactical movement of the war:

> The ten oldest companies of Grenadiers and the ten oldest companies of light Infantry, (exclusive of the Regiments lately landed) the 5th and 38th Regiments, to parade half after eleven o'Clock, with their Arms, Ammunition, Blankets, and provisions ordered to be cooked this morning, they will march by files to the long wharf.[49]

The mistaken image of British soldiers marching up Bunker Hill laden with knapsacks seems to have begun with one of the first British histories of the war, published in 1794. Charles Stedman, who served in America but was not at Bunker Hill, wrote that the troops were 'encumbered with three days provisions, their knapsacks on their backs' and estimated their total burden at 125 pounds. Even if knapsacks had been carried, other contemporary accounts estimate the British soldier's full load of knapsack, blanket, provisions, and arms at about 60 pounds; regardless, the embarkation order makes it clear that knapsacks were not

49 TNA:WO 36/1: general orders, 17 June 1775.

carried. A later author who expressly intended to rectify misconceptions about the battle repeated the error, going so far as to present the embarkation order but then suggest that the British troops were 'in heavy marching order, each man encumbered with a superfluous weight estimated at nearly one hundred pounds.' Stedman's error has been reinforced by historians who have taken descriptions of especially harsh campaigns to be representative of the typical mode of operation.[50]

The grenadiers and light infantry landed first and formed, the grenadiers in a line facing the rail-fence breastwork extended from the redoubt down to the shore, the light infantry in a column for their advance along the beach to the right. Two regiments formed on the left facing the redoubt. While the grenadiers advanced with deliberate slowness as a distraction, the light infantry trotted along the narrow beach, expecting it to provide an avenue around the end of the rail fence breastwork, the 23rd's company in the lead, followed by the 4th's, 10th's, 52nd's, 43rd's, 65th's, 59th's, 47th's, 38th's, and the 5th's in the rear. Unbeknownst to them, their foes had built a barrier across the beach and manned it. When the light infantry neared this unexpected obstacle, a hail of fire from behind it inflicted heavy casualties and the confines of the beach, with water on the right and embankment on the left, afforded no alternative but retreat. This check was the undoing of British plans and the remainder of the action was conducted extemporaneously.

It is not clear when the grenadiers became aware of the failure of the flanking movement, but they fatefully continued advancing towards the breastworks. Progress was perilously slow, not because of 'superfluous weight' or rigid marching, but because of a series of fences, brick kilns, enclosures and other obstructions. The fences could not be quickly broken down, so the grenadiers had to climb over each one, preventing the rapid assault they would normally have maintained in the face of an enemy. 'A piece of swampy ground, some brick-kilns, and several small fields enclosed by strong paling were in front of the redoubt about one hundred yards,' remembered Martin Hunter, an ensign in the 52nd Regiment that was also in the action; he wrote that this was the area where many of the losses occurred, 'for as soon as we got up to the works we were not nearly so much exposed to their fire, as we were then in some degree covered.'[51]

The slow and irregular advance brought about a danger even greater than hostile fire. The battered light infantry battalion, having withdrawn from the barricade on the beach, reformed into a line near their initial staging area. The shape of the coastline put them behind the advancing grenadier battalion. From this disadvantageous position they opened fire. The distance was too great to have any material effect on the enemy, but for the grenadier battalion it was disastrous. In a letter dated three days after the battle, Abercrombie

50 Charles Stedman, *The History of the Origin, Progress and Termination of the American War* (London: by the author, 1794), p.128; John Burgoyne, *A State of The Expedition From Canada, as Laid Before The House of Commons, by Lieutenant-general Burgoyne, and Verified by Evidence; with a Collection of Authentic Documents …* (London: J. Almon, 1780), p.148; Murdock, *Bunker Hill Notes and Queries*, pp.14, 27. In the last stages of Burgoyne's 1777 campaign soldiers were forced to carry their knapsacks, adding to the overall hardship, but a contemporary account presents it as a contrast to conditions earlier in the campaign when wagons or boats transported the knapsacks. Don N. Hagist, *A British Soldier's Story: Roger Lamb's Narrative of the American Revolution* (Baraboo, WI: Ballindalloch Press, 2005), pp.xxxv, 42.

51 Martin Hunter, *The Journal of Gen. Sir Martin Hunter* (Edinburgh: Edinburgh Press, 1894), pp.10–11.

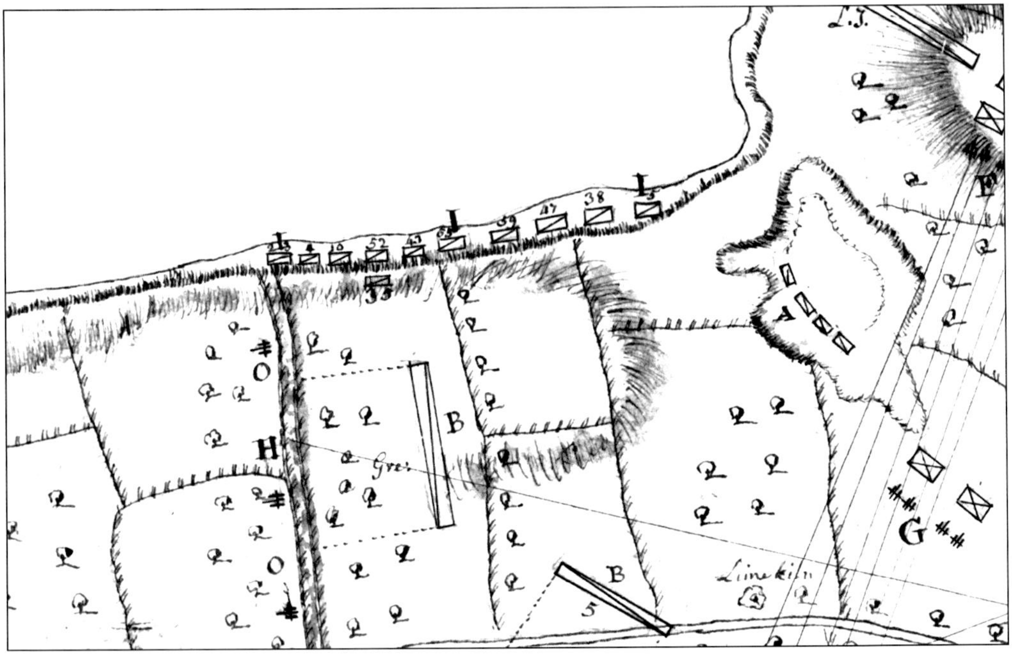

Detail from the map of the Battle of Bunker Hill, showing the arrangement of the light infantry companies as they advanced along the beach, and the obstacles faced by the grenadiers as they trudged up the slope. (Library of Congress)

wrote that 'our Light Infantry killed many of the Grenadiers.' After ordering them to desist, the friendly fire abated for eight or 10 minutes, but then the light infantry 'gave me a plumper & killed two officers & 3 private'; he used the vernacular 'plumper' to refer to a volley of lead.[52] Another unnamed officer wrote that although the light infantry rallied after being pushed back from the barricade they were 'in such consternation that they fired at random, and unfortunately killed several of their officers.' Abercrombie himself was among the wounded.[53]

This friendly fire incident is occasionally mentioned by historians, but its importance is largely overlooked. It calls into question not only British discipline at this early stage of the war, but also American marksmanship. The disproportionate casualties in this battle are sometimes used as evidence of the effectiveness of American firepower. That some of the casualties were inflicted by friendly fire means that American musketry was that much less lethal. There are no precise figures on the total number of friendly fire casualties, but Abercrombie's description of a volley that killed five men allows us to estimate the proportion of wounded at around 20 based on the overall casualty figures for the battle of 226 dead

52 Center for Kentish Studies (CKS): U1350 080/3: Amherst Mss., Abercrombie to Jeffrey Amherst, 20 June 1775; *Edinburgh Advertiser*, 11 August 1775. 'To plump; to strike or shoot. He pulled out his pops and plumped him; he drew out his pistols and shot him.' Eric Partridge (ed.), *A Classical Dictionary of the Vulgar Tongue* (New York: Dorset Press, 1992), p.265.

53 *Edinburgh Advertiser*, 11 August 1775.

and 828 wounded. Abercrombie implies that more were struck previously, and there may have been other casualties of which he was not aware.

There are several possible explanations for the light infantry firing into their own men. While the light infantry was composed of trusted and experienced soldiers, several years of peace may have diminished their discipline and operational readiness. Only a few of the men were recently transferred into the light infantry to recruit losses sustained on 19 April, but their unfamiliarity with officers and comrades may have diminished overall discipline. The withering fire from the barricade threw the light infantry – at least the lead companies in the column – into confusion and inflicted significant casualties. Some soldiers may have been overly determined to inflict punishment on the rebels that had handled them so roughly in April and again this day. Regardless of the reason, after the action Abercrombie wrote, 'Our men must be drilled before they are Carryed to action again.'[54]

In spite of withering fire enemy fire, and the additional friendly fire, the grenadiers finally attained their objective. Captain George Harris, leading the 5th Regiment's grenadier company, wrote that his company reached 'their fortifications, which I had twice mounted, encouraging the men to follow me, and was ascending a third time, when a ball grazed the top of my head, and I fell, deprived of sense and motion.'[55] Lieutenant Francis, Lord Rawdon, in the same company, 'received a shot through a cat-skin cap that he wore that day,' and later remarked on 'how narrowly he had escaped being shot through the head.'[56] He nonetheless caught his falling captain and ordered four soldiers to carry him to a safe place. 'Three of them were wounded,' recalled Harris, 'while performing this office (one afterwards died of his wounds), but they succeeded in placing me under some trees out of the reach of the balls.' He was then taken to the waterside; 'our blankets had been flung away during the engagement; luckily there was one belonging to a man in the boat, in which wrapping me up and laying me in the bottom, they conveyed me safely to my quarters.'[57]

Besides the flank companies of the 'ten oldest companies' of light infantry and grenadiers in the initial landing, the companies of the 35th and 63rd joined the battle later in the day. At least 18 grenadier officers were killed or wounded in the battle, as were five light infantry officers. All three officers in the 4th Regiment's grenadier company were wounded, as were the three officers of the 23rd's and 47th's grenadiers. In the 10th Regiment, all six flank company officers were wounded, one of whom soon died. Lieutenant General Gage's report on the battle enumerated casualties by regiment; the numbers align closely with deaths recorded on muster rolls, which generally do not record wounded.[58] Comparing the two sources makes it clear that the grenadiers suffered nearly twice as many killed as the light infantry. Most of the light infantry casualties probably occurred early in the action when they were in column on the beach, but no company appears to have suffered so many killed that we can assume they were at the head of the column. The grenadiers, on the other hand, advanced in a line – to the extent that a line could be maintained on the uneven terrain – and their companies suffered accordingly. Lieutenant

54 CKS: U1350 080/3: Abercrombie to Amherst, 20 June 1775.
55 W.H. Wilkin (ed.), *Some British Soldiers in America* (London: H. Rees, 1914), 1777.
56 Hunter, *Journal*, p.11.
57 Wilkin, *Some British Soldiers*, pp.177–178.
58 *The Remembrancer*, Vol. 1, p.99; TNA: WO 12: muster rolls of the various regiments.

Rawdon of the 5th Regiment (for which no 1775 muster rolls survive) wrote, 'only eleven of our grenadier company are left.'[59]

Table 2.1: Soldiers Killed and Wounded on 17 June 1775, from Lieutenant General Gage's report and muster rolls

Regiment	Grenadiers killed	LI killed	Total killed in flank companies	Total wounded in flank companies
4th	9	4	13	31
5th	Unknown	Unknown	Unknown	Unknown
10th	3	4	7	40
18th (grenadiers only)	3	-	3	7
23rd	10	4	14	38
35th	7	7	14	Unknown
38th	3	7	10	Unknown
43rd	5	2	7	Unknown
47th	8	0	8	Unknown
52nd	6	6	12	Unknown
59th	6	4	10	25
63rd	2	5	9	Unknown
65th	Unknown	Unknown	9	27

Lieutenant General Gages report lists total killed and wounded from each regiment, but not by company. Muster rolls denote killed but not wounded. No muster rolls are available for the 5th Regiment and the Marines.

The report is dated 25 June; the numbers of men killed includes those who, according to the muster rolls, died between 17 June and 25 June.

The 23rd Regiment's muster rolls record 12 corporals, drummers and privates killed, but Gage's report lists 11. Gage's report says a sergeant of the 63rd Regiment was killed, but the muster rolls do not indicate one.

Most of the wounded officers and men recovered in the following months, but muster rolls record deaths of a few grenadiers and light infantrymen in each regiment during July and August. Captain Harris was attended by a surgeon who cut open his skull to relieve pressure. 'Before the callous was formed,' he wrote, 'they indulged me with the gratification of a singular curiosity – fixing looking-glasses so as to give me a sight of my own brain.' He later quipped, 'They still every day peep at my brain, which, all things considered, is not an unlucky circumstance, as it may convince you and the rest of the world that I have such a thing.'[60] Lieutenant Colonel Abercrombie was not so lucky. A bullet from the light infantry went through the middle of his right thigh, inflicting what Major General William Howe called 'only a flesh wound.'[61] But the shot that came from behind had hit Abercrombie 'with

59 Francis Bickley (ed.), *Report on the Manuscripts of the late Reginald Rawdon Hastings, Esq.* (London: Historical Manuscripts Commission, 1934), p.155, Francis, Lord Rawdon, to his uncle, 20 June 1775.

60 Wilkin, *Some British Soldiers*, p.178.

61 John Fortescue (ed.), *Correspondence of King George III,* (New York: McMillan & Co., 1927), Vol.3, p.223, William Howe to King George III, 24 June 1775.

such power from its proximity, as to force a pen case which he had in his side pocket, along with it into his thigh, from the lodgment of the ball it could readily be extracted – but part of the pen case being got so far it baffled the art of the surgeons.'[62] Complicating matter was that, according to Howe, he was 'said to have been in a very bad habit of body.'[63] Three days after the battle Abercrombie wrote that 'all the Doctors agree that wound Looks well but it has not Begun to desist yet,' but he was nonetheless in such a state of convalescence that he dictated the letter to his servant. In spite of the good prognosis, the wound proved fatal; he died on 22 June.[64]

A few wounded soldiers who recovered and served well into the next decade mentioned wounds from Bunker Hill when they were discharged. The 4th Regiment's grenadier Samuel Lewis, a butcher from Dunster, Somerset, who had joined the army in 1763 at the age of 21, was wounded in the ankle. Kilkenny native Sergeant Alexander McLean of the 38th's grenadiers, who had joined the army in 1765 at the age of 23, was wounded in the left arm. And Matthew Haymer of the 23rd's grenadiers, wounded twice on 19 April, was wounded yet again, this time in the right shoulder.[65]

* * *

Having driven the rebels off the peninsula and secured their objective, Bunker Hill, the soldiers immediately began fortifying their hard-won position. They had been outnumbered to begin with; now, having sustained casualties amounting to half the attacking force and about 15 percent of the total strength of the Boston garrison, taking a strong defensive stance was crucial. After the day's great exertion, the troops spent the first night on the open ground, those who had not thrown off their blankets during the battle having some scant shelter. The grenadier battalion, depleted though it was, took post in the most advanced entrenchment for the first 24 hours, relieved the next day by the light infantry battalion, and then by other regiments in turn. One third of each corps' strength was at labour every four hours, the men keeping their arms near at hand in case of alarm, Major General Howe giving orders that he 'expects the Men will perform the labour require'd of them with Chearfulness and Alacrity.'[66]

Major Edward Mitchell of the 5th Regiment took command of the grenadier battalion on 19 June, replacing the mortally wounded Abercrombie. Although wounded men from the flank battalions were detached from their regiments for operational purposes, their regiments were responsible for providing them with clean clothing and other needs while they recovered in army hospitals. Twenty-four grenadiers are known to have died during the two months following the battle, as well as 17 light infantrymen. A few others in each battalion

62 *Edinburgh Advertiser*, 18 August 1775.

63 Fortescue (ed.), *Correspondence of King George III,* Vol.3, p.223, Howe to King George III, 24 June 1775.

64 CKS: U1350 080/3: Abercrombie to Amherst, 20 June 1775; TNA: WO 12: muster rolls, 22nd Regiment.

65 TNA: WO 121/4/273, WO 121/26/190 and WO 121/8/92: discharges of Samuel Lewis; Alexander McLean, and Matthew Haymer respectively.

66 Stevens (ed.), *General Sir William Howe's Orderly Book*, pp.3–4.

were transferred back into their regiments during the same period. The muster rolls that record these deaths and transfers do not give the reasons, but presumably most were due to wounds. Replacing them meant transferring men from the regiments' battalion companies. On 1 August regiments were ordered to put their flank companies 'on an equality, as to numbers, with the Battalion Companies as soon as possible.' Because the strength of each regiment was below the full complement, each flank company ended up with 28 to 30 soldiers rather than the nominal 36.[67]

The flank companies of the 10 regiments that participated in the fighting on 19 April and again on 17 June had suffered significantly. Getting them ready to fight again would take some time, but the war's fortunes provided that time – no further offensive operations were undertaken out of Boston. The majority of the wounded men recovered and were back in the ranks by the end of the year. The flank companies of the 4th, 10th and 23rd Regiments, for example, had each mustered their full complement of five non-commissioned officers and 36 private soldiers at the beginning of 1775. The 4th Regiment's two companies lost six men killed on 19 April, and another 14 killed and 35 wounded on 17 June. At the end of the year, 41 of those private soldiers were still in the two companies, 19 grenadiers and 22 light infantrymen (including three who had advanced to non-commissioned ranks). The 10th Regiment's two companies lost just two on 19 April, and seven killed and 46 wounded on 17 June; at the end of the year 38 of the private soldiers remained. For the 23rd Regiment, three were lost on 19 April, and another 14 killed and 42 wounded on 17 June; but by the end of the year, a full 43 were still in the ranks. For each regiment, some men were discharged or transferred to the battalion companies after 17 June, but most soldiers healed well enough to return to the ranks of the flank companies. The numbers were similar in other regiments; at the end of 1775, the flank companies of all of the regiments involved in the year's battles still had, typically, at least one and usually two of the same officers, three or four of the same non-commissioned officers, and 20 (plus or minus two or three) of the same private soldiers that they'd had at the beginning of the year.[68]

After the battle on 17 June, the flank battalions were strengthened by the addition of companies from seven newly-arrived regiments; the 35th, 49th and 63rd Regiments (which had arrived just before the battle), and the 22nd, 40th, 44th and 45th Regiments at the end of June. All of these new companies except those of the 63rd initially remained in Boston, the grenadiers under the command of Major Mitchell and the light infantry under Major Thomas Musgrave of the 64th Regiment, while Lieutenant Colonel James Agnew of the 44th took command of the grenadier battalion on Charlestown Neck.[69] The days and weeks passed in a rigorous duty rotation, half the time as guards – often posted within sniping distance of rebel lines – and half at hard labour, digging, building, hauling, toiling to construct a large redoubt with its associated outworks, trenches, platforms and gun emplacements, strong enough to stop any assault the rebels might undertake.

With manpower limited and no imminent offensive operations, the flank battalion soldiers were not exempt from this labour. 'Youl please excuse this Scrawl,' wrote Lieutenant

67 Stevens (ed.), *General Sir William Howe's Orderly Book*, pp.11, 59; TNA: Wo 12, muster rolls for the several regiments. No rolls are known to exist for the 5th Regiment or the Marines during this period, so the casualties from their companies are not known.

68 TNA: WO 12: muster rolls of the several regiments.

69 TNA: WO 36/1: general orders, 16 and 17 June, 17 July 1775.

William Braco Gordon of the 52nd Regiment in a letter home on 7 July, 'when a man has no more Baggage then what he can conveniently carry on his back many conveniencys are not to be expected which is really my situation at present. Our duty is very fatiguing, every second day on Guard and always sleep in our Cloaths which I have done every night since the day before the action.'[70] 'Remember poor me three thousand miles off, "my lodging on the cold ground,"' wrote 4th Regiment light infantry Lieutenant William Glanville Evelyn on 7 October, using the title of a popular song to describe his situation. 'Now and then -ducking- at the whistling of a twenty-four pounder,' he continued, 'one of which came a few days ago into our camp, went through one of our tents, and fairly took the crown out of one of the King's Own Grenadier's hats. His head was not in it. Now, Sir, there's nothing reconciles being shot at to one, so much as being paid for it.'[71]

In December three more regiments arrived in Boston from Great Britain, the 17th, 27th and 55th, further bolstering the flank battalions. The regiments that arrived in June had been inspected the previous summer, and their inspection returns enumerate the nationalities, ages and length of service of men in each company. From the time of inspection in the summer 1774 to the time of embarkation in spring 1775, changes occurred – men were transferred in and out of the flank companies – so that the inspection return data is not fully representative of the companies as they were in Boston. In most regiments the turnover was only a few men, for example, the 44th Regiment's grenadiers lost four men, and added four new ones, from January through May 1775; their light infantry lost and replaced five. The three regiments that arrived in Boston at the end of 1775 had been inspected that summer and had little turnover in their flank companies before embarking, so their inspection data more accurately reflects the state of the companies in Boston.[72]

Table 2.2: Age distribution of 10 grenadier companies, summer 1774 (summer 1775 for 17th, 27th and 55th Regiments)

Years	17th	22nd	27th	35th	40th	44th	45th	49th	55th	63rd
50								1		
45	2	1	1	1	1	1				
40	1	1	3	1	4	3		4	2	
35	4	5	5	2	6	4	3	2	3	9
30	5	6	7	7	4	6	7	7	5	10
25	14	11	13	23	11	11	13	18	16	19
20	18	18	13	6	14	19	20	10	14	2
18		2	2	2	5		1		3	2

Data from TNA: WO 27: inspection returns.

70 NRS: GD 225/1044, William Braco Gordon to unknown, 7 July 1775. Gordon wrote that he was with the light infantry, but the regiment's muster rolls list him with the grenadier company.

71 G.D. Scull (ed.), *Memoir and Letters of Captain W. Glanville Evelyn, of the 4th Regiment, ('King's Own,') from North America, 1774–1776*, (Oxford: Parker & Co., 1879), p.70.

72 TNA: WO 27/32 and WO 27/35: inspection returns of the several regiments.

Table 2.3: Age distribution of 10 light infantry companies, summer 1774 (summer 1775 for 17th, 27th and 55th Regiments)

Years	17th	22nd	27th	35th	40th	44th	45th	49th	55th	63rd
45									1	
40		1			1	4			1	
35	2	1	2		1	4		3	7	4
30	9	11	2	1		3	6	1	11	3
25	19	22	24	25	15	17	19	19	13	25
20	18	7	12	13	25	13	16	14	10	6
18	1		2	3			1	1		2

Data from TNA: WO 27: inspection returns.

Table 2.4: Service of men in 10 grenadier companies, summer 1774 (summer 1775 for 17th, 27th and 55th Regiments)

Years	17th	22nd	27th	35th	40th	44th	45th	49th	55th	63rd
25					1	2				
20	5	2	9	4	9	2	3	1	3	1
15	3	3	1		8	2	2	7	1	7
10		3	5	3	2		1	3	8	4
8	1	7	2	8	1	7	5	3	3	1
7	15	8	9	9	1	2	9	7	9	10
6	9	4	5	4	4	3	10	4		5
5	1	5	4	4	3	8	8	2	11	
4	3	3		2	6	11	3	3	1	5
3	2	4	4	3	1	2	2		3	6
2	1	3	2	4	5	4		2	2	2
1	4	1	3	1	3	1	1	4	2	2

Data from TNA: WO 27: inspection returns.

Table 2.5: Service of men in 10 light infantry companies, summer 1774 (summer 1775 for 17th, 27th and 55th Regiments)

Years	17th	22nd	27th	35th	40th	44th	45th	49th	55th	63rd
25						1				
20	2	2	2		3	6			4	
15	1	1			1		4	5	1	5
10	1			3			1	1	12	1
8	15	13	2	18		2		3	5	5
7	9		9	4	3	2	7	4	6	4
6	2	7	9	2	4	3	12	1	7	3
5	2	7	8	2	5	7	5		3	3
4	4	3	4	5	15	3	6	17	1	11

Years	17th	22nd	27th	35th	40th	44th	45th	49th	55th	63rd
3	1	7	2	3	3	12		1	3	4
2	1	1	4	4	3	2	3	1	1	1
1	3	1	2	1	5	3	4	5		3

Data from TNA: WO 27: inspection returns.

Table 2.6: Nationality of men in 10 grenadier companies, summer 1774 (summer 1775 for 17th, 27th and 55th Regiments)

	17th	22nd	27th	35th	40th	44th	45th	49th	55th	63rd
English	32	27	21	33	18	17	28	18	16	34
Scottish	3	10	3	3	12	12	16	17	23	2
Irish	9	6	20	5	14	13		11	4	6
Foreign		1		1		2				

Figures for English include the Welsh.
Data from TNA: WO 27: inspection returns.

Table 2.7: Nationality of men in 10 light infantry companies, summer 1774 (summer 1775 for 17th, 27th and 55th Regiments)

	17th	22nd	27th	35th	40th	44th	45th	49th	55th	63rd
English	30	23	25	35	16	17	14	16	13	24
Scottish	7	14		5	19	19	20	8	23	9
Irish	4	5	17	2	7	4	8	13	7	5
Foreign						1		1		2

Figures for English include the Welsh.
Data from TNA: WO 27: inspection returns.

In November, word reached Boston that the War Office had authorized an increase in strength for regiments on service in America. One sergeant, one drummer and 18 private soldiers were added to each company, resulting in a nominal strength of three sergeants, three corporals, two drummers and 54 privates. It would be nearly a year before enough recruits arrived in America for regiments to reach these numbers; for the time being, flank companies were barely able to attain the peacetime strength of 36 private men. The 18th and 59th Regiments were sent back to Britain, but before departing their fit men were drafted – transferred – into other regiments; for the most part, flank company soldiers from these two regiments went into flank companies of others. For example, the 5th Regiment's grenadiers brought on four men from the 59th's grenadier company, and the 5th's light infantry added five from the 59th's light infantry; each regiment received drafts in proportion to their own needs, so numbers to each regiment differed.

Throughout the second half of 1775 and the first months of 1776 duty was rigorous with every part of Boston being close to a front line, fuel and provisions replenishable only by sea. Soldiers succumbed to sickness and skulking enemies, a few skirmishes occurred, but there was no major fighting in Massachusetts after 17 June. Boston was evacuated on 17 March 1776 in a hasty embarkation covered by the flank battalions that were the last to leave. The army sailed to Halifax, Nova Scotia, to regroup, await reinforcements, and prepare for a new campaign. After an inauspicious first year of war, the flank companies would soon be transformed into an offensive juggernaut that would spearhead a stunning series of British victories.

3

Attacking the Proper Way: New York and New Jersey, 1776–1777

When Howe's army abandoned Boston, another British army was at sea, making its way from Ireland towards the North Carolina coast. The intention was to end the rebellion in the southern colonies, particularly North and South Carolina, where loyalist sentiment was believed to be strong. Seven British regiments, the 15th, 28th, 33rd, 37th, 46th, 54th and 57th, departed Ireland early in 1776. Typical of British regiments bound for America early in the war, they were anxious to put down the rebellion; Captain James Murray of the 57th Regiment wrote as he was preparing for departure, 'We are all in great spirits here, as to myself being appointed to the Light Infantry I have got a double barrel fusee and propose shooting 7 Americans a week exclusive of women and children.'[1]

Each of the regiments had been inspected in the early summer of 1775. Data from these returns gives a rough idea of the age, experience and nationality of the soldiers in each regiment's flank companies, but, as with the regiments sent to Boston, there were changes between the inspections and embarkation half a year later. Besides the usual transfers of men into and out of the flank companies, each regiment took on more soldiers to reach the peacetime full strength of 36 private soldiers – they had already added a third sergeant to meet wartime strength, but, like regiments already in America, would require much longer to approach the wartime strength of two drummers and 54 privates. To reach 36 private men per company, new soldiers included some recruits but also a substantial number of drafts – experienced men transferred from regiments remaining in Great Britain and Ireland.

The changes were significant. After the 1775 inspection the grenadier company of the 28th Regiment, for example, discharged one man, sent three to the regiment's battalion companies, lost two to death and another to desertion; they took in five men from the battalion, five recruits, and five men from the 1st and 2nd Regiments of Horse, men who left their higher-paying cavalry regiments to serve overseas in the infantry. This difference of 22 men between the inspection and embarkation certainly changed the demographics of the company. Belfast native John Galispie, a wheelwright before he joined the 2nd Horse in 1770 at the age of 19, was one of at least 11 Irishmen who joined the 28th's grenadiers in August and September

1 Eric Robson (ed.), *Letters from America, 1773 to 1780*, (New York: Barnes & Noble, 1950), p.29.

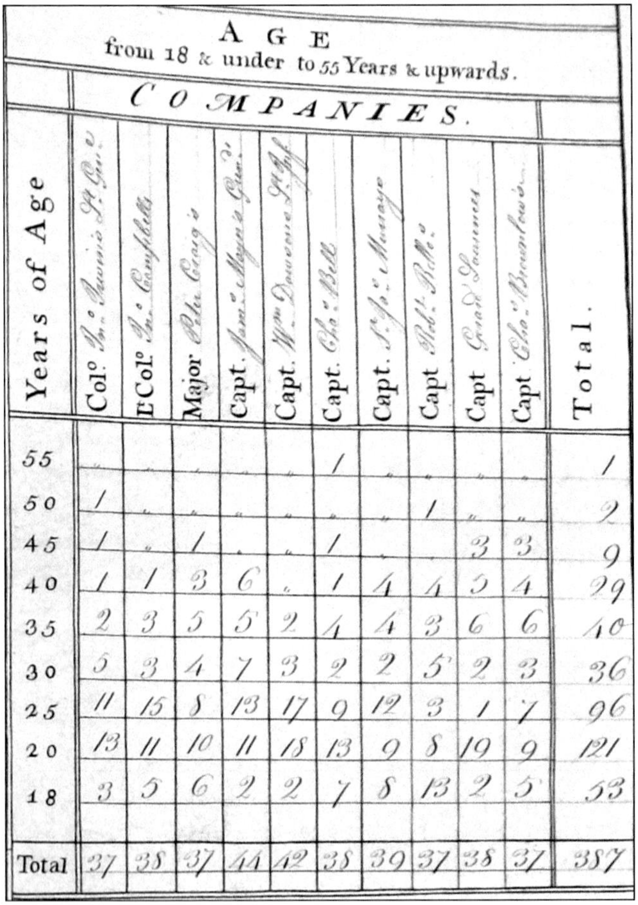

AGE from 18 & under to 55 Years & upwards.

Years of Age	Col°	Lt Col°	Major	Capt.	Capt.	Capt.	Capt.	Capt	Capt	Capt	Total.
	COMPANIES.										
55						1					1
50	1							1			2
45	1		1			1			3	3	9
40	1	1	3	6		1	4	4	5	4	29
35	2	3	5	5	2	4	4	3	6	6	40
30	5	3	4	7	3	2	2	5	2	3	36
25	11	15	8	13	17	9	12	3	1	7	96
20	13	11	10	11	18	13	9	8	19	9	121
18	3	5	6	2	2	7	8	13	2	5	53
Total	37	38	37	44	42	38	39	37	38	37	387

Age distribution in the 57th Regiment before they embarked for America. Detail from Inspection Return, 57th Regiment of Foot, WO 27/35. (The National Archives)

1775, a company that had no Irish soldiers when inspected (Table 3.5).[2] This means that the inspection return data is only a vague approximation of the actual composition of these regiments when they arrived in America.

Lieutenant General Sir Henry Clinton sailed from Boston to meet and take command of this force, taking with him the light infantry companies of the 4th and 44th Regiments. When he met the fleet from Britain off the Carolina coast, he learned that it had been scattered by storms; some transports were missing, among them the *Argo* carrying three companies of the 46th Regiment, including the grenadiers. The light infantry company of the 33rd Regiment fared much better, getting a taste of battle when their transport fell in with an enemy cargo vessel, gave chase, and after an exchange of fire took it as a prize.[3]

A series of events led Clinton, after several inconsequential landings and re-embarkations, to take this army to Charleston, South Carolina, where he hoped to secure the seaward approach to the city by capturing the incomplete Fort Moultrie on Sullivan's Island.[4] It was mid-June when British troops landed on an adjacent island named Long Island, little more than a sandbar. On 23 June, anticipating a coordinated attack on the fort by the army and navy, Clinton gave orders that set the tone not only for this assault, but for many to come:

2 TNA: WO 27/32: inspection return 28th Regiment; WO 12: muster rolls of the several regiments; WO 121/13/276, discharge of John Galispie.

3 *Edinburgh Advertiser*, 30 July 1776.

4 William B. Willcox (ed.), *The American Rebellion; Sir Henry Clinton's Narrative of His Campaigns, 1775–1782* (New Haven, CT: Yale University Press, 1954), p.29.

Table 3.1: Age distribution of seven grenadier companies, summer 1775

Years	15th	28th	33rd	37th	46th	54th	57th
45						3	
40	3	2	2	2	2	14	6
35	2	7	8	3	3	4	5
30	7	6	10	8	6	11	7
25	15	12	11	14	16	7	13
20	17	15	10	15	15	1	11
18		2	3	2	2		2
Under 18						1	

Data from TNA: WO 27: inspection returns.

Table 3.2: Age distribution of seven light infantry companies, summer 1775

Years	15th	28th	33rd	37th	46th	54th	57th
35	1	4	2	1		7	2
30	1	7	3	3	4	14	3
25	20	19	17	11	20	14	17
20	16	10	18	26	16	1	18
18	3	2	1	1	2		2

Data from TNA: WO 27: inspection returns.

Table 3.3: Service of men in seven grenadier companies, summer 1775

Years	15th	28th	33rd	37th	46th	54th	57th
25						3	
20	4	3	3		4	15	3
15	2	2	9	11	4	2	8
10	2	7		5	1	5	1
8	1	3	7	3	2		1
7		5		2	5		6
6	15	8	11		8	3	5
5	5	5	5	7	10	8	7
4	1	4		6	5		3
3	6	6	3	7	1		2
2	7			3	3		6
1	1	1	6		7	5	2

Data from TNA: WO 27: inspection returns.

Table 3.4: Service of men in seven light infantry companies, summer 1775

Years	15th	28th	33rd	37th	46th	54th	57th
20	1	4		2	1	5	2
15	1	4	4	4		6	
10	1		2	1		1	
8		1	3	1	10	1	4
7		6	2	1	7	1	5
6	6	7	3	21	9	9	10
5	8	9	2	11	6	10	13
4	10	2	7	9	3		4
3	10	9	12	9	2		3
2	1		4	2	4		1
1	3		2			3	

Data from TNA: WO 27: inspection returns.

Table 3.5: Nationality of men in seven grenadier companies, summer 1775

	15th	28th	33rd	37th	46th	54th	57th
English	18	42	40	32	33	31	23
Scottish	10	1		7		6	6
Irish	16		4	5	10	3	15
Foreign		1			1	1	

Figures for English include the Welsh.
Data from TNA: WO 27: inspection returns.

Table 3.6: Nationality of men in seven light infantry companies, summer 1775

	15th	28th	33rd	37th	46th	54th	57th
English	28	39	34	32	21	26	18
Scottish	4			5	3	6	15
Irish	9	3	7	5	18	4	9
Foreign							

Figures for English include the Welsh.
Data from TNA: WO 27: inspection returns.

> The Soldier will now Consider that he is Opposed by an Undisciplined Rabble, if he will make use of the Advantages which military discipline have given him, if he will be silent, steady & observant of the Orders of his Officer there cannot be a Doubt of Victory. The Officers Commanding Regiments will never Order their men to Fire, when they can use the Bayonet.[5]

5 WLC: 6912/14-32: Eyre Coote Orderly Book, general orders 23 June 1776.

The grenadiers and light infantry prepared to lead an attack on the rear of the fort while the navy bombarded it from the sea. The plan was to wade from one island to the other, but the channel between them proved too deep to ford. On 28 June, when the navy commenced their attack, it became clear that too few boats were available to ferry enough troops across to secure a landing. The soldiers watched from their sandy island as the naval bombardment failed to reduce the fort, leaving several ships damaged and one lost.[6] The army remained encamped on their sandbar until late July, when they finally re-boarded their transports and sailed for New York to join the army on Staten Island.

SERVICE. from 1 Year & under to 35 & upwards.											
Years	Companies as above.										Total
35	„	„	„	„	„	„	„	„	„	„	„
30	1	„	„	„	„	1	„	„	„	„	2
25	„	„	„	„	„	„	„	„	„	„	„
20	3	2	„	3	2	2	„	„	1	8	21
15	1	3	11	8	„	5	7	9	10	2	56
10	„	1	„	1	„	1	1	3	2	„	9
8	„	2	„	1	4	1	„	„	„	1	9
7	4	5	1	6	5	„	3	3	2	„	29
6	6	6	3	5	10	3	4	2	4	3	46
5	7	4	3	7	13	3	4	4	2	4	51
4	2	3	6	3	4	7	6	3	3	6	43
3	3	3	1	2	3	3	3	2	6	5	31
2	3	5	1	6	1	4	1	4	1	2	28
1	7	4	11	2	„	8	10	7	7	6	62
Total	37	35	37	44	42	38	39	37	38	37	387

Length of service in each of the 57th Regiment's 10 companies before they embarked for America. The grenadier company is fourth from the left; the light infantry is fifth from the left. Detail from Inspection Return, 57th Regiment of Foot, WO 27/35. (The National Archives)

* * *

Meanwhile, transports from Boston flowed into Halifax harbour at the beginning of April 1776. Accommodating large numbers in a small town consumed the first week, finding and fitting up buildings for barracks, making arrangements for cutting and distributing firewood, sorting out where and how provisions would be distributed, and the myriad tasks necessary for supporting over 10,000 troops, over 2,000 military wives and children, and a few thousand civilians who had fled with the army. By the second week, it was time to begin the serious business of preparing for a new campaign.

On 13 April eight light infantry companies – the 17th, 22nd, 27th, 35th, 40th, 45th, 49th and 64th – exercised together under Major Thomas Musgrave on Citadel Hill overlooking the town. On 17 April the light companies of the 5th, 10th, 23rd, 38th, 43rd, 52nd, 55th and 63rd did the same, again under Musgrave, having been delayed for two days by weather.

6 For a full account of the battle see Rick Atkinson, *The British are Coming: the War for America, Lexington to Princeton, 1775–1777* (New York: Henry Holt and Company, 2019), chapter 14.

Musgrave then trained the grenadier companies, those of the 4th, 10th, 17th, 23rd, 35th, 40th, 44th, 49th, 55th, 64th and 65th on 18 April, and those of the 5th, 22nd, 27th, 43rd, 45th, 52nd, 63rd and two battalions of Marines on the 20th. On 21 April, the first group of eight light infantry companies exercised again, and this time a brigade consisting of the battalion companies of the 22nd, 43rd and 63rd exercised at the same time under Lieutenant General Hugh, Earl Percy. The 27th, 55th and 64th Regiments, with the remainder of the light infantry companies, followed suit on 27 April. Percy had been training brigades of three battalions at a time during the preceding days when the flank companies were not training; the orders for 21 April do not state whether the light infantry and the brigade worked together or separately on that day.[7]

Nothing was recorded of the specific training given to the flank companies. They may have learned the exercise taught by Howe at Sarum in 1774 (Appendix V), or a somewhat simplified version published in 1778 (Appendix VI). The fundamentals of both exercises are the same: companies formed in two ranks, that is, two rows of men one behind the other. Instead of standing shoulder-to-shoulder, men stood two feet apart, and they learned to extend that interval to four feet, and to 10 feet. Advancing and retreating in lines while maintaining these intervals was not easy, but flank company soldiers had already mastered close-order work and were chosen for their experience and aptitude for adaptability. They learned to collapse their lines into a column two-men wide by having the men at the centre of the line move forward while those to the left and right fell in behind them; they practiced forming on the left or the right rather than on the centre. Using similar techniques, the line could re-form facing to the left or the right of its previous direction. These manoeuvres were practiced at a marching pace, at a quick march, and at a run. The result was fluid, fast movement effective on uneven and obstructed ground, maintaining the linear or columnar integrity of each company and of larger formations.[8]

On 26 May, General Howe directed the grenadiers and regiments to form three deep instead of two deep, with intervals of 18 inches between the files.[9] The reason for the change was not stated, nor its impact on the efficient movements that had presumably already been taught using two-ranks formations; it is possible that three ranks had been used during the training that commenced in April, and was therefore prescribed in general orders at the end of May. Regardless, the three-rank formation would not remain in use for long.

On 11 May Howe ordered regiments to transfer men to bring their grenadier and light infantry companies up to full peacetime strength of 36 private soldiers.[10] On the 17th, for reasons not stated, the two grenadier companies of the Marines were increased in size to 45 'rank and file,' meaning corporals and private soldiers, per company.[11]

7 Stevens (ed.), *General Sir William Howe's Orderly Book*, pp.251–254, 256.

8 NAM: 6807-157-6: 'Discipline established by Major General Howe for Light Infantry in Battalion'; Houlding, *Fit for Service*, pp.336–337; John Williamson, *The Elements of Military Arrangement, comprehending the Tactick, Exercise, Manoevres, and Discipline of the British Infantry* (London: printed for the author, 1781), pp.111–119.

9 Stevens (ed.), *General Sir William Howe's Orderly Book*, p.294.

10 Stevens (ed.), *General Sir William Howe's Orderly Book*, p.269. The order reads '39,' including corporals in the number.

11 Stevens (ed.), *General Sir William Howe's Orderly Book*, p.277.

On 14 May, Howe created new flank battalions. The 1st and 2nd Battalions of Grenadiers were each composed of 10 companies, those from the older 10 regiments forming the first battalion, and those from the younger eight regiments, and the two Marines battalions, forming the second battalion.[12] The light infantry battalions were similar, but with nine companies each, containing no light infantry from the Marines.

1st Battalion of Grenadiers
Lt. Col. William Meadows, 55th Regiment; Maj. Edward Mitchel, 5th Regiment
5th, 17th, 23rd, 35th, 40th, 38th, 27th, 22nd, 10th, 4th

2nd Battalion of Grenadiers
Lt. Col. Henry Monckton, 45th Regiment; Maj. Charles Stuart, 43rd Regiment
44th, 49th, 55th, 64th, 2nd Marines, 1st Marines, 63rd, 52nd, 45th, 43rd

1st Battalion of Light Infantry
Maj. Thomas Musgrave, 64th Regiment; Maj. Thomas Dundas, 63rd Regiment
5th, 17th, 23rd, 35th, 38th, 27th, 22nd, 10th, 4th

2nd Battalion of Light Infantry
Maj. John Maitland, Marines; Maj. Turner Straubenzee, 17th Regiment
43rd, 45th, 52nd, 63rd, 64th, 55th, 49th, 44th, 40th

The newly-formed light infantry battalions paraded at 9:00 a.m. on 15 May, and the grenadier battalions on the 17th. Over the next several days staff officers were appointed to these battalions so that they had staffs similar to regiments: for the grenadiers, George Fowler, the quartermaster of the 38th Regiment, became adjutant to the 1st Battalion and Lieutenant John Vevers of the Marines became adjutant to the 2nd Battalion; Sergeant Peter Williamson of the 4th Regiment's grenadier company was appointed quartermaster to the 1st Battalion and Sergeant James Richardson of the 45th's grenadiers quartermaster to the 2nd.[13] To perform medical services which, in a regular regiment, were handled by a surgeon and surgeon's mate, the army's general hospital contributed a hospital mate to each battalion: Thomas Walker and John McCullough to the 1st and 2nd Battalions of Grenadiers, and John Handyside and James Whiteman to the 1st and 2nd Battalions of Light Infantry.[14] Each infantry brigade had a staff officer called the extra major of brigade to assist the brigadier in command; the two pairs of flank battalions, although not designated as brigades, were also given extra majors of brigade, Captain John Lewis of the 64th Regiment for the light infantry and Captain Thomas Moncrieffe of the 59th for the grenadiers.[15] The transport *Argo*, with the grenadiers and two other companies of the 46th Regiment, came into Halifax on 18 May; she had been separated from the fleet bound to the Carolinas and was blown to Antigua,

12 Stevens (ed.), *General Sir William Howe's Orderly Book*, pp.272–273.
13 Stevens (ed.), *General Sir William Howe's Orderly Book*, pp.279, 282.
14 Stevens (ed.), *General Sir William Howe's Orderly Book*, p.291.
15 Stevens (ed.), *General Sir William Howe's Orderly Book*, pp.278, 288.

from which she then sailed to Halifax.[16] Howe did not incorporate the 46th's grenadiers into a battalion.

Orders on 24 May directed that gun flints be distributed to the army, essential for creating the spark that ignited the priming charge in a flintlock musket. The ordnance office provided enough for each man to receive two flints; in addition, the deputy quartermaster general provided each regiment with another flint per battalion man, and two for each grenadier and light infantryman, 'which they are desired to take the greatest care of as they are of a better sort.'[17] The extra flint for each flank company soldier foretold the critical role they would play in the upcoming campaign.

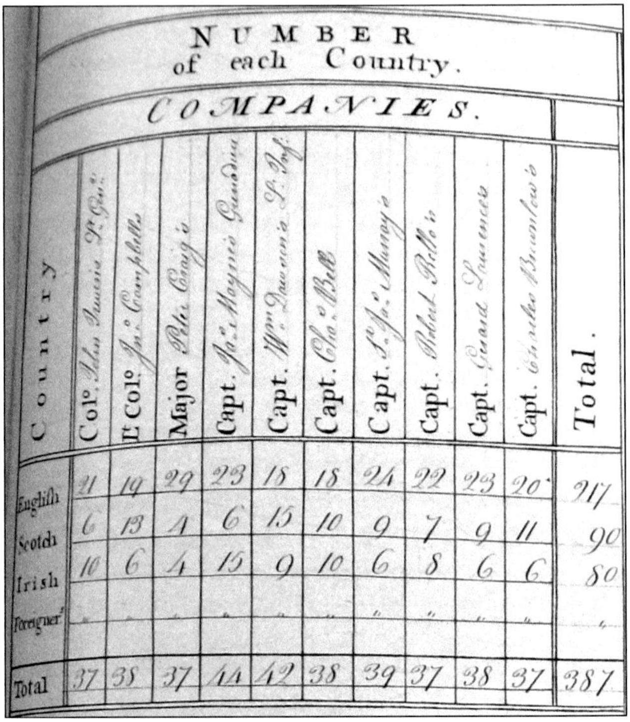

NUMBER of each Country.

Country	COMPANIES.										Total.
	Colo.	Lt Colo.	Major	Capt.	Capt.	Capt.	Capt.	Capt.	Capt.	Capt.	
English	21	19	29	23	18	18	24	22	23	20	217
Scotch	6	13	4	6	15	10	9	7	9	11	90
Irish	10	6	4	15	9	10	6	8	6	6	80
Foreigners	-	-	-	-	-	-	-	-	-	-	-
Total	37	38	37	44	42	38	39	37	38	37	387

Nationalities in the 57th Regiment before they embarked for America. Detail from Inspection Return, 57th Regiment of Foot, WO 27/35. (The National Archives)

The musket used by the army was called a land pattern firelock, the latter term referring to the flintlock ignition. Popular 1770s and 1780s vernacular used phrases such as 'take Brown Bess on your shoulders' and 'hug brown Bess' to describe enlisting in the army, usage which in later decades evolved into naming these firelocks Brown Bess.[18] The design of these weapons evolved in various ways throughout the eighteenth century, and infantry regiments usually received new arms every 10 years or so. Some regiments in American in 1776 were armed with the pattern of musket first used in 1756, with barrels 46 inches long, while others had a newer model first issued in 1769 with a 42-inch barrel. Light infantry companies; having been created and equipped in 1771, all had the shorter 1769-pattern guns.[19] With companies from various regiments, the grenadier

16 William James Morgan et. al. (eds), *Naval Documents of the American Revolution* (Washington, DC: Government Printing Office, 1964–2019), Vol.5, p.149.

17 Stevens (ed.), *General Sir William Howe's Orderly Book*, p.291. The 59th Regiment had been drafted and returned to Great Britain at the end of 1775, but Moncrief, already in a staff position, remained in America.

18 *Connecticut Courant*, 9 April 1771 (take Brown Bess on your shoulders); Partridge (ed.), *A Classical Dictionary of the Vulgar Tongue*, p.54; Samuel Collings, artist, *The Recruiting Serjeant – or, Brown Bess Sooner Than Bigg Belly'd Betty* (1786), Lewis Walpole Library.

19 Don N. Hagist and Erik Goldstein, 'Short Land Muskets for the British Light Infantry in America,' *Man at Arms* (December 2009), pp.18–25.

battalions had a mix of 1756 and 1769 pattern guns, a non-uniformity that Howe corrected, even though both used the same calibre ammunition. He ordered grenadier companies armed with shorter guns to turn them in to the ordnance store in exchange for longer ones, of which the army apparently had a sufficient supply.[20]

When transport ships were assigned for the next voyage in orders on 18 May, the newly-created flank battalions travelled together, the 1st Battalion of Light Infantry divided among three vessels, *James & William*, *Grand Duke of Russia* and *William*; the 2nd Battalion on *Ranger*, *Betty Stevenson* and *Betty Higgins*; the 1st Battalion of Grenadiers on *Symmetry*, *Friendship* and *Whitby*; and the 2nd Battalion on *Ocean*, *Hartfield* and *Saville*. Embarkation was still weeks away, and preparations continued, including stowing 50 fascines – tightly-bound bundles of saplings six feet long – on each transport 'upon their Quarters,' useful to make each vessel more defensible should it stray from the fleet and to build fortifications immediately after the army landed.[21]

The army prepared to sail on 5 June, but delays in final preparations such as getting provisions on board transports delayed departure until 9 June.[22] As they left port and headed southwest, transports from Great Britain carrying companies of the 42nd and 71st Regiments of Foot joined the fleet, a few at a time. These were highland regiments, the 42nd a long-standing corps and the 71st newly-raised for the war in America. The structure of these regiments was different from the other infantry regiments in General Howe's army. The 42nd had 10 companies, including one of grenadiers and one of light infantry, but each company had an additional lieutenant for a total of four officers each, five sergeants and corporals rather than three of each, bagpipers instead of fifers, and 100 private soldiers. The 71st used the same structure, but consisted of two battalions, that is, 20 companies including two each of grenadiers and light infantry. Misfortune met them at sea. Scattered by storms, several transports were captured by rebel privateers, leaving both regiments under strength.[23] General Howe would determine their place in the army later.

* * *

It took the fleet 20 days to reach the waters off Sandy Hook, the spit of land off the coast of New Jersey that formed the western shore of the entrance to New York harbour. A few ships got separated during the voyage, including a light infantry transport, but overall the passage was uneventful.[24] Howe gave orders on 29 June to prepare for landing on Staten Island, reminding the troops that they came to protect the inhabitants who were 'known to be well affected to Government' and had 'suffered great depredations from the Rebels.' He called on the 'superior discipline and humanity of the troops' to treat people and property well, and

20 Anon. (ed.), 'British Army Orders,' *Collections of the New York Historical Society for the year 1883* (New York: New York Historical Society, 1884), pp.374–375, general orders, 29 and 30 May 1776.

21 Stevens (ed.), *General Sir William Howe's Orderly Book*, p.294.

22 Anon. (ed.), 'Journals of Lieut.-Col. Stephen Kemble,' in *Collections of the New York Historical Society for the year 1883* (New York: New York Historical Society, 1884), p.76; John B. Hattendorff (ed.), *A Redcoat in America: The Diaries of Lieutenant William Bamford, 1757–1765 and 1776* (Warwick: Helion, 2019), p.195.

23 William James Morgan et. al. (eds), *Naval Documents*, Vol.5, pp.619–621.

24 Kemble, 'Journals,' p.78.

gave particular admonishment against plunder.[25] On 2 July flat boats brought ashore the light infantry, then the grenadiers supported by two light 3-pounder field guns with each battalion, and then the first brigade, followed by the remaining brigades in turn. Each man landed with his firelock and bayonet, 60 rounds of ammunition, three days of provisions, a blanket, and a canteen filled with a mixture of rum and water. Knapsacks, tents and other baggage could wait. The canteens, issued out only the day before, were in such short supply that the brigades received only 150 for each battalion, but the flank battalions received one for each man, a testament to the importance of these elite troops. 'The men to be as sparing as possible with their Grogg, as there is a great scarcity of water on the coast and they must expect no supply for many hours,' cautioned General Howe, adding an order to maintain 'the greatest silence' in getting into and out of the boats, as 'it is impossible to preserve good order & security without it.'[26]

The landing was unopposed, and the flank battalions lay 'on their arms that night,' fully clothed in their blankets, on the open ground.[27] The next day the troops went into quarters – barns, outbuildings, whatever vacant structures were available – around the island. The light infantry quartered along the road from the Dutch Church, on the shore opposite Paulus Hook on the north side of the island, to Richmond, the principal town roughly in the middle of the island; the grenadiers quartered in Richmond. For the remainder of July and the first weeks of August, the army regained its land legs and settled in, both securing the island and preparing to move yet again. Officers made arrangements for hiring wagons to transport provisions, the army fixed prices for purchasing local foodstuffs, work parties began erecting fortifications and attending to other military engineering tasks. Occasional shots were exchanged between soldiers on shore and boats in the narrow passage between the island and the New Jersey shore. Soldiers explored the island in their free time, and some got into mischief. Almost immediately after landing, in spite of orders against plunder, men of the 17th Regiment's light infantry company broke open a cellar, 'from whence they took out wine & were drunk when ordered to march.' Twelve of them were tried by general court martial (military courts often tried several men at once, if accused of the same crime), the findings of which were announced on 9 July: nine were acquitted, but John Ryland, Archibald Chisholm and David Henry were found guilty; Ryland was sentenced to receive 300 lashes, and the other two to 500. General Howe, 'in consideration of some circumstances in favor of Archibald Chisholm and David Henry,' remitted their punishments. Ryland, born in Norwich, Norfolk in 1748 had been a peruke (wig) maker before enlisting in 1767. He joined the light infantry company in 1775. After receiving his lashes, he was sent back to the battalion and replaced by another man.[28]

Another trial sat on 1 August to try three cases, the second of which involved two grenadiers from the 46th Regiment. John Riley and James Barry had committed a 'robbery on

25 TNA: WO 36/5: general orders, 26 June 1776.

26 TNA: WO 36/5: general orders, 30 June and 1 July 1776.

27 Charles Stuart, *New Records of the American Revolution: The Letters, Manuscripts and Documents sent by Lieut.-General Sir Charles Stuart to his Father, the Earl of Bute, 1775–79* (London: L. Kashnor, 1927), p.9.

28 TNA: WO 36/5: general orders, 4 and 9 June 1776; WO 121/14/413: discharge of John Ryland; WO 12: muster rolls, 17th Regiment.

the highway' the previous week. The victim recognized the robbers as grenadiers 'from the wings on their coats, and their size.' No evidence was presented against Riley, and he was acquitted, but Barry, 'a very large, big man, not only tall, but well set, a hoarse strong voice' who had served in the 2nd Regiment of Horse for nine years before he 'turn'd out as a Volunteer to come to America' was found guilty and sentenced to 1,000 lashes, a typical punished for this type of crime.[29]

On 1 August, the army from South Carolina under Lieutenant General Clinton dropped anchor off of Staten Island, and its seven regiments landed the next day.[30] With them came Captain Francis, Lord Rawdon, a veteran of Bunker Hill who was now an aide-de-camp to Clinton. He sent a letter home on 5 August that described life on Staten Island in terms intended to entertain the recipient. Included was a passage that has since been widely used, and taken out of context, to assert that British soldiers terrorized inhabitants everywhere they went:

> The fair nymphs of this isle are in wonderful tribulation, as the fresh meat that our men have got here has made them as riotous as satyrs. A girl cannot step into the bushes to pluck a rose without running the most imminent risk being ravished, and they are so little accustomed to these vigorous methods that they don't bear them with the proper resignation, and of consequence we have most entertaining courts-martial every day. A girl of this island made a complaint the other day to Lord Percy of her being deflowered, as she said, by some grenadiers. Lord Percy asked her how she knew them to be grenadiers, as it happened in the dark. 'Oh, good God,' cried she, 'they could be nothing else, and if your Lordship will examine I am sure you will find it so.'[31]

Rawdon had been on Staten Island for only five days when he wrote this, and his statement about courts-martial is not supported by other evidence. Rape was a capital offense, and as such required a general court martial rather than a lower-level regimental trial. Orderly books record outcomes of general courts, and describe only six trials on Staten Island from the time the army landed to the time the letter was written. Regimental trials may have occurred if the charge was assault rather than rape, but Rawdon, on the general's staff, would be unlikely to attend these internal regimental affairs.[32] He probably learned of one of 1 August trials in which a soldier of the 40th Regiment murdered a fellow soldier

29 TNA: WO 71/82: trial of John Riley and James Barry, pp.388–402. Barry was listed as 'sick in hospital' on muster rolls prepared on 29 April 1777, but he appears to have recovered by the time of the next rolls prepared on 3 February 1778. He died on 23 April 1778 of unknown causes. WO 12: muster rolls, 46th Regiment.

30 Kemble, 'Journals,' p.83.

31 Francis Bickley (ed.), *Report on the Manuscripts*, Rawdon to his uncle, 4 August 1776, p.179.

32 No records of regimental trials survive for regiments on Staten Island in July and August. Out of some 1,400 trials in six regiments and detachments in other places between 1773 and 1785, only one trial was for rape. Regimental court martial records for the 3rd, 36th, 67th and 68th Regiments. Parliamentary Archives, Houses of Parliament (PA): HL/PO/JO/10/7/544: Return of Courts Martial held in Ireland, 1 August 1774 – 10 January 1778. Public Archives of Canada (PAC): MG23, K6(2): Punishment Book of the 44th Regiment. Stephen Baule and Don Hagist, 'The Regimental Punishment

(not a grenadier) who had sexually assaulted his wife, but that trial did not involve local residents;[33] the only case that did was the highway robbery case described above. Although there is no evidence of the 'entertaining courts-martial' that Rawdon wrote of, frequent admonishments against plunder in general orders foretold recurring problems that would forever tarnish the reputation of the British Army in America.

The grenadiers and light infantry companies of the seven regiments from South Carolina remained 'under the command of the officers appointed to them by Lieut. General Clinton,' becoming the 3rd Battalion of Light Infantry and the 3rd Battalion of Grenadiers, the latter taking in the grenadier company of the 46th that had arrived with Howe the previous month. Major Francis Marsh of the 43rd Regiment took command of the new grenadier battalion; Major Henry Johnson of the 28th Regiment took the new light infantry battalion, with Lieutenant Ralph Glenstans of the 28th's light infantry company as adjutant and a sergeant of the 28th as quartermaster.[34] On 20 August commanders of regiments with companies in this battalion were directed to 'to make Good the deficient Arms & Accoutrements of their Respective Companies immediately in the best manner they are able,' which may have meant taking muskets and bayonets from battalion companies if there were not enough spares to insure that the light infantry companies were fully equipped with weapons in good order.[35] The 28th's light infantry company, apparently lacking cartridge boxes to supplement their pouches, obtained 'Forty Cartridge Boxes containing 18 rounds ball Cartridges each' from artillery stores.[36]

On 6 August, a battalion of grenadiers was formed of companies from the highland regiments. The grenadier company of the 1st Battalion 71st Regiment had been captured at sea, but a new company was formed of men from the regiment's battalion companies. The three companies of grenadiers from the 42nd and 71st Regiments, equivalent in strength to six companies from other regiments, became the 4th Battalion of Grenadiers, under Major Charles Stuart of the 43rd Regiment (his former post in the 2nd Battalion of Grenadiers left vacant for the time being); Lieutenant John Peebles of the 42nd's grenadiers was appointed adjutant, and Sergeant Alan Stewart of the same company became quartermaster.[37] Both of the 71st's light infantry companies had been captured at sea, but the 42nd's company joined the 1st Battalion of Light Infantry. Brigadier General Alexander Leslie took command of the three light infantry battalions, and the grenadier battalions joined the 33rd and 42nd Regiments to form a 'corps de reserve' commanded by Lieutenant General Charles, Earl Cornwallis.[38] All of the components of the army were together.

Back in May, Howe had ordered the army to form 'three deep' with intervals of 18 inches between files. On 22 July he changed this to two ranks without specifying the interval, but on 1 August he issued the general order that would characterized British infantry tactics, with

Book of the Boston Detachments of the Royal Irish Regiment and 65th Regiment, 1774–75,' *Journal of Army Historical Research* 88 (2010), pp.5–18.

33 TNA: WO 71/82: Trial of William Norrington, pp.377–388.

34 TNA: WO 36/5: general orders, 2, 5 and 7 August. The sergeant's name is illegible and doesn't appear to correspond to any sergeants on the muster rolls. WO12: muster rolls, 28th Regiment.

35 TNA: WO 36/5: general orders, 20 August 1776.

36 TNA: WO 36/5: general orders, 11 August 1776.

37 TNA: WO 36/5: general orders, 5 and 16 August.

38 TNA: WO 36/5: general orders, 6 and 9 August 1776.

few exceptions, for the remainder of the war: 'The Infantry of the Army without exception is ordered upon all occasions to form two Deep, with the Files at 18 Inches Interval till further orders.'[39] Gone were the three-rank, close-order formations described in the standard drill manual, replaced by formations that gave greater freedom of movement to each man and covered a much wider frontage – figuring the width of each soldier to be about two feet, a company of 36 men standing elbow-to-elbow in three ranks was about 24 feet wide, while the same company formed into two ranks at 18-inch intervals spanned about 60 feet, with room for each man to manoeuvre around obstacles as the line advanced.

There was a cost in depth. Lieutenant General Clinton called the open-order, two-deep line a 'loose, flimsy order' which could easily be thrown into confusion by a sudden, strong response from the enemy.[40] At this early stage of the war, though, there was no fear of such a response from a newly-raised rebel army that included some combat veterans from previous wars but which had not operated as a cohesive force in open battle. Howe was confident that the superior resolve of his well-trained men would allow his thin, open formations to rush quickly upon an enemy that lacked the discipline to stand fast in the face of an onslaught.

German regiments, collectively called Hessians even though they came from several German states, landed on Staten Island in August, as did the Brigade of Guards, a 1,000 man force composed of volunteers from each of Britain's three regiments of Foot Guards. The 65th Regiment, which had been in Nova Scotia and Boston since 1767, was sent home, as was the 50th, just arrived in Staten Island after years in the West Indies; their fit men were drafted into other regiments, some into flank companies: three grenadiers from the 65th Regiment went into the 4th's grenadier company, and two others to the 63rd; the 50th Regiment contributed one grenadier to the 4th and 63rd, and four to the 43rd, as well as three light infantrymen to the 4th; and so forth.[41]

General Howe established an order of battle that had the three battalions of light infantry as the vanguard – the 1st Battalion on the right, the 2nd Battalion on the left, and the 3rd Battalion in the centre. In the reserve, the 1st and 3rd Battalions of Grenadiers were on the right, the 2nd and 4th on the left, and the 33rd and 42nd Regiments in the centre. Between these were three lines of infantry brigades, artillery and other corps. Although 'reserve' suggests being held in the rear, when the army moved from unthreatened Staten Island across a narrow stretch of water to rebel-held Long Island, the advance guard and the reserve went first, troops capable of effecting a landing and securing a beachhead for the remainder of the army. They formed at 4:00 a.m. of 22 August and embarked in boats provided by the Royal Navy, as usual carrying only arms, ammunition, blankets, three days provisions, and canteens filled with rum and water. Rather than move directly across the channel, they slipped south and landed at Gravesend Bay, on open land well away from rebel positions. The landing was unopposed. The first wave of troops moved inland to the west while the navy ferried the remainder of the army. Having secured the landing, tents, camp kettles and knapsacks were ferried from Staten Island; officers were ordered to bring as little baggage as possible and to use the same type of tents as the soldiers. An exception was the

39 TNA: WO 36/5: general orders, 1 August 1776.

40 Wilcox (ed.), *The American Rebellion*, p.247.

41 TNA: WO 12: muster rolls for the various regiments; for a comprehensive discussion of recruiting and drafting, and changes in regimental establishment, see Hagist, *Noble Volunteers*, pp.97–112.

light infantry, directed to have no tents at all, 'as they may expect to be in constant motion.'[42] By 25 August over 20,000 British, German and a few companies of loyalist soldiers were in place, facing a rebel army only about half the size but holding fortified high ground. There were some minor skirmishes; the day after the initial landing, John Galispie, who had left the 2nd Regiment of Horse to join the 28th Regiment's grenadier company a year before, was wounded in his left hand near the village of Flatbush.[43]

* * *

The battle that ensued not only validated Howe's decision to form flank battalions and rely on thin, open-order lines, but also set the tone for British campaigning during the next five years. The British forces were encamped in a line facing to the north towards a line of rebel-held hills. At 8:00 p.m. on 26 August, the entire army struck their tents and prepared to march, the soldiers carrying only canteens, camp kettles and provisions in addition to arms and ammunition. General orders cautioned, 'The Men are not to Load till ordered by their respective Commanding Officers & the greatest Silent Attention to be Observ'd by the Troops.' A contingent of cavalry, the light infantry and grenadier battalions marched out on a road to the east, followed by a substantial portion of the army. They marched by half-companies, each regiment also sending out a flanking party consisting eight non-commissioned officers and 32 men.[44] The column turned north to an unguarded pass east of rebel positions, then turned again onto the westbound road, seizing a few rebel sentries in the darkness. Captain James Murray, leading the 57th Regiment's light infantry company, remembered the march being:

> as disagreeable a one as I remember to have passed in the course of my campaigning. I had been up three out of the five preceding nights. We dragged on at the most tedious pace from sunset till 3 o'clock in the morning, halting every minute just long enough to drop asleep, and to be disturbed again in order to proceed twenty yards in the same manner. The night was colder too than I remember to have felt, so that by day break my stock of patience began to run very low.[45]

As dawn broke, the remainder of the British army opened fire and began a slow, calculated advance towards rebel lines in the hills, knowing their opponents had the advantage of high ground and woods for cover. For a time, the advance met stiff resistance from an enemy well prepared to defend against a frontal assault. Large in scale though this assault was, it was a diversion. The British flanking column, led by the light infantry, was soon behind the eastern end of the rebel lines, and the sound of gunfire from that direction triggered a rout. 'About a mile before we came to Bedford saw the Rebels on our left,' wrote a staff officer with the flanking column, 'the light infantry ordered to attack them, which they did with success, and drove them every way; the grenadiers and brigades continued the road to

42 TNA: WO 36/5: general orders, 20–22 and 24 August 1776.
43 TNA: WO 121/13/276: discharge of John Galispie.
44 TNA: WO 36/5: general orders, 26 August 1776.
45 Robson (ed.), *Letters*, p.33.

Brookland.'[46] Captain Murray wrote, 'The Light Infantry who were first engaged dashed in as fast as foot could carry. The scoundrels were driven into the wood and out of the wood, where they had supposed that we would never venture to engage them.'[47] By nightfall, a stunning victory had been achieved by the army that had seen such disastrous results at Bunker Hill the previous year. At a cost of just over 300 casualties, General Howe's army had killed some 300, wounded over 800, and captured almost 1,100 of their opponents. 'This was entirely owing to our Men attacking them the proper Way. The moment the Rebels fired our Men rushed on them with their Bayonets & never gave them Time to load again. Our Men behaved themselves like British Troops fighting for a good cause,' reflected a British general.[48]

Before the victory was complete, some flank companies experienced tense moments. Captain Murray described terrain that favoured the enemy, 'entirely after their own heart covered with woods and hedges, from which they gave us several very heavy fires.' Captain William Dansey's light company from the 33rd Regiment, in the 3rd Battalion of Light Infantry, appears to have operated with some autonomy which nearly caused their destruction. Dansey wrote that he 'led my Company into the very thick of them and had a most miraculous Escape.' He explained that he, with 'five or six of my men got into the Wood among them.' He found himself confronted with American riflemen who 'jump'd up within Ten yards and fired upon us, which did us no harm, I ordered my Men to get behind the Trees and return it which they did and kill'd the Rebel Captain within Twenty Yards of me. The Rebels gave us a second fire that came all round us.' The man on his right was killed, the man on his left wounded; 'upon seeing us surrounded, I called to my Men to run to the first Wall they cou'd find and we all set off, some into some short Bushes others straight across a Field,' retreating to a wall they had previously climbed over. 'In running across the field we were exposed the Fire of 300 Men we had literally run out of the skirmish and they calling me to surrender I stop'd twice to look behind me and saw the Riflemen.' Throwing himself over the wall, Dansey banged his leg and thought he had been hit. Safe for the moment behind the wall, he took stock of his company, which had lost three killed and six wounded in what he recalled to be about three minutes of intense fighting; one of his lieutenants, Richard Cotton, 'got a graze upon the shoulder.' In the nick of time three more light infantry companies and a grenadier battalion came to their assistance and routed their riflemen, capturing some from whom Dansey learned their numbers and casualties. In a letter home, he described the danger: 'The only map I can give a person how the Balls flew about me whilst running over that small Field is suppose yourself under a large Apple Tree full of ripe Fruit and a person is in the Tree Shaking as hard as they can, how thick the Apples will drop about you and perhaps not one hit you.' Elias Broadbent, Edward Ogden and James Wilson of the 33rd Regiment were the only men of the 3rd Battalion of Light Infantry killed that day, and another six in the battalion were wounded including Lieutenant Cotton. [49]

46 Kemble, 'Journals,' p.85.
47 Robson (ed.), *Letters*, p.33.
48 Percy, *Letters*, p.68.
49 Robson (ed.), *Letters*, p.33; Paul Dansey (ed.), *Captured Rebel Flag: The Letters of Captain William Dansey, 33rd Regiment of Foot, 1776–1777* (Godmanchester: Ken Trotman Press, 2010), pp.14–16;

A private soldier in a battalion company of the 49th Regiment wrote that his regiment's light infantry company, in the 2nd Battalion:

> fell in with a large body of them to the right in a large wood to the left of Bedford, and a smart engagement ensued, which lasted for some time. Our light Infantry Company after the Rebels giving way and being repulsed, unawares, came in with a small Breast-work almost covered with Bushes; in which the Enemy had two Pieces of Cannon. The Company brought one Piece off, but being far inferior to the Rebels, who rallied a second time upon them; so that they could not bring the second piece of Cannon off, it was carried away by the Enemy. They had the Captain slightly wounded, one man killed upon the spot, and another died of his wounds in a few hours after; besides 6 men wounded.[50]

The 49th's muster rolls show that William Hickey and John Sutliff of the 49th's light infantry were killed that day. Also, in the 2nd Battalion of Light Infantry, William Bolar and John Deady of the 44th were killed; 31 were wounded, including Lieutenant John Weir of the 43rd Regiment. The 1st Battalion of Light Infantry reportedly lost four killed, but only two are enumerated on available muster rolls, John Knight of the 4th Regiment and Adam Brindle of the 38th; 24 were wounded including the battalion's commander, Major Thomas Musgrave. Captain Evelyn wrote that six of his men in the 4th Regiment's light company were killed or wounded.[51]

Captain George Harris, commanding the 5th Regiment's company in the 1st Battalion of Grenadiers, had a much less intense experience than the light infantry: 'We have had what some call a battle, but if it deserves that name, it was the pleasantest I ever heard of, as we had not received more than a dozen shot from the enemy, when they ran away with the utmost precipitation.'[52] His battalion suffered only one man killed, James Mason of the 22nd Regiment's company, and four wounded. Major Stuart of the 4th Battalion of Grenadiers wrote that 'I was ordered to draw up my Highland Grenadiers on the right of the Grenadiers, by doing which one of the squares blocked and my men were gauled very much, 17 were killed and wounded, and I received a slight scratch upon my hip with a musket ball, which for three or four days was inconvenient, but at present is quite well.'[53] An officer of the 71st's grenadiers confirmed the 4th Battalion's posting on the right, and wrote that to avoid rebel cannon fire the highlanders 'clapt every shot on our back and charged our pieces, and then fired on our knees, and then down to our backs again, thus loading and firing.'[54] Casualties for the 4th Battalion were reported as one killed, 12 wounded and one missing. The 3rd Battalion, to the left of the 1st, had only a single man wounded. The 2nd Battalion,

---

TNA: WO 12: muster rolls, 33rd Regiment; Thomas Warren Field, *The Battle of Long Island* (Brooklyn, NY: Long Island Historical Society, 1869), pp.416–419, return of British casualties.

50 Joseph Lee Boyle (ed.), *From Redcoat to Rebel: The Thomas Sullivan Journal* (Bowie, MD: Heritage Books, 1997), p.50.

51 Field, *The Battle of Long Island*, pp.416–419; TNA: WO 12: muster rolls; Evelyn, *Letters*, p.89.

52 Wilkin, *Some British Soldiers*, pp.183–184.

53 Stuart, *New Records*, p.10.

54 *North British Intelligencer*, 4 December 1776.

on the far left, suffered most among the grenadiers. The company of the 52nd Regiment and one of those of the Marines had a particularly bad encounter, related by Captain Murray of the 57th Light Infantry: 'Two companies suffered by an unfortunate mistake which might have created a good deal of confusion. They took a large body of the rebels dressed in blue for the Hessians, and received a fire from them at a very small distance, before they discovered their mistake.'[55] The battalion had 12 killed including Captain Thomas Williamson of the 52nd and Captain George Logan of the Marines.[56] Muster rolls identify privates Michael Hurley of the 44th, James McDonell of the 52nd and Thomas Brinon of the 52nd killed; no rolls are known to survive for the Marines' grenadier companies, who may have accounted for the remainder of the dead. Commanding officer Lieutenant Colonel Henry Monckton was among the battalion's 38 wounded, 'shot through the Body,' according to another officer writing five days later, 'but is in a fair way of Recovery.'[57] Also wounded was Captain Andrew Brown of the 44th, who died on 4 October. The 2nd Battalion also lost Lieutenant John Ragg and 21 men of the Marines who were 'detached to a rising ground, and the Enemy surrounded them before the Battalion could come to their assistance; they carried them prisoners.'[58]

Nightfall saw the rebel army, still numerically strong in spite of the crushing defeat, in a second line of fortified positions on Brooklyn Heights. Their backs to the East River separating Long Island from Manhattan, they had no easy retreat but their defences were strong. General Howe's army, although victorious, needed time to regroup after a long day of rapid marches and furious fighting. Rather than immediately attempting to storm the rebel works, which could result in significant casualties, Howe chose to make 'regular approaches,' establishing lines facing the works and digging trenches to move gradually closer.

What had the makings of a prolonged siege quickly ended when the rebels managed a stealthy retreat to Manhattan during the night of 29–30 August, aided by morning fog that covered the last of their flight. For Howe's army, the pursuit was over for the moment.

* * *

The day after the battle the two companies of Marines grenadiers, having lost two officers and a substantial number of men, were combined into a single company under Captain Thomas Averne.[59] On 29 August, Lieutenant Colonel Robert Abercromby of the 37th Regiment took command of the 2nd Battalion of Grenadiers, taking over for the wounded Lieutenant Colonel Monckton; Major Thomas Dilkes of the 49th was appointed major to the battalion four days later, replacing Major Charles Stuart who had taken command of the 4th Battalion.[60] With no more opposition on Long Island, the army regrouped for the next objective, the city of New York. The grenadiers and light infantry encamped at Hell Gate, the north-western extreme of Long Island in the area of present-day Astoria Park, for

55 Robson (ed.), *Letters*, p.33.
56 Field, *The Battle of Long Island*, pp.416–419.
57 Ballindalloch Castle (BC): James Grant Papers: James Grant to Edward Harvey.
58 Sullivan, *From Redcoat to Rebel*, p.50.
59 TNA: WO 36/5: general orders, 28 August 1776.
60 TNA: WO 36/5: general orders, 29 August and 2 September 1776.

the next several days. Captain Harris in the 1st Battalion of Grenadiers related his living conditions on Long Island: 'Colonel Medows is my commanding officer, and this I consider one of the pleasantest things that ever happened to me. We sleep together in a soldiers' tent, which, when well littered down with straw, we consider quite a luxury.'[61] There was no immediate need to replace casualties in the flank battalions; many of the wounds were minor, according to an officer, 'the Light Infantry & Grenadiers chiefly in their Hands & Arms, which is not easily accounted for.'[62]

In the 4th Battalion of Grenadiers, the officers and soldiers of the newly-raised 71st Regiment offered disciplinary challenges for their battalion commander. Major Stuart addressed them in orders of 2 September, stating that he was 'extremely sorry to be under the necessity of reminding the Officers that a Battalion newly form'd required their Strictest care & Attention,' and asserting that 'No Officer whatever to quit the Camp without mentioning it to the Major.' He continued:

> It having been represented that men from the 71st Companys taken away Articles from, & otherwise ill treated several persons near this Encampment, the Commanding Officer requests that the Officers make diligent search to discover said offenders & that they pay such Attention to their non Commission Officers and Men as may prevent them in future from being guilty of the like infamous practices.[63]

Turning to health, hygiene, and basic military procedures, Stuart reminded his officers that the duty of the officer of the day was 'to Visit the Men before Roll Calling see that their Tents are made clean the Straw taken out & air'd the Canvass roll'd up – They will also see that the Messes are properly regulated & that the Men are fed by tattoo.'[64] By 13 September Stuart saw fit to order rolls to be called every half hour, suggesting that absence had become a significant problem.[65]

The light infantry were kept busier than the grenadiers. On 10 September the 1st and 2nd Battalions took to boats to Montresor's Island and Buchanan Island (today a single island, Randall's Island) at the mouth of the Harlem River that divided upper Manhattan Island from the mainland. It was only lightly defended; Lieutenant Henry Stirke of the 10th Regiment's light infantry recorded, 'one of the Rebel Centrys fired three times at the boat I was in, before he Retreated, and wounded (I fear mortally) a man of my Company.' Another officer, not with the attacking force, wrote that the sentry fired three times and wounded two men, 'both by one ball.' During the next two days an additional brigade joined them on the islands, making it the obvious stepping-stone for the army to cross to Manhattan.[66]

61 Mackenzie, *Diary*, p.40.
62 BC: James Grant Papers: James Grant to Edward Harvey, 2 September 1776.
63 NRS: Papers of John Peebles: orderly book, 4th Battalion of Grenadiers, general orders, 2 September, 1776.
64 NRS: Papers of John Peebles: orderly book, 4th Battalion of Grenadiers, general orders, 2 September, 1776.
65 NRS: Papers of John Peebles: orderly book, 4th Battalion of Grenadiers, general orders, 13 September, 1776.
66 Henry Stirke, 'A British Officer's Revolutionary War Journal, 1776–1778,' *Maryland Historical Magazine* 56 (June 1961), p.158; Mackenzie, *Diary*, pp.43–44. Stirke noted that the man died 'a few days after'; the only man of the company to die in this time frame was John Rook, on 28 September. TNA: WO 12: muster rolls, 10th Regiment.

On 13 September, General Howe gave orders for the impending assault on American positions protecting the city of New York:

> An attack upon the Enemy being shortly intended, the soldiers are reminded of their evident superiority on the 27th August, by charging the Rebels with their Bayonets, even in the Woods where they thought themselves invincible. They now place their security in slight breastworks of the weakest construction & which are to be carried with little loss by the same high spirited manner of attack. The General therefore recommends it to the troops an entire dependence on their Bayonets, with which they will ever command that success their bravery so well deserves[67]

The next evening, troops from Long Island converged on Newtown Creek, a waterway that emptied into the river between Long Island and Manhattan. Carrying only arms, blankets and two days' provisions, at 6:00 a.m. on 15 September the light infantry and grenadier battalions, three battalions of German grenadiers and the corps of jägers boarded 60 flat-boats in the creek, 'and lay on their Oars at the mouth of it, until all was ready.' Five warships moved into position opposite the creek and anchored close to the Manhattan shore, their cannon facing entrenchments the rebels had dug along the shoreline. At 10:00 a.m. the flat-boats rowed south to a point closer to the city and joined another group of boats carrying troops and artillery. American troops repositioned to oppose them at a likely landing place near the city. Just before 11:00 a.m., the warships opened fire, pummelling American entrenchments for 90 minutes, driving away defenders who had not already moved to oppose the troops in boats.[68]

The deception was complete. At noon the flatboats pushed off, but rather than drive straight across the river, they took advantage of wind and a strong tidal current to stream north for about a half-hour, passing behind the cannonading ships, then turning towards land at Kip's Bay. The three battalions of light infantry landed first in an unlikely spot, 'a high and steep rock,' which they clambered up and secured the adjacent beach for the rest of the troops to land.[69] The grenadiers and Brigade of Guards quickly landed, and the fast-moving flank battalions 'rush'd for wood and took possession of a hill about a mile from the spot where we landed.'[70] By 5:00 p.m. the entire army had landed, established positions at McGowan's Pass, seven miles north of the city, and sent troops south to secure the city itself. The routed American defenders fled to Harlem Heights further north on the island. There was still consolidation to do, but the operation had effectively taken the city of New York without loss. The grenadier battalions were fired upon by 'a few stragglers,' wounding

67 TNA: WO 36/5: general orders, 13 September 1776.

68 TNA: WO 36/5: general orders, 14 September 1776; Mackenzie, *Diary*, pp.46–47. General orders were to carry blankets and provisions, but the reserve corps which included the grenadier battalions were directed, 'to carry their provision with them, but it is left to the discretion of the Commanding Officers of Corps whether the men should carry their Blankets or leave them with the Tents.' NRS: GD 21/492/2: Orderly book, 4th Battalion of Grenadiers, in John Peebles Diary, Cunninghame of Thornton Papers, general orders, 14 September 1776.

69 Mackenzie, *Diary*, p.47; Evelyn, *Letters*, p.84.

70 Stuart, *New Records*, p.11.

Major General John Vaughan but causing no other casualties.[71] Howe's recommendation to rely solely on charging with bayonets proved to be outstandingly effective. Misdirecting the enemy as to the landing place, and the dramatic and devastating naval bombardment, had made it easy for professional soldiers to drive away an already confused and panicked foe.

* * *

Having marched with only their weapons, provisions and blankets, the troops settled down for the night in whatever accommodations they could find. Men of the 1st Battalion of Grenadiers found knapsacks and other equipment abandoned by fleeing Americans; according to Captain Harris, 'Their blankets were a great prize, as several of our men had thrown off their's on the 27th, when pursuing the enemy. Here they amply made up their losses.' He described how he and his fellow officers of the 5th Regiment's grenadier company dealt with the Spartan conditions at the end of the day:

> We … placed our piquets, borrowed a sheep, killed, cooked, and ate some of it, and then went to sleep on a gate, which we took the liberty of throwing off its hinges, covering our feet with an American tent, for which we should have cut poles and pitched, had it not been so dark. Give me such living as we enjoy at present, such a hut and such company, and I would not care three farthings if we stayed all the winter, for though the mornings and evenings are cold, yet the sun is so hot as to oblige me to put up a blanket as a screen.[72]

The next day, Howe put the light infantry, the reserve, two British and two German brigades under the command of Lieutenant General Henry Clinton. Clinton posted two 3-pounder field pieces with the 1st Battalion of Light Infantry and two 6-pounders with the 1st Battalion of Grenadiers, and ordered the troops to move into positions spanning the island, the light infantry on the left, or west, closest to the Hudson River.[73] In taking these positions, the light infantry's zeal nearly got the better of them.

In the morning 'a Party of the enemy showed themselves' at a house in front of the lines. Two companies of light infantry, apparently the 33rd Regiment's and one other, 'engaged and drove a very Superior Body to a great distance.'[74] Sensing another rout, Brigadier General Leslie sent more companies of the 3rd Battalion in pursuit. 'The enemy appeared in open view,' wrote an American officer soon after the battle, 'and in the most insulting manner sounded their bugle horns as is usual after a fox chase. I never felt such a sensation before, it seemed to crown our disgrace.'[75] The lights followed their quarry into woods 'with more ardor than discretion,' and suddenly found themselves dangerously close to enemy lines on Harlem Heights, far forward of friendly forces.[76] Seeing an opportunity, American

71 Mackenzie, *Diary*, pp.48–49.
72 Wilkin, *Some British Soldiers*, pp.185–186.
73 NRS: Papers of John Peebles: orderly book, 4th Battalion of Grenadiers, general orders, 16 September 1776.
74 Kemble, 'Journal,' p.89.
75 Joseph Reed to his wife, 17 September 1776, *Magazine of American History*, Vol. 4 (1880), p.370.
76 Evelyn, *Letters*, p.85.

forces quickly moved to surround the impetuous but vastly-outnumbered light infantry, and a firefight ensued. Leslie ordered the rest of the light infantry forward, but they could do nothing more than support their comrades; still outnumbered, they were soon 'smartly engaged, hemmed in and almost surrounded.'[77]

Captain Harris company wrote that the 1st Battalion of Grenadiers 'were ordered to stand to our arms at 11 a.m., and were instantly trotted about three miles (without a halt to draw breath)' to support the beleaguered light infantry. Artillery pieces came with the grenadiers, as did the 42nd Regiment. This allowed the light infantry to retreat, after which British forces retired more or less to their original positions. Recalling his own head wound from the Battle of Bunker Hill, Captain Harris wrote, 'A man in my company had his hat shot through nearly in the direction of my wound, but the ball merely raised the skin.' Richard Burly of the 46th's grenadiers, in the 3rd Battalion, was the only grenadier killed that day; Captain Harris, to their right in the 1st Battalion, described his death: 'in the battalion on our left a man was shot so dead when lying on the ground, that the next man did not perceive it, but when he got up to stand to his arms, kicked his comrade, thinking he was asleep, and then found, to his great surprise, that he was quite dead, a ball having entered under the ear, and very little blood having issued from it.'[78]

A battalion company officer wrote about Captain Mathew Johnson's handling of the 46th Regiment's light infantry company in this battle:

> Johnson and his Company behaved amazingly, he goes thro his manavers by a whistle for which he has often been laughed at, they either form to right or left or squat or rise by a particular whistle which his men are as well acquainted with as the Battalion with the word of Command, he being used to Woods fighting and having a quick Eye had his Company down in the moment of the Enemies present & up again at the advantegious moment for their fire, killed several and had not one of his Company hurt during the whole time he drove the Enemy before him, but upon the retreat tho' managed in the coolest manner he had Seven Wounded, not one of whom would suffer themselves to be taken precipitately off and some continued their fire after being severely wounded.[79]

Captain Johnson's company was in the 3rd Battalion of Light Infantry, which may not have had an opportunity to learn the same manoeuvres and procedures taught to the other two light battalions in Halifax, perhaps accounting for Captain Johnson's distinctive procedures.

Captain Harris offered an amusing anecdote about the servant who diligently attempted to prepare a meal for the officers of the 1st Battalion of Grenadiers in spite of the unfolding action, and the return to relative normalcy when it was over:

77 Stuart, *New Records*, p.11; see also Mackenzie, *Diary*, p.52; Dansey (ed.), *Letters*, p.17. No writer identified the companies that pushed too far forward; Evelyn and Mackenzie wrote 'a few companies' and 'some of the Companies,' while Kemble wrote 'two Companies.' Dansey wrote that 'the Light Infantry were chiefly concern'd and my Company among the first of them.'

78 Wilkin, *Some British Soldiers*, pp.186–187; TNA: WO 12: muster rolls, 46th Regiment.

79 WLC: Loftus Cliffe Papers: Loftus Cliffe to 'Jack,' 21 September 1776.

> Before we started in the morning, our dinner, consisting of a goose and a piece of mutton, had been put on the fire. The moment we marched, our domestic deposited the above-named delicacies on a chaise and followed us with it to our ground. When the fight was over, he again hung the goose to the fire, but the poor bird had scarcely been half done, when we were ordered to return to our station. There we again commenced cooking, and, though without dish, plate, or knife, did ample justice to our fare, which we washed down with bad rum and water, and then composed ourselves to rest on our friendly gate.[80]

This action in which 'nothing was intended or gained' cost 14 dead including a sergeant of the 45th's light infantry and several private soldiers of different companies, and around 100 wounded including several officers.[81] Major Stuart of the 4th Battalion of Grenadiers lost 'three men of my Batt. Wounded, and, what was more singular, my dog as he was lying by me.'[82] The pursuit 'without proper precautions or support,' 'gave the General a good deal of concern.'[83] In the next day's general orders Howe expressed 'the highest opinion of the bravery' of the troops that 'beat back a very superior body of the Rebels,' but saw fit to add an admonition:

> But at the same time he finds himself under a necessity of disapproving a want of attention in the light companies pursing the Rebels without that proper direction, to be observed where there are not troops to support.[84]

It would not be last time that the light infantry, accustomed to superiority, rushed on their foe 'with more zeal than prudence.'[85]

* * *

With their enemy entrenched on the northern end of a narrow island, Howe had no avenue of attack other than a costly frontal assault, and he recognized that even a successful assault would leave an easy path of retreat for the Americans to the northeast. Another flanking movement was needed, one that took time to organize and effect. After strengthening his

---

80 Wilkin, *Some British Soldiers*, p.187.

81 Mackenzie, *Diary*, p.52. Casualty figures vary; Kemble gave the most detailed tabulation, listing one sergeant and 13 privates killed, two majors, two captains, seven lieutenants and ensigns, five sergeants, three drummers and 138 men wounded. Muster rolls, which indicate killed but not wounded, show only three killed in the light infantry, the sergeant of the 45th, a private of the 33rd and a private of the 15th, and one man killed in a battalion company of the 42nd Regiment. Dansey confirmed that only one man of his company was killed, and an officer, a sergeant and another man wounded, 'but not bad.' Men who died during the next few days may have died of wounds from this battle, but muster rolls do not indicate cause of death, only the date. Kemble, 'Journals,' p.89; Dansey, *Letters*, p.17; TNA: WO 12: muster rolls, 33rd Regiment, 45th Regiment, 46th Regiments.

82 Stuart, *New Records*, p.11.

83 Mackenzie, *Diary*, p.52.

84 TNA: WO 35/5: general orders, 17 September 1776.

85 Stuart, *New Records*, p.11.

lines on Manhattan, at the beginning of October he pulled the light infantry and grenadiers off to the east, replacing them with other troops. The light infantry, having no tents, 'cantoned in the farm houses and Barns near Bloomingdale.' Howe ordered regiments to bring their light infantry companies up to full strength, but muster rolls confirm only a few that did – the 10th, 44th and 57th Regiments transferring one man each, and the 45th, 46th and 49th two men each; possibly transfers by other regiments were recorded at a later date.[86]

Throughout September, the 4th Battalion of Grenadiers, composed of companies from the 42nd and 71st Regiments, had been dogged by illness, particularly the companies of the 71st. Major Stuart, gave orders on 19 September suggesting the causes:

> By the Number of Sick men that have lately been sent to the Hospital & those that daily complain, the Commanding Officer has great reason to fear that the Battalion in a few weeks will be incapable of doing duty, to prevent which disgrace falling upon a Corps of Grenadiers it is the Majors orders that a NonCommissioned Officer per Company see that the Men bathe or wash their feet thrice a Week. The Commanding Officers of Companys to be answerable that this order is comply'd with – An Officer of a Company to visit the Messes of their respective Companys daily & to Specify in a Written Report if the Messes are properly regulated & provisions Cook'd.[87]

On 2 October, Stuart addressed another disciplinary problem, this time with men relieved from picket duty:

> It having been represented to the Major that yesterday Evening the Picquet of the 4th Battalion Refused to be march'd home & contrary to the express desire & order of the Captain who commanded them ran irregularly to their Tents in consequence of which it is the Majors Orders that the Captains reprove their several Companies for their insolent & disobedient behavior, & acquaint them with the Enormity of the Crime.[88]

The problems continued nonetheless, particularly illness. On 8 October General Howe ordered the battalion disbanded, sending the 71st's two companies, 'being very sickly,' to their regiment, while the 42nd's joined the 3rd Battalion of Grenadiers. The 3rd Battalion had been smaller than the 1st and 2nd, with only seven companies; companies in the 42nd Regiment were twice the size of companies in other regiments, so the addition of the 42nd's company brought the 3rd Battalion much closer to the strength of the two 10-company battalions. Major Stuart, commander of the 4th Battalion, was posted instead as major to the 3rd Battalion.[89]

86 Mackenzie, *Diary*, p.68; TNA: WO 36/5: general orders, 2 October 1776; WO 12: muster rolls. Muster rolls were maintained for administrative purposes and often do not reflect actual dates of transfers.
87 NRS: Papers of John Peebles: orderly book, 4th Battalion of Grenadiers, general orders, 19 September 1776.
88 NRS: Papers of John Peebles: orderly book, 4th Battalion of Grenadiers general orders, 2 October 1776.
89 General orders, 8 October 1776, Anon. (ed.), 'British Army Orders,' p.385.

The bulk of the army struck tents and prepared to march at 6:00 p.m. on 11 October. They marched at 10:00 p.m., embarked in boats along the eastern shore near the city, and rode the tide through the waterway called Hell Gate to a peninsula called Throg's Neck or Frog's Neck, protruding from the mainland into Long Island sound, where they landed unopposed, the light infantry once again first ashore. The intention was to quickly move north towards White Plains, outflanking the American army on Manhattan, but an obstacle arose immediately. The neck was separated from the mainland by a narrow strait, and the single bridge across had been destroyed. Rebel troops had fortified the mainland side, making it impractical to cross. Captain Dansey's description of the ensuing action implies that the light infantry battalions formed in the expected manner, the 1st Battalion on the right, the 2nd on the left and the 3rd in the centre. Dansey wrote that he was in command his own company and one other – probably the 15th's, whose captain and one lieutenant were wounded at Harlem Heights, and which was next to Dansey's on the right flank of the 3rd Battalion. The formation put these companies closest to the enemy on the other side of the water, near the road that led to the now-destroyed bridge. Dansey wrote that '150 or 200 Riflemen' were 200 yards away, 'better cover'd than we were having a house a Mill and a Wall.' The enemy 'got the first fire at us before I saw them, I bid my Men cover themselves with the Trees and Rocks and turn out Volunteers among the Soldiers to go to the nearest Trees to the Riflemen and keep up the Fire.' Rifle-armed German Jägers came up in support 'but did not stay above an hour;' Dansey's men continued to exchange fire with the rebels 'for upwards of seven hours at their favorite distance of 200 Yards.' He wrote with pride:

> I continued the popping fire at them and they at us, we had the Satisfaction of knocking several of them down and had not a Man hurt. This kind of popping continued two or three Days between the Light Infantry and Riflemen across the Water 'till we had kill'd an Officer of theirs besides several men and had not one of ours wounded, and they at last fairly gave up firing finding themselves beat in their own way, which shew'd a cool Soldier with a good Firelock was beyond a Rifleman with all his Skill.[90]

Howe had a different opinion of this sniping, admonishing in orders, 'as nothing can mark the Unsteadiness of the Troops more than the frequent and useless firing of the advanced posts, the Commander in Chief flatters himself it is unnecessary to remind the Army of the superiority they must have in Discipline over the Enemy opposed to them.'[91]

Unable to move off of Throg's neck, Howe determined on landing at a different location. The army on the neck decamped at midnight and boarded boats early in the morning of 17 October. They landed at about 8:30 a.m., once again unopposed, at Pell's Point just a couple of miles up the coast, where a road led inland. Once ashore the 1st Battalion of Light Infantry led the way, followed by the 3rd and then the 2nd Battalions; two 3-pounder cannon accompanied each battalion. Following them was the 1st Battalion of Grenadiers, then the 3rd and 2nd Battalions, each with two 6-pounders. German grenadiers and other

90 Dansey (ed.), *Letters*, pp.19–20.

91 General orders, 15 October 1776, Anon. (ed.), 'British Army Orders,' p.389.

troops followed. Loyalist soldiers from the newly-raised Queen's Rangers, commanded by Major Robert Rogers, were detached to assist handling the artillery in the flank battalions, five men to each 3-pounder and eight to each 6-pounder, presumably providing manual labour to move the guns quickly; they were relieved from this duty on 22 October.[92]

Major Stuart, with the grenadiers, wrote that 'the rebels not expecting us, we proceeded near 3 miles unmolested, until the Lt. Infantry coming to the great road which leads from New York to New England they had a slight brush.'[93] For the 1st Battalion of Light Infantry, this 'brush' was severe. Typical of the region, the 'great road' was lined by stone walls, one of which concealed rebels who by this time were indeed expecting the advancing British troops. Captain Stirke of the 10th's light infantry described receiving 'a very heavy fire, as we march'd up a Hill, from behind Stone Walls, pickets &c.' He said the battalion 'push'd the Rebels from fence to fence, without being Sustain'd, 'till about 2 O'Clock when a battalion of Hessian Grenadiers came up' and they gained high ground.[94] Killed on the spot were Sergeant Thomas Beale of the 22nd Regiment, Thomas Jones of the 27th and Thomas Goosney of the 35th. Sergeant William Boarman of the 10th was wounded and died two days later; two other sergeants, a drummer and 23 soldiers were wounded.[95] Major Thomas Musgrave, leading the battalion, was wounded, as were Captain William Glanville Evelyn of the 4th Regiment and Lieutenant Archibald Rutherford of the 22nd. Evelyn's wound was severe; taking him for dead, an impetuous American soldier 'leaped over the wall and took a hat and canteen' from him.[96] The stricken officer was 'carried to New York, and after suffering Amputation soon expired, to the great regret of all that knew him as a soldier or friend.'[97] Captain Harris of the grenadiers attributed the loss, once again, to the light infantry's 'too great haste to attack,' adding, 'The Grenadiers did not suffer, being only exposed to the fire of the American batteries, which were very ill served.'[98]

Lieutenant Colonel Monckton recovered from his wounds of 27 August and on 23 October took command of the 2nd Battalion of Grenadiers, allowing Lieutenant Colonel Abercromby to assume command of the 1st Battalion of Light Infantry, replacing the wounded Musgrave.[99] The army moved inland and consolidated its position, but found their opponents once more occupying advantageous ground, this time the hilly area called White Plains. The army assaulted these positions on 28 October in the Battle of White Plains; the positions were such that, according to Captain Harris, 'here, for the first time, we were tranquil spectators of the fight, except, indeed, as far as our anxiety for our friends and comrades was concerned.'[100] Lieutenant Martin Hunter, in the 52nd's light infantry, remembered that late in the day, 'The Light Infantry and Grenadiers who could not be brought into action at the beginning, now came up, and pursued the enemy quite through their camp.'[101]

92 General orders, 18 and 22 October 1776, Anon. (ed.), 'British Army Orders,' pp.391–392, 394.
93 Stuart, *New Records*, p.12.
94 Stirke, 'British Officer's Revolutionary War Journal,' p.160.
95 TNA: WO 12: muster rolls, 22nd, 27th and 35th Regiments.
96 Evelyn, *Letters*, pp.10–11.
97 George Inman, 'George Inman's Narrative of the American Revolution,' *Pennsylvania Magazine of History and Biography*, Vol.7, No. 3 (1883), p.239.
98 Wilkin, *Some British Soldiers*, p.189.
99 General orders, 23 October 1776, Anon. (ed.), 'British Army Orders,' p.395.
100 Wilkin, *Some British Soldiers*, p.189.
101 Hunter, *Journal*, p.19.

Over the next weeks, the armies manoeuvred with occasional skirmishes but no significant actions for the flank battalions. American forces either withdrew to New Jersey or consolidated at Fort Washington, a citadel with extensive outworks on high ground at the northern end of Manhattan. On 16 November, General Howe launched a four-pronged assault on the position. A German brigade advanced from Kingsbridge against the northern approach to the fort. Once their initial position was secure, the Brigade of Guards and the 1st and 2nd Battalions of Light Infantry, carrying only arms, blankets and one day's provisions, crossed the Harlem River in boats to attack an artillery battery on the shore east of the fort; to their left the 42nd Regiment also crossed, while British and German brigades approached the fort from the south.[102] After assembling at 4:00 a.m., the light infantry landed 'at 12 at Noon, the tide not permitting it sooner, and by some neglect not foreseen before.'[103] Lieutenant Hunter, in the 2nd Battalion of Light Infantry, remembered the dangerous river crossing: 'The Light Infantry landed under so very heavy a fire of cannon and musketry that the sailors quitted their oars and lay down in the bottom of the boats. In this situation we must have remained exposed to the enemy's fire had not the soldiers taken the oars and pulled us on shore. The instant we landed the enemy retreated to Fort Washington.'[104] In spite of the heavy fire the light infantry did not lose a single man, and 'The Guards and Light Infantry drove all before them.'[105] The fort's garrison soon surrendered, and the 2nd Battalion of Light Infantry occupied the post. An American officer, writing some years later, wrote of verbal abuse the prisoners sustained from their captors: 'This chiefly proceeded from the officers of the light infantry; for the most part, young and insolent puppies, whose worthlessness was apparently their recommendation to a service, which placed them in the post of danger, and in the way of becoming food for powder, their most appropriate destination next to that of the gallows.'[106]

The next day the 3rd Battalions of Grenadiers and Light Infantry were sent towards the City of New York to encamp, awaiting a new expedition. The other flank battalions soon embarked on their most dramatic endeavour so far, led by Lieutenant General Cornwallis. Opposite Fort Washington on the New Jersey side of the Hudson River stood Fort Lee, at the top of 500-foot cliffs that stretched for miles along the riverbank, making the Hudson a seemingly impenetrable barrier. At 9:00 p.m. on 19 November, two grenadier and two light infantry battalions, the Brigade of Guards, the 33rd and 42nd Regiments, three battalions of German grenadiers, artillery and some other troops, took blankets and provisions and boarded boats. 'After passing a very disagreeable night in the Flat boats, under a thick heavy rain,' according to Captain Stirke of the 10th Regiment's light infantry, they proceeded upriver to a landing about six miles north of Fort Lee, where a narrow footpath led up the cliffs. The light infantry battalions landed first, at daybreak, led by the companies of the 10th and 17th Regiments, 'with orders to push up the hill, with as much expedition as possible to take post, and maintain it, 'till sustain'd,' wrote Stirke. Within a few hours, four

102 General orders, 15 November 1776, Anon. (ed.), 'British Army Orders,' p.408.

103 Kemble, 'Journal,' p.99.

104 Hunter, *Journal*, p.20.

105 Stirke, 'British Officer's Revolutionary War Journal,' p.164; Mackenzie, *Diary*, p.108.

106 Alexander Graydon, *Memoirs of a Life, Chiefly Passed in Pennsylvania* (Harrisburg: John Wyeth, 1811), p.184.

thousand men with cannons, 'which were oblig'd to be drawn up almost a Precipice, above a half mile in length, by men, as it was impassable for Horses,' were established at the top of cliffs that the rebels had assumed secured their position.[107] Two miles to the west flowed the Hackensack River, parallel to the Hudson; Lieutenant General Cornwallis's corps quickly marched south towards Fort Lee, but the fort's garrison, alerted of the surprise attack just in time, managed to escape across the only available bridge over the Hackensack at New Bridge. Fort Lee was secured without loss; the troops lay on their arms that night. At 9:00 a.m. the next morning the 2nd Battalion of Light Infantry and 2nd Battalion of Grenadiers, with a German chasseur company, 'made so rapid a march as to secure the New Bridge on the Hackinsack River from being destroyed by the enemy in their precipitate retreat.'[108] They faced almost no opposition and captured substantial amounts of military stores including, according to Captain William Hale of the 45th's grenadiers, '11 pipes of Madeira which were distributed to the troops, each officer had a gallon.'[109]

Over the next two weeks Cornwallis pursued the fleeing foe across New Jersey, taking advantage of the flank battalions' speed supported by dragoons, but their quarry managed time and again to escape, razing bridges to buy time, the light infantry often arriving just in time to see the enemy rear guard flee. The army moved in two columns to Acquakenack (present-day Passaic) on the 26th, where the flank battalions, 33rd and 42nd Regiments in the right column forded the Passaic River, causing opposition to flee and allowing the left column with the Brigade of Guards and German grenadiers to cross using a captured sloop. The next day they pushed into Newark and 'were cantoned, the Enemy had evacuated it only in the Morning & had left their Quarters in great haste; we found the Rooms in the Houses very unclean from the filth and dirt of the Rebel Troops.'[110] The flank battalions pushed on through Elizabeth, Woodbridge, Amboy, and arrived in Brunswick by 1 December where 'on our appearing on the heights before the Town, the Rebels began to abandon it, with all ye expedition possible. We fired on them a Cross the River, from our field pieces, which was return'd for sometime. As the Rebels took care to demolish part of the bridge, we cou'd not prevent their Carrying off some of their stores &c.' After taking some time to regroup, and joined by additional brigades, the flank battalions pressed on to Princeton, where again they saw their foes 'destroying a bridge, which they effected, before we cou'd drive them off.' They moved into Trenton the next day unopposed, but as they halted on the bank of the Delaware River, they 'receiv'd a very heavy Cannonade from the opposite side of the River' which killed a dragoon and an artilleryman, and wounded a soldier in the 27th Regiment's light infantry company.[111] 'We marched four days after them, but they outran our Light Infantry, indeed they seem to have forgotten every thing but running,' wrote Captain Hale; 'We pursued them to a ferry and found the boats burnt or carried off, which was no small disappointment as it was a forced march of 14 miles all night, and we had but six hours halt during the preceeding days.'[112] Captain Harris of the grenadiers complained that 'We

107 Stirke, 'British Officer's Revolutionary War Journal,' pp.164–165.
108 Firestone Library (FL), Princeton University: Thomas Glyn Journal: 20 and 21 November 1776.
109 Wilkin, *Some British Soldiers*, p.220.
110 FL: Thomas Glyn Journal: 26 and 28 November 1776.
111 Stirke, 'British Officer's Revolutionary War Journal,' p.166.
112 Wilkin, *Some British Soldiers*, pp.217–218.

now pursued the enemy much too slowly for our wishes,' but wisely added, 'it is not for us subordinates to comment on the movements of our commanders, of which we are in general very incompetent judges. Warped by passion, we consider only visible objects, and forget the thousand latent wheels by which a great army moves.'[113] The American army had been unable to put up any credible resistance, but had nonetheless effected a successful retreat; their final stroke was to remove every single boat the from the east bank of the Delaware, leaving no possibility for further British pursuit. The campaign season was over. It was time to establish winter quarters.

* * *

The British troops were ready for a period of rest. Grenadier Captain Hale wrote of 'numbers of the men wanting shoes, having marched great part of the way barefoot; yet so eager was their desire of overtaking the flying enemy, that not a single complaint was uttered.' Quarters for British troops in New Jersey were designated in towns along the route from Trenton to New York – a German brigade in Trenton, another at Bordentown, the British light infantry battalions and another brigade in Princeton, the British grenadiers in Brunswick. Having marched with only minimal baggage, officers and soldiers struggled to make their accommodations comfortable. Captain Hale complained in a letter home, 'I have neither bed or baggage; my clothes are all on my back and I am often obliged to wrap my cloak and blanket round me while I get my rags mended; we have no butter, wine or vegetables, though a Market is promised. A room is allotted me in this Town, with only three doors in it, papered and well furnished, eight Mahogany chairs, the bottoms compose my bed, a book-case and tables are the principal ornaments.' He ended by saying that although he owed many other letters, he had only two more sheets of paper which he needed for military reports, was using ink borrowed from a fellow officer, and despaired of how he would seal the letter because 'where wafers are to be procured is beyond my comprehension, nothing of the kind in town.'[114]

Howe gave orders on 20 December for regimental commanders to 'keep up their flank Companies level with those of the Battalion.'[115] Throughout this campaign the flank companies had operated at a nominal strength of 36 private soldiers per company, the companies of the 42nd and 71st Regiments excepted, which were much larger at 96 private men. Recruits and drafts had poured into New York throughout the fall, allowing the regiments' battalion companies to be brought closer to the new strength of 54 private men, so it was time to send suitable men to the flank companies, but getting them to New Jersey would take time.

Losses in the flank battalions had been few. From the time of the battle on 27 August the three grenadier battalions had lost only 30 men dead of all causes (exclusive of the Marines and 71st Regiment, for whom no muster rolls are known to survive for this period); 19 had been transferred out, presumably due to wounds or other disability. The light infantry battalions lost 35 dead and 15 transferred out, plus two deserters – Thomas Farrier of the 54th

113 Wilkin, *Some British Soldiers*, p.190.

114 Wilkin, *Some British Soldiers*, pp.218–220.

115 General orders, 20 December 1776, Anon. (ed.), 'British Army Orders,' p.426.

at the beginning of November, and Thomas Ridley of the 40th in mid-December.[116] Many of the wounded recovered sufficiently to return to their companies, such as 42nd Regiment grenadier Duncan McGraw from Killearn in Ross and Cromarty, Scotland, 32 years old, wounded through the jaw on 27 August; grenadier John Ingram of the 63rd, a 34-year-old barber from St. James Parish in Taunton, Somerset, wounded in the hand, right leg and left thigh in the same battle; 44th light infantryman James Panton, a 35-year-old weaver from Fordice, Banffshire, wounded at Harlem Heights on 16 September; and 29-year-old William Strath of the 63rd's light infantry, from Jervis, Aberdeenshire, wounded in the right arm the same day.[117] They would rejoin the fight, a fight that came sooner than anyone expected.

116 TNA: WO 12: muster rolls for the various regiments.

117 TNA: WO 121/7/58, WO 121/1/370, WO 121/10/91, WO 121/1/65: Discharges of Duncan McGraw, John Ingram, James Panton, and William Strath respectively.

4

'Much harassed during the winter': New Jersey, 1777

The British soldiers in New Jersey had just begun to settle in to winter quarters when, on Christmas Day in 1776, General George Washington led an American attack that surprised the German garrison in Trenton, capturing most. The other garrisons spread among towns between Trenton and New York went on alert, but none were near enough, or strong enough, to independently counterattack. For many British officers, having been on campaign for four months, settling in to garrison meant taking leave to go to New York to obtain personal baggage and necessities for troops under their command. Lieutenant General Cornwallis had already boarded a ship to return to England for the winter. During the final week of 1776 they scrambled to return to their regiments, battalions and companies, preparing to once again go on the offensive during a normally militarily quiet season.

By 1 January 1777 Cornwallis was back in command of the British troops in New Jersey, and on the move to dislodge the rebel army from the that side of the Delaware. George Harris, captain of the 5th Regiment's company in the 1st Battalion of Grenadiers, remembered marching with the Brigade of Guards and the grenadier battalions from quarters in Brunswick through Princeton, where for the entire week between 26 December and the new year the light infantry battalions had expected to be the next target of the rebel incursion. 'Our children, as we call the light infantry, welcomed us, one and all crying: "Let them come!" "Lead us to them, we are sure of being supported!"'[1] That night the Guards and grenadiers 'occupied the Barns in the Environs of the Town.'[2]

At 8:00 a.m. the next morning they were on the march again – the two British light infantry battalions and two grenadier battalions, the Brigade of Guards, and a German brigade, with jägers, dragoons and artillery. Skirmishing with an American rearguard slowed the move to Trenton, but no British writer detailed which troops engaged them – the flank battalions, the Brigade of Guards, German chasseurs (men picked men from German infantry regiments to serve as light infantry) and dismounted British dragoons were all well-versed in skirmishing. By the time the British column pushed through Trenton and arrived at Assunpink Creek, which flowed through a gully and formed a significant barrier,

1 Wilkin, *Some British Soldiers*, p.192.
2 FL: Thomas Glyn Journal: 1 January 1777.

daylight was waning. Cornwallis's troops made three attempts to force a crossing of the only bridge but were thwarted each time. American accounts call this a significant battle, but British participants recorded it as only a skirmish with few casualties. As darkness fell, with the two armies in sight of each other, Cornwallis was confident that a morning assault would rout the American incursion. The men in the flank battalions 'remained all night lying upon our arms, in expectation that he would attack us,' recalled Lieutenant Hunter of the 52nd Regiment's light infantry.[3]

Another group from the British grenadiers and light infantry was in the area. Some officers hurrying to join their companies were tasked with shepherding replacements and recovered convalescents from New York to the flank battalions. One of them, Lieutenant Hale of the 45th's grenadiers, wrote that they arrived in Brunswick on 1 January 1777 only to find the battalions 'had marched to Trenton, of which the rebels were in possession.' He continued, 'We followed the next day with an escort of drafts and Recruits for the Grenadiers and Light Infantry' numbering about 80 men; besides Hale, Captain John Hatfield of the 43rd's grenadiers, Captain Thomas Williamson of the 52nd's grenadiers and Lieutenant John Campbell of the 44th's light infantry are known to have been with this detachment. They reached Princeton the next day, where the 17th, 40th and 55th Regiments and some mounted and dismounted troopers of the 16th Light Dragoons were posted.[4]

The next morning eight battalion companies of the 17th Regiment marched out of Princeton along with a portion of the 55th, the dismounted dragoons, and the little corps of flank battalion men, led by the 17th's Lieutenant Colonel Charles Mawhood. Unbeknownst to them, or to Cornwallis, the rebel army near Trenton had slipped away during the night, not to escape across the Delaware, but to circle inland and north to attack the garrison of Princeton. The two forces met in the morning south of Princeton when a party of dismounted dragoons 'discovered a Column of the rebel Army, as they were marching thro' a wood on the left Flank,' according to a dragoon officer.[5] Alerted to the enemy's presence, Mawhood's men 'drew up on a woody eminence and looked at them for a considerable time, during which Col. Mawhood had two choices ... either to retire back to Princetown,' wrote Lieutenant Hale, 'or push on to Maidenhead.' But the rebels, far more numerous, were gaining ground on Mawhood's left flank, pushing past them. Seeing the danger to the troops in Princeton, 'we sent off the 55th to alarm the 40th, and then marched down with 330 to attack 8000 drawn up in regular order, and strongly posted in an orchard covered with some Barns,' remembered Hale; 'The advanced guard of 800 reserved their fire till we advanced within 40 yards, and then gave us a very heavy discharge, which brought down 7 of my platoon at once, the rest, being recruits, gave way.' By 'recruits,' Hale appears to refer to men transferring into flank companies rather than men recently arrived from Great Britain; although selected for suitability to serve in the flank battalions, being from different regiments they may have fled because of a lack of cohesion or familiarity with the officers commanding them.[6]

3 FL: Thomas Glyn Journal: 2 January 1777; Hunter, *Journal*, p.24. Muster rolls do not indicate any grenadiers or light infantry killed on 2 January.
4 Wilkin, *Some British Soldiers*, pp.221–222.
5 TNA: WO 71/87: trial of Cornet Henry Evatt, pp.343–361.
6 Wilkin, *Some British Soldiers*, p.223.

Hale remained determined: 'I rallied them with some difficulty, and brought them on with bayonets, the Rebels poured in a second fire, and killed Captain Williams of the 52nd Grenadiers and Leslie of the 17th which Regiment advanced in a most excellent order, and at length we drove them through the railings, barns and orchards, back on their main body which also fell into confusion.' Hale's description suggests that the flank company detachment operated like battalion troops in concert with the 17th Regiment rather than in the more typical fashion of flank companies, a logical disposition given the composite nature of the detachment. Hale continued, 'We kept possession of the orchard for 20 minutes, turning one of their own guns upon them; during this time they discovered our weakness, and brought three pieces of Cannon in play on our right with grape and case, but our nearness, 100 yards, saved us greatly.' Recognizing that they were too weak to press a further attack – by this time, according to Hale, only about 240 men remained fighting – and in great danger of being surrounded, 'a resolution was taken to retreat, i.e., run away as fast as we could.' Mawhood's force lost about 100 men, '15 out of 80 Grenadiers and a Captain,' wrote Hale, adding, 'I was shot through my coat, and received a Contusion on the leg, but am now well and able to walk.'[7]

While this was going on, the flank battalions and Brigade of Guards made their way from Trenton back towards the fighting with all possible speed. But it was not fast enough. The rebel army pushed through Princeton, took a number of prisoners from the 40th and 55th Regiments, and continued north. Cornwallis's troops pursued; Lieutenant Hunter of the 52nd's light infantry recalled, 'We only halted two hours at Princetown,

Engraving on the escutcheon of a 1756 pattern firelock shows that it was used by grenadier company of the 22nd Regiment of Foot. This regiment received 1769 pattern arms in 1774; this gun is probably among those exchanged for 1756 pattern arms in Halifax in 1776. (Private collection)

7 Wilkin, *Some British Soldiers*, pp.223–224.

and continued our march all night in hopes of coming up with Washington, but he was too far before us.'[8] The grenadiers and light infantrymen with Mawhood joined their battalions as they passed through, and continued with them all the way back to their original quarters. An officer of the Guards described the overnight march from Princeton to Brunswick: 'We marched at five in the Evening a very hard frost & Snow on the ground, the Bridge at Kingston being demolished occasioned some delay, Our Men were so fatigued having had nothing to eat for two Days & no rest that with difficulty we accomplished this March of eighteen Miles.'[9] Lieutenant Hunter described the miserable march in more detail:

> I never experienced such a disagreeable night's march in my life. It was as dark as possible, and a very cold hard frost, and the horses being tired, the guns got on so slowly that we did not arrive at Brunswick before ten the next morning. We had been eighteen hours in marching sixteen miles. On our arrival at Brunswick we expected to have gone into barracks with the Grenadiers, but we were very much disappointed. The men were quartered in barns, and the officers of three Companies in one room, without anything to eat but salt pork, and half the battalion ordered on piquet on a bleak hill without any cover but some paling and straw made into a shed, a large fire at our feet – one side roasted and the other frozen. I shall never forget it.[10]

Grenadier Lieutenant Hale, with the detachment of drafts and recovered men, wrote, 'We went 20 miles round that day to join our troops and marched all the following night to Brunswick, in all upwards of 40 miles without halting two hours,' adding, 'I am as well pleased as you can be at my slight hurt at Princetown, for with all my enthusiasm I have not the least quarrel with a whole skin, and shall think myself obliged to the Rebels for entertaining the same sentiments.'[11]

Muster rolls indicate four grenadiers killed on 3 January besides Captain Williamson of the 52nd: John Letham of the 10th, George Gillan and William Stephenson of the 44th, and Benjamin Cuper of the 64th. In the light infantry, Charles Martin of the 10th was killed. Among the wounded grenadiers was 26-year-old Benjamin Noble from Sandwich, Bedfordshire, a draft for the 44th Regiment who had already served for 11 years in the 14th Regiment of Foot and had been wounded twice previously, once on the island of St. Vincent during the Carib War of 1773, and again in 1775 at the Battle of Great Bridge in Virginia.[12]

* * *

Once again the army attempted to settle in to winter quarters, the British and German grenadiers in Brunswick, the light infantry 'on the road leading from Brunswick to the Bridge at Rariton' in whatever available buildings they could find.[13] Lieutenant Hale resignedly

8 Hunter, *Journal*, p.25.
9 FL: Thomas Glyn Journal: 3 January 1777.
10 Hunter, *Journal*, p.25.
11 Wilkin, *Some British Soldiers*, pp.224–225.
12 TNA: WO 12: muster rolls of the various regiments; WO 121/10/94: discharge of Benjamin Noble.
13 FL: Thomas Glyn Journal: 3 January 1777.

wrote, 'our quarters are now contracted and bad enough in reason, but we may live in them,' while Lieutenant Hunter gave a more vivid view of the Spartan accommodations: 'The Light Infantry were in barns the whole winter, and 12 officers in a small room, lying upon straw, and a very genteel Royalist family in an inner room, the only way out of which was through ours. In this situation we remained for the winter.'[14] Captain Charles Cochrane, who took over the 4th Regiment's light infantry company after Captain Evelyn was killed the previous October, described similar conditions that he endured with fellow officers of his battalion; in March, he wrote:

> We have had rather a disagreeable winter of it. The light infantry, with which corps I am, have been much harassed during the winter, and are miserably ill lodged; my whole company, which consists of 53 men, are obliged to live in one small room, and I am in a pigeon-hole, with 11 officers, where we eat, drink, and sleep. I don't believe a man of this army, ever since the affair of Tronton, where the fatal security of the Hessians brought us into that sad scrape, have had their clothes off; for my part, except one fortnight, I have not been uncased these ten months. I have a Galloway plaid, which Jack sent me; this, a blanket, and a skin of a bear, is my principle baggage and bed. It is the healthiest and most agreeable life in the world, could one divest themselves of reflection, and have no eye towards futurity, or the main chance.[15]

To make matters worse, the defeat of the Trenton garrison breathed life and vigour into the American rebellion, making every British post in New Jersey seem vulnerable. Cornwallis ordered the troops to form at their alarm posts half an hour before daybreak each morning and remain under arms until sunrise; the men were to keep their arms near them and 'never quit their accoutrements.' The general tried to soften the drudgery by contrasting it with the alternative: 'Lord Cornwallis is thoroughly sensible of the great fatigue which the Troops have suffered yet he flatters himself if a glorious Opportunity should happen of attacking the Enemy they will exert themselves upon that occasion, not thinking an unexpected March a hardship.'[16]

Under normal circumstances garrisons like those in New Jersey purchased food from the region's farms, but this too changed after the rebel incursion in December. The people of New Jersey largely abandoned British interests, causing for the troops a 'want of fresh Provisions; which the Country People tho well paid would not bring in.' Officers could, at significant personal expense, procure some goods from New York brought on sloops that worked their way up the Raritan River, a dangerous route given the rebel sentiment in the area. The soldiers had no such luxury – 'the soldiers were kept on Salt Provisions.'[17] To sustain soldiers and horses, it was necessary to forage from the farms and fields in the countryside, expeditions that required wagons, men to gather goods, and troops to protect

14 Wilkin, *Some British Soldiers*, p.224; Hunter, *Journal*, pp.25–26.

15 James Paterson, *History of the County of Ayr: with a Genealogical Account of the Families of Ayrshire* (Edinburgh: Thomas George Stevenson, 1852), Vol.2, p.28.

16 FL: Thomas Glyn Journal: 4 January 1777.

17 FL: Thomas Glyn Journal: 9 January 1777.

them from attack. 'The whole army for the greatest part of the winter always turned out an hour before daybreak, and drew up in line in expectation of being attacked,' remembered Lieutenant Hunter; 'This was a most harassing winter for the troops at Brunswick. They were on piquet every third night, and generally marched out five or six miles twice every week to cover foraging parties.'[18] Some relief came on 28 January when turning out before daybreak was temporarily suspended, but soldiers still were required to be accoutred and ready in their quarters.[19] In the words of Lieutenant Stirke of the 10th Regiment, 'The Light Infantry took post at the Bridge of Brunswick, about a mile above the Town; where we spent a very disagreeable winter, continually harass'd in Observing the motions of the Enemy, collecting forage &c.'[20]

Several foraging expeditions became skirmishes and battles, with no impact on the course of the war but dangerous for the participants. On 1 February the 1st Battalions of Grenadiers and Light Infantry, with some German grenadiers and two troops of light dragoons were covering a foraging party when they were 'attacked by 1,000 of the enemy from Morristown with two artillery pieces,' according to a Guards officer; 'our troops with the loss of one Officer and 16 Private obliged the Enemy to retire with many killed, & returned with the Forage which was procured beyond Piscataway. The enemy were so well apprized of our movements, as to be in force wherever we appeared, notwithstanding the Orders were given but a few hours before the Troops moved.'[21] Killed was Lieutenant George Augustus Cunningham of the 22nd Regiment, who had transferred from the regiment's battalion into the light infantry to replace Lieutenant Rutherford wounded the previous October.[22]

The next day, Cornwallis admonished in orders that because 'Several Men of the 2d Battalion of Light Infantry and some other Corps having been lately taken by the Enemy, by stragling beyond the outposts of the Army,' sentries were in the future to fire upon any soldier 'attempting to go beyond them without a proper pass.' Battalion commanders and company captains were directed to prevent men leaving their quarters; 'he hopes the Soldiers have too much spirit to risk a long and shameful Captivity for the hopes of procuring any trifling temporary Conveniencies.'[23] Frequent foraging expeditions only accentuated the temptation to procure 'trifling temporary conveniencies,' a practice of which opportunistic soldiers had already shown aptitude. Writing many years after the war of his time in New Jersey, Lieutenant Hunter made light of his company's proclivity for plundering:

> The 52nd Light Infantry were famous providers. They were good hands at a Grab. Grab was a favourite expression among the Light Infantry, and meant any plunder taken by force; a Lob when you got it without any opposition, and I am very certain there never was a more expert set than the Light Infantry at either grab,

18 Hunter, *Journal*, pp.25–26.
19 FL: Thomas Glyn Journal: 28 January 1777.
20 Stirke, 'British Officer's Revolutionary War Journal,' p.167.
21 FL: Thomas Glyn Journal: 1 February 1777.
22 Stirke, 'British Officer's Revolutionary War Journal,' p.167; TNA: WO 12: muster rolls, 22nd Regiment. Rutherford remained listed as a battalion company officer on the muster rolls but was serving with the light infantry.
23 FL: Thomas Glyn Journal: 2 February 1777.

> lob, or gutting a house. The Grenadiers used to call us their children, and when we got more plunder than we wanted we always supplied our fathers.[24]

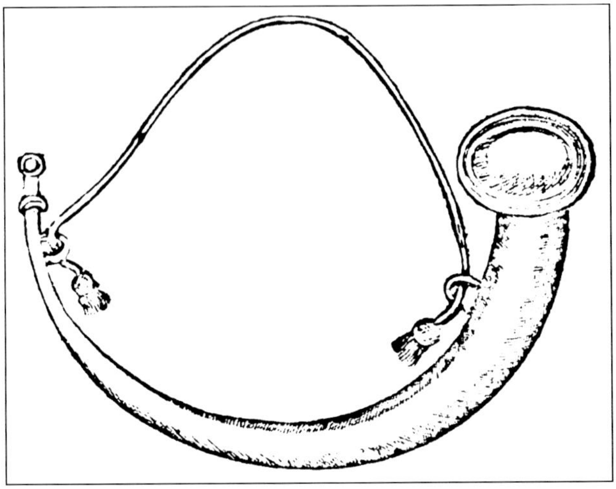

Bugle horn typical of those used by light infantry and dragoons, as shown in Robert Hinde, *The Discipline of the Light Horse* (London: W. Owen, 1778), p.207.

General Howe recognized the risk in these exploits, which led to an untold number of men being captured. Soldiers straying from quarters posed another risk as well: the 52nd Regiment's light infantry company recorded three soldiers – William Harvey, Dennis Carroll, and Dennis Kennedy – as having deserted on 31 January.[25]

Hard duty, cold weather and bad quarters took their toll in the form of further desertions, a dramatic change from the flank battalions' zeal during the previous campaign. The 4th's light infantry lost Patrick McConnell and James Lees on 14 January; three of 52nd's lights followed at the beginning of February. After the orders of 2 February, losses to desertion were few: Charles Chambers of the 4th on 21 February, Drummer John Fisher of the 28th on 21 April, and Drummer John McCaully of the 46th on 27 April. For the grenadiers, on the other hand, desertion worsened. Not a single man absconded from the grenadier battalions until 10 February, when John Buchan of the 44th deserted. Over the next three months 19 others followed, four from companies in the 1st Battalion including a sergeant of the 23rd Regiment, and 15 from companies in the 2nd Battalion, seven of them were from the 44th's company. The other British brigades quartered in New Jersey also suffered significant desertion during the early months of 1777, particularly among recruits.[26]

The 3rd Battalions of Grenadiers and Light Infantry had sailed with the expedition to occupy Rhode Island late the previous year. Finding no opposition, and with no offensive operations expected from there, the flank battalions were recalled by General Howe to join the forces in New Jersey – minus the flank companies of the 54th Regiment, which remained in the Rhode Island garrison. The flank battalions sailed from Rhode Island to New York, where they prepared for winter quarters in New Jersey the way they would normally prepare for a summer campaign: 'got our heavy Baggage ashore & lodged in the store,' wrote Lieutenant John Peebles of the 42nd Regiment's grenadier company, 'filled the

24 Hunter, *Journal*, p.27.
25 TNA: WO 12: muster rolls, 52nd Regiment.
26 TNA: WO 12: muster rolls; Ira D. Gruber (ed.), *John Peebles' American War: the Diary of a Scottish Grenadier, 1776–1782* (Mechanicsburg, PA: Stackpole Books, for the Army Records Society, 1998), p.110.

portmanteau with Campaign articles & left all the rest of my Baggage (except the Canteen Box & my Bedding).'[27] In the middle of February their transports sailed into the mouth of the Raritan River and anchored near Amboy, on the New Jersey shore adjacent to the southern tip of Staten Island. 'Here we are likely to stay for some time as there is no Room for us on Shore till Sir William Howe thinks proper we should fight for it,' wrote Captain William Dansey of the 33rd's light infantry on 17 February, 'for my part I had rather stay on board this time of Year than fight for bad Quarters.'[28]

Living on ships did not prevent these battalions from participating in the frequent foraging forays. Captain James Murray of the 57th Regiment wrote to relatives in Scotland on 25 February that the weather was 'much more severe than you can have any idea of even in the remotest regions of Perthshire,' but the army was nonetheless 'fighting away as if it was the month of July, which is in my humble opinion as great an incongruity as wearing point ruffles or eating hot rolls and butter at the season.' He referred to the expeditions into the country as 'a pretty amusement known by the name of foraging or fighting for our daily bread,' continuing, 'As the rascals are skulking about the whole country, it is impossible to move with any degree of safety with out a pretty large escort, and even then you are exposed to a dirty kind of tiraillerie, which is more noisy indeed than dangerous,' although he admitted that sometimes it was 'a little troublesome.' His battalion had already been on two such expeditions since arriving two weeks previously. On 20 February the 3rd Battalion of Light Infantry with two other battalions escorted General Howe, just arrived from New York, inland to other British posts. After leaving him with troops from the next post, Murray wrote that they 'fell in with 3 or 400 of the Rebels upon our return; after exchanging a few shots in which there was one man of our battalion wounded, they thought proper to retire, to my great joy and satisfaction for I was very cold and very hungry.'[29]

Lieutenant Peebles prepared his grenadier company for service on shore, despite not knowing when they would disembark. He inspected arms and ammunition, seeing that each man had 60 rounds of cartridges and two spare flints, and that firelocks were in good working order. His company 'got out the new cloathing & put it on the men just as it is, having no time to get it fitted,' referring to the usual winter activity of the regiment's tailors fitting annually-issued coats and waistcoats to each soldier; 'it is in general too little for the men, set the Taylors to work to put on hooks & Eyes & turn up the corner of the skirt which is all that can be done at present.' The battalion's grenadier caps had been left in storage in New York and men were sent to retrieve them. On 21 February 'The Troops from Rhode Island took a walk ashore' to get exercise.[30]

The first major operation for the 3rd Battalion of Light Infantry and 3rd Battalion of Grenadiers came on 23 February. They set out in the morning with three British regiments, about 1,500 men altogether, led by Lieutenant Colonel Mawhood. After six or eight miles, the force divided; Lieutenant Colonel Mungo Campbell of the 52nd Regiment took four grenadier companies including those of the 28th and 42nd, four companies of the 37th Regiment, the 52nd Regiment, and the 57th's light infantry company; they went in column

27 Gruber (ed.), *Diary*, pp.89, 92–93.
28 Dansey (ed.), *Letters*, p.21.
29 Robson (ed.), *Letters*, pp.38–39.
30 Gruber (ed.), *Diary*, pp.94–95.

to the left, while the remainder went with Mawhood hoping, according to Captain Murray, 'to surprise, surround and extirpate' a rebel post to the northwest.[31] Lieutenant Peebles 'was order'd with 20 men to be the advance guard,' and soon spotted enemy troops. Peebles informed Campbell; 'Very well says he I'll manouvre them,' and sent Peebles's advance guard forward to 'the edge of a wood' while the rest of the detachment formed for battle. The enemy withdrew from sight, so Peebles took his little force of grenadiers forward assuming that the rest of the detachment was also coming. But he was mistaken; they took another route. Peebles' detachment met more opponents who, seeing his small, unsupported force, 'sent out about 30 or 40 to bring us on to engage.' Peebles moved forward against them, 'receiv'd their fire from behind a fence,' then 'moved on to a fence in front & ordered my men to fire, which we continued to do at each other for a few minutes when they gave way,' this time because the rest of the British detachment came up in support. Two grenadiers were wounded, and Peebles remarked, 'I don't think we hit above 3 or 4' of the enemy. He took his little force towards another small enemy party, 'form'd & gave them a platton & two or 3 rounds after,' presumably meaning one volley by his platoon followed by a few rounds of independent firing.[32]

Peebles' advance guard rejoined Campbell's column, when their 'attention was awakened with a rattling of small arms upon our right, which we soon discovered to be our other Division driving the enemy before them.' Discovering a large enemy force in the woods, Campbell sent Peebles and his men, now only 14 or 15, to a fence at the edge of the woods where they 'kept up as much fire as we could.' The grenadier and light infantry companies came up in support, 'but began their fire at too great a distance; when they got up to the fence they soon found themselves gall'd by a fire on their right,' according to Peebles. They expected support from the 37th and 52nd, but none came; they withdrew, except for Peebles and his little party, who did not hear the order. He 'remain'd at my post till I had not one man left near me,' and although he was an officer, his situation was desperate enough that he 'fired away all my Cartridges.' As the enemy closed in he 'took to my heels & ran back to the Company under heavy fire.' Finally, the 52nd Regiment, after being stymied by conflicting orders from Mawhood and Campbell, 'came down at last' and 'gave a heavy volley into the wood which cleared it of the Rebels,' allowing the wounded to be cared for and removed from the area.[33]

As the two columns reunited and headed back towards their quarters, 'the men much fatigued & harassed a great many of them quite knock'd up,' rebels skirmished with the rear guard of grenadier companies. 'We were at last obliged to halt & fire some Cannon amongst them which set them a scampering,' wrote Peebles, but later on 'we found a large body of them in a wood posted to oppose us in front.'[34] Captain Murray wrote of this next opposition, 'You may believe by this time the men were pretty much fatigued; it is impossible to conceive what life and spirits was communicated to the breasts of every one upon

31 Robson (ed.), *Letters*, p.39.

32 Gruber (ed.), *Diary*, p.96. Murray's and Peebles' accounts generally agree, with some minor differences concerning which companies were in action in which places.

33 Robson (ed.), *Letters*, pp.39–40; Gruber (ed.), *Diary*, pp.96–97.

34 Gruber (ed.), *Diary*, p.98.

the first appearance of the attack.'[35] Peebles described the quick, and final, action: 'upon discovering them we fired a few pieces of Cannon into the wood and then formed a line in front which moved on to the wood & pour'd in their fire,' then 'this front line moved on to charge them. They fired some scattering shots in going off which did little hurt,' and the column was finally able to return to Amboy, arriving after nightfall, 'much fatigued.'[36] Murray summed up:

> The remaining part of the day was by no means agreeable. We had marched at least 28 or 30 miles over fences woods and ditches every step up to the ankles in mud or snow, and some part of it at run. My company in particular had not halted a single instant since we left the parade, et qui pis etait we had not had a morsel that day. Night came on, the men fainting every instant from the fatigue they had undergone.[37]

Two light infantry officers offered lighthearted views of the day's dangers, expressing a level of ease that belies the fact that, because they had both been on the expedition to Rhode Island, they had seen no significant fighting since the attack on Fort Washington the previous November, and the minor action on 20 February. Captain Dansey of the 33rd wrote, 'I flatter myself with understanding fighting the Rebels so well now that I am not in half the danger I was in at first and mind a Shooting match with them no more than a Days Cockshooting,' and continued,

> you know I was never a famous Shot but I made a very good one in the Skirmish we had on the 23d. of last month, of which I wrote Mr. Gwillim an Account, a Fellow jum'd from behind a Bush very near me ran behind a Tree and presented at us, I up with my Fuzee and knock'd him as quick as a Cockshooter wou'd a Cock, so don't fear me, who never was cool enough at home to kill a Woodcock, yet now am got cool enough to shoot a Man, I think I shall make one of the coolest Shooters in the Country when I return.[38]

Both Dansey and Captain Murray compared the affair to a hunt, Murray writing, 'I enjoyed this affair upon the whole, at least equal to a fox chase,' and Dansey sentimentally assuring his family in England, 'no doubts, no hopes or Fears ever disturb our Rest when we get any, if we hear from our Friends at home we are completely happy and as to War's Alarms they are now come so familiar that a Day's Yankie Hunting is no more minded than a Day's Fox Hunting, at both Diversions a Broken Bone may be got.'[39]

This fight cost the flank battalions more than just a few broken bones. Captain Murray remembered, 'The fire was prodigiously heavy at one time but per favour of some pretty large trees, which by a good deal of practice we have learnt to make a proper use of, my Company

35 Robson (ed.), *Letters*, p.40.
36 Gruber (ed.), *Diary*, pp.98–99.
37 Robson (ed.), *Letters*, pp.40–41.
38 Dansey (ed.), *Letters*, pp.23–24.
39 Robson (ed.), *Letters*, p.40; Dansey (ed.), *Letters*, p.23.

suffered very little,' although he lost 'one of the officers most dreadfully wounded and two men … one of them I fear very dangerously.'[40] Captain Dansey asked friends to 'send word to Ludlow that Drummer Peach, Son to a Miller at Ludlow, one of my first Herefordshire Recruits, was missing in the Skirmish of the 23d. Feb. last and is supposed to be taken Prisoner,' and gave no indication of other losses in his company.[41] The 42nd's grenadiers were less fortunate, losing a man killed, 22 wounded and both drummers missing; overall, 69 were killed and wounded, and six missing. Lieutenant Peebles visited the wounded from his company frequently during the next week, writing on 24 February, 'saw the wounded men several of them in a very dangerous way poor fellows, what pity it is to throw away such men as these on such shabby ill managed occasions;' on the 25th, 'Geo. Munro one of our wounded died this morning;' the next day, 'saw our wounded men dress'd, most of them very bad wounds indeed, Carr, Wm. McIntosh & Miller & Srgt. McPherson I am afraid wont live.' William Miller died the next morning. On 2 March Peebles saw 'several of the wounded men very bad, of McIntosh & Carr I have very little hopes poor fellows, I never saw men more patient & resign'd than they are.' On the 10 March he wrote, 'the Wounded are all doing well except Wm. McIntosh who is just dying – Jno. Car holds it out surpizingly, all the rest are in a good way.' William McIntosh died the next morning, John Carr held out for over three more months, finally expiring on 5 July, but Sergeant Angus McPherson defied expectations and recovered fully, serving in the 42nd Regiment's grenadier company for the rest of the war.[42]

Lieutenant Peebles recorded that this expedition was discussed among officers for the next several days, and Lieutenant Colonel Campbell even asked Peebles and Captain Charles Graham, commander of the 42nd's grenadier company, why they had not been supported, a question that these officers certainly were not in a position – on the battlefield or afterwards – to answer. Campbell went so far as to hold a court of inquiry which determined that orders were not communicated properly. During the campaign in 1776, flank companies had at least twice suffered because they advanced with too much zeal and outpaced their support; this time, they advanced in accordance with orders but their support did not follow. Regardless of the cause, these actions demonstrated that the fast-moving, open-order formations of the flank battalions were risky, requiring constant and careful coordination to prevent parties from becoming isolated and outnumbered, especially when the enemy 'received better information of our intentions,' according to Captain Murray, 'almost as soon as we began to march.'[43]

Except for these excursions, duty in the garrisons was routine but difficult due to poor, crowded quarters and bad weather. On 27 February the 3rd Battalion of Grenadiers, still on ships in the Raritan River, 'went ashore this morning to stretch their limbs & to get the ship cleaned.' The 3rd Battalions of Light Infantry and Grenadiers went foraging again the next day, accompanied by two 6-pounder field pieces, this time only three miles into the country. Hay and straw were loaded into wagons 'whilst the Troops were posted all around to defend

40 Robson (ed.), *Letters*, p.40. He did not identify the officer; Lieutenant George Monoux retired from the 57th's light infantry a week after the battle. TNA: WO 12: muster rolls, 57th Regiment.
41 Dansey (ed.), *Letters*, p.24.
42 Gruber (ed.), *Diary*, pp.98–100, 102; TNA: WO 12: muster rolls, 42nd Regiment.
43 Gruber (ed.), *Diary*, pp.98–100, Robson (ed.), *Letters*, p.39.

them,' wrote Peebles, but there was no opposition this time. The following week they formed up for another expedition but were thwarted by a snowstorm; they went again the next day and gathered salt hay successfully with no opposition.[44]

The cramped quarters began to affect the soldiers' health. On 5 March the grenadier companies of the 33rd and 37th Regiments moved to a different ship, easing crowding somewhat, and on 7 March the 3rd Battalion of Grenadiers began a routine of parading on the beach for an hour or two on every morning that weather permitted. Some of Lieutenant Peebles' men were ill with the flux and the ship needed cleaning, 'for I never saw anything so dirty'; the hours each morning afforded some time for cleaning, except on several days that snow or rain confined the men on board. By 19 March 'an ugly fever' had 'seized upon a good many both in Town & transports of which several have died.'[45]

Expeditions on 8 and 10 March were uneventful, Peebles wrote of the latter that the flank battalions 'filed off to the right & posted themselves on the Short Hills & high grounds' to cover forage wagons. On 16 March the 3rd Battalions of Light Infantry and Grenadiers marched at 1:00 a.m. with an expedition of 2,000 men; they encountered opposition at daybreak that fled after exchanging a few shots, and on the way back 'a parcel of the rascals came on our rear & kept up a scattered popping fire for a good while with the Light Bobs,' wrote Peebles. Major Henry Johnson, commanding the 3rd Battalion of Light Infantry, was among the three or four wounded. Arriving at quarters well after dark, the march left the men 'a good deal fatigued' not just from duration and distance, but because the season left the roads and ground 'very soft & deep.' They nonetheless went on two similar expeditions in the next week.[46]

It was finally time for shipboard battalions to move into land quarters on 26 March. They put baggage and sick men on sloops to sail up the Raritan while the rest marched, arriving at Brunswick in the early afternoon. There, the two battalions were disbanded and the companies distributed among the 1st and 2nd Battalions of Light Infantry and Grenadiers – the companies of the 15th, 28th, 33rd and 37th going to the 1st Battalions, those of the 42nd, 46th and 57th to the 2nd Battalions.[47] Assuming that the newly-joined companies were integrated into their battalions in order of seniority, from the flanks to the centre as they had been arranged in Halifax in 1776, the battalions when formed into line were arranged like this:

1st Battalion of Grenadiers
5th, 15th, 22nd, 27th, 33rd, 37th, 40th, 38th, 35th, 28th, 23rd, 17th, 10th, 4th
2nd Battalion of Grenadiers
43rd, 45th, 49th, 52nd, 57th, 64th, 63rd, 55th, Marines, 46th, 44th, 42nd

1st Battalion of Light Infantry
5th, 15th, 22nd, 27th, 33rd, 37th, 38th, 35th, 28th, 23rd, 17th, 10th, 4th
2nd Battalion of Light Infantry
42nd, 44th, 46th, 52nd, 57th, 64th, 63rd, 55th, 49th, 45th, 43rd, 40th

44 Gruber (ed.), *Diary*, pp.99–100.
45 Gruber (ed.), *Diary*, pp.101–102, 104.
46 Gruber (ed.), *Diary*, pp.101–105.
47 Gruber (ed.), *Diary*, pp.106.

No contemporary information has been found to confirm this arrangement, and it is entirely possible that the new companies were added in a different way – in the centre of each battalion, for example –to maintain better continuity among the existing companies.

Lieutenant Peebles sent a man to New York to purchase canvas for two pairs of trousers for each man in his company, a typical preparation for summer campaigns in America – and a bigger change for his highlanders, whose dress uniform included a kilt, than for other British regiments that wore woollen breeches as their regimental uniform. 'This Place quite full of troops,' he wrote, 'the duty easy & the Post quiet.' The grenadiers were quartered in store houses, their officers in 'Empty Dwelling Houses.'[48] Captain Dansey wrote from Piscataway, just north of New Brunswick and closer to the enemy, 'we came into Quarters in this District, where we expect to enjoy a Month or Six Weeks rest before we take the Field.'[49]

The rest lasted only two and a half weeks. As the weather warmed, 'The Rebels like other venomous Animals of this Continent begin to turn out of their lurking holes and harass us with small scouting Parties,' wrote Captain Dansey.[50] On 12 April the light infantry battalions, the 1st Battalion of Grenadiers and two troops of light horse paraded at 9:00 p.m. and marched northwest along the south side of the Raritan. Some hours later the Brigade of Guards, a brigade of infantry and a party of jägers marched north. Just before daybreak the flank battalions turned north, fording the river to attack 'a Nest of them' at Bound Brook; the northbound column turned west to attack at the same time. The light infantry and jägers made contact with enemy sentries and 'drove them with precipitation to the Village where the alarm was spread & they took to their heels'; British troops captured about 100 men, three field pieces, some cattle and wagonloads of flour, destroyed fortifications, and seized the papers of an American general who fled. The flank battalions lost one killed and two wounded, the other column had three wounded; they were back in quarters by 10:00 a.m., 'a good deal fatigued,' according to Lieutenant Peebles.[51] On 15 April General Howe sent word that he was 'highly pleased with their Behaviour on that occasion' and gave 'his thanks for their Silence and Attention during the March, and for their Spirit when they arrived at the Enemys Quarters.'[52]

On 20 April Captain Dansey wrote a vivid description of his exploits in one of these actions without stating which one, an indication of the frequency with which the flank battalions were called upon to undertake these missions, and the diminished sense of danger induced by frequent exposure to the enemy:

> the Light Infantry are in the most danger, that is of being wounded in the Arms for we have learn'd from the Rebels to cover our Bodies if there's a Tree or a Rail near us. I faced two hundred of the Rebels with my Company only in a Wood, for two minuits, myself not twenty Yards from some of them and received all their Fire our Friends thought we were cut to pieces another Company join'd me and I drove the Rebels and had only one man wounded in the Arm, we kill'd six and wounded

48 Gruber (ed.), *Diary*, pp.105–107.
49 Dansey (ed.), *Letters*, p.25.
50 Dansey (ed.), *Letters*, p.26.
51 Gruber (ed.), *Diary*, p.109.
52 FL: Thomas Glyn Journal: 12 and 15 April 1777.

> sixteen of them. I was so near as to call to them "by God my Lads we have you now" in hopes they would be bullied to surrender but that wou'd not do they answer'd me with heavy fire, however when I got my men to the trees round about me and the other Company coming up to my Support, I bullied them another way, seeing them snug behind the Trees and showing no disposition to run, and too many of them to charge as we were rather too thin I cried as loud as I cou'd hollow that they might be sure to hear me "by God Soldiers they run, have at them my brave Boys" which had the desired effect, one thought the other run and they all set off as if the D–l drove them we clear'd the Wood of them and they never travelled themselves within Shot again that Day. I tell you this Story as it really happen'd that you may be less afraid of the Dangers I undergo as I now pretty well understand how to encounter them.[53]

Many times during the winter and spring New Jersey garrison towns were attacked; the flank battalions and individual flank companies were seldom involved in these defensive actions unless in their immediate area. One such event occurred on 10 May, when a large force attacked the 42nd Regiment's quarters in Piscataway. Some light infantry companies – no writer identified which ones – exhibited 'spirited behavior' in helping drive off the assault, but with the misfortune of inflicting a friendly-fire casualty: Major Duncan McPherson of the 42nd was 'slightly wounded in the head by a Light Infantry Man.'[54] The next day, the troops in New Jersey received uplifting news that the King had learned of their success in the previous year's campaign, and was 'pleased to express his Royal Approbation of the Ability and Conduct displayed by Lord Cornwallis in his March through jersey in December last, and of the exemplary Steadiness which was manifested by the Troops under his Lordships Command,' a compliment read to the army in general orders.[55]

On 17 May, the troops moved out of winter quarters and into encampments, taking advantage of warmer weather. On the 26th, the 1st Battalion of Light Infantry and a party of the 16th Light Dragoons marched out at 2:00 a.m. towards Bound Brook to probe enemy positions. After daylight they engaged hostile troops, but 'finding the Enemy were still in force after some skirmishing took post on some rising Ground.' The Brigade of Guards came up in support, forming behind the light infantry. The enemy brought up artillery, and British troops responded by putting the rising ground between themselves and the enemy. When the cannonade began, 'we were ordered to lay down & being covered by the Ground, no loss ensued except Major General Grant having his horse shot dead under him.' British field pieces soon returned fire, causing the enemy to retreat 'with great precipitation,' and the British force returned to their encampments.[56] The general's horse was the only casualty, prompting Lieutenant Hale to write, 'I wish it had been the General instead of the horse, no man can be more detested.'[57]

More regiments came into the area in early June in preparation for a new campaign. Some regiments added replacements to their flank companies; on 8 June the 40th's commanding

53 Dansey (ed.), *Letters*, p.27.
54 Gruber (ed.), *Diary*, p.111.
55 FL: Thomas Glyn Journal: 10 and 11 May 1777.
56 FL: Thomas Glyn Journal: 17 and 26 May 1777.
57 Wilkin, *Some British Soldiers*, p.226.

Engineer officer Archibald Robertson included a reclining light infantryman wearing a round hat, jacket and trousers in *View from Staten Island 2nd July 1777*, after the arduous winter and spring in New Jersey. (New York Public Library)

officer ordered company commanders to 'to turn out this Evening at Roll Call two of the properest men they have of a twelve months standing as Soldiers in the Regiment for the Light Infantry that Captain Wolfe may Chuse out the Number he wants to Compleat his Company to 50 Rank And File.' With eight battalion companies, Captain William Wolfe had 16 men to choose from, and selected eight.[58]

Three times in early June the army pushed deeper into New Jersey, only to retire again to their original posts, attempting to draw their enemy out of the mountains that sheltered them in the northwest part of the state, each series of skirmishes failing to bring about a pivotal action. Later in the month General Howe made further manoeuvres, feinting retreat, attempting encirclement, trying assorted movements to bring on a pitched battle. The light infantry played significant roles in actions on the 23rd and 26th, in the latter of which 'The Light Troops of the Right Column were in constant skirmish the whole Day,' wrote Major General James Grant.[59] Captain Dansey, now with the 1st Battalion of Light Infantry, wrote, 'the Affair was mostly with our Battalion of Light Infantry and thank God my usual Luck attended me.'[60] When the army finally left New Jersey on the last day of June, the flank battalions formed the rear guard.[61]

58 LOC: George Washington Papers: orderly book, 40th Regiment, regimental orders, 8 June 1777, Regiment; TNA: WO 12: muster rolls, 40th Regiment.
59 BC: James Grant Papers: James Grant to Edward Harvey, 10 July 1777.
60 Dansey (ed.), *Letters*, p.28.
61 General orders, 30 June 1777, Anon. (ed.), 'British Army Orders,' p.455.

5

'Never more eager to press forward': Quebec and New York, 1776–1777

Back in the spring 1776, while General Howe arranged his army in Halifax, another force cruised past in the Atlantic, skirted Nova Scotia, and sailed into the St. Lawrence River. Rebel forces had invaded the province of Quebec in the waning months of 1775, capturing the two thinly-spread British regiments defending posts from Lake Champlain to Montreal, and laying siege to Quebec, the Canadian capital and lynchpin of the colony. Nine infantry regiments – the 9th, 20th, 21st, 24th, 29th, 31st, 34th, 53rd, and 62nd – led by General John Burgoyne left Great Britain in March 1776 to relieve the siege or retake the city if necessary. The 47th Regiment, part of Howe's army in Halifax, was detached and joined Burgoyne's force.

Each Quebec-bound regiment was close to the established strength of 54 private men per company. Attaining this strength between the increase in establishment ordered in the summer 1775 and embarkation in 1776 had required a great deal of recruiting and drafting, meaning that the regiments as a whole had substantial numbers of recruits – but their flank companies were composed almost entirely of experienced soldiers, drawing men from their own regiments' battalion companies and suitable drafts from other corps. When the 9th Regiment was inspected in mid-1775, for example, half their grenadiers and almost two-thirds of their light infantry had been in the army for over five years; between that time and embarkation, each company added six recruits and 12 drafted men to attain their increased strength. While most of the 9th's drafts came from the 32nd Regiment, three grenadiers and two light infantrymen were volunteers from cavalry regiments.[1] The 62nd's grenadiers took on 10 men drafted from the cavalry, while their light infantry added three.[2]

The 21st, 29th, 31st and 34th Regiments had been in North America as recently as 1773, albeit not in Canada. The 31st and 34th took part in the Carib War in 1772 and 1773, and their ranks included many veterans of that conflict; at least 18 of the 31st's grenadiers and 14 of their light infantry had fought there.[3] Some 30 soldiers in the 29th's flank companies

1 TNA: WO 27/35: inspection return, 9th Regiment, 17 July 1775; WO 12: muster rolls, 9th Regiment, 8th Dragoons, 12th Light Dragoons, 13th Light Dragoons.

2 TNA: WO 12: muster rolls, 62nd Regiment, 2nd Horse, 5th Dragoons, 9th Dragoons, 12th Light Dragoons, 13th Light Dragoons, 18th Light Dragoons.

3 TNA: WO 12: muster rolls, 31st Regiment.

had been in the regiment in March 1770 when the famous Boston Massacre occurred, including three who were tried for murder and acquitted in its aftermath – John Carroll, now a sergeant in the grenadier company, William McAuley, now a grenadier corporal, and William Warren, light infantry private.[4]

The first ships to reach Quebec, carrying a portion of the 29th Regiment, arrived in early May. The first troops to land included the grenadier company, and the very presence of a relief force caused the city's besiegers to flee.[5] Over the next two weeks the remainder of the 29th arrived, followed by the 47th. The 29th's light infantry and grenadiers, and the entire 47th, boarded again and continued up the St. Lawrence, reaching Trois Riviéres on 22 May. There they dropped anchors and remained on board, awaiting the rest of the army now led by General Guy Carleton, commander in chief of British forces in Quebec. The entire army was at Trois Riviéres, some on ships and some ashore, by 7 June. On the 8th, they were attacked by a substantial American force, but rapidly outmanoeuvred their adversaries in a swift action that left the British masters of the field. The following day it was back onto the transports to continue pursuit of the fleeing rebel forces.[6]

The next day General Carleton organized his army into brigades. He detached the grenadiers and light infantry from their regiments and formed two flank battalions, the grenadiers commanded by Major John Dyke Acland of the 20th Regiment, the light infantry led by Major Alexander, Earl of Balcarres of the 53rd. With the 24th Regiment, the two flank battalions formed the advance corps of the army commanded by Brigadier General Simon Fraser. They embarked on the 10 June, found favourable winds to proceed up the river on the 14th, arriving that evening at Sorel where the Richelieu River joins the St. Lawrence, the location of a substantial fort. The grenadiers and light infantry immediately disembarked, landing by 9:00 p.m., only to find the fort abandoned. They 'lay all night on their arms,' anticipating a march in the morning.[7]

Part of the army went by the St. Lawrence towards Montreal, while the advance corps and six artillery pieces stepped off at 9:00 a.m. on the 15th on the banks of the Richelieu, marching towards Chambly. Led by General Burgoyne, they covered about 18 miles that day, a march that 'notwithstanding the great heat of the day and the fatigue the men underwent the night before, they executed with great cheerfulness.' The months on transports, however, had left them unprepared for such exertion, and they spent the next day resting, then proceeded another 16 miles on the 17th. All the while their quarry fled just hours ahead of them. On 18 June the march began at 2:00 a.m., to arrive at the fort at Chambly by 9:00 a.m., but the fort had been abandoned and burned. The next objective was St. John's

4 TNA: WO 12: muster rolls, 29th Regiment. William Warren had been in the grenadier company in March 1770, but transferred to the light infantry when that company was created the following year. The two grenadiers convicted in the 1770 trial, Mathew Kilroy and Hugh Montgomery, were discharged before embarkation and received pensions. WO 116/7: Examinations of Invalid Soldiers, 22 February 1776, Pension Admission Book.

5 Elizabeth Cometti (ed.), *The American Journals of Lt. John Enys* (Blue Mountain Lake, NY: Adirondack Museum, 1976), p.12

6 Cometti (ed.), *American Journals*, p.15.

7 William Digby, 'Some Account of the American War Between Great Britain and Her Colonies, 1776', in James Phinney Baxter, *The British Invasion from the North* (Albany, NY: Joel Munsell's Sons, 1887), p.115

where another fort stood. When about two miles away, knowing the enemy rear guard was near, Burgoyne ordered three light infantry companies ahead; they trotted the remaining distance, but found the fort abandoned and afire. The rest of the army arrived after dark and lay on their arms that night.[8] 'The Men notwithstanding so fatiguing a March of near fifty Miles, were in good Spirits, & never more eager to press forward,' wrote an aide-de-camp.[9] 'Thus was Canada saved,' recalled Lieutenant William Digby of the 53rd's grenadiers, 'with much less trouble than was expected on our embarking from Great Britain.'[10]

Knowing there were cannon-armed enemy vessels on the lake, the British army in Montreal and Chambly assembled naval forces of their own, schooners and gunboats and a three-masted ship, all brought from Montreal over portages to the Richelieu.[11] While this work proceeded it was time for the army, which had been on the move almost constantly since disembarking, to drill and exercise. 'Regiments to be under Arms in their several Cantonments for two hours, and no more in the cool of every Morning to prepare themselves for active Service,' directed General Carleton on 29 June; 'No Exercise need be practiced, except Loading, Levelling, charging with Bayonets, and marching, in which it is meant to comprehend changing front by Divisions, and by Files; suffering the Regiment to break and form upon one given point, either by a file from Right, Left or Centre.' Simple movements for rapid manoeuvre, to bring bullets and bayonets against poorly-trained opponents. Carleton included one instruction identical to that given by General Howe on Staten Island in August: 'The Order of forming is to be at two deep, and the Files 18 Inches asunder.'[12] Firing was practiced mostly with blanks, allowing only 20 ball cartridges for each recruit and 10 for other soldiers, 'expended for firing at marks or otherwise' at the discretion brigade commanders.[13] No procedures specific to the grenadiers or light infantry have been found. Each regiment procured paper, powder and ball to produce 100 cartridges per man, not all to be carried by each man but to be stored in small barrels or boxes covered with painted canvas to prevent damage from dampness.[14]

Soldiers practiced working with bateaux and flat-bottomed boats, 'embarking, rowing, landing, and forming with celerity' as well as 'boarding boats, or armed vessels, that they may be expert in those exercises should the Rebels be foolish enough to attempt opposition on either element.'[15] Batteaux were fitted with 'two planks … to be fitted with Cross Pieces to prevent slipping, and to serve as Gang-Boards,' and soldiers practiced embarking and disembarking wearing haversacks and knapsacks. The planks, after embarkation, were laid along each side of the batteau, 'and as large a proportion of Men, as can sit without interrupting the Rowers, are to be seated upon them fore and aft, and are to be practiced to give

8 Digby, 'Some Account', pp.116–118.

9 Ronald F. Kingsley (ed.), 'Letters to Lord Polwarth from Sir Francis-Carr Clerke, Aide-de-Camp to General John Burgoyne,' *New York History* Vol.79, no. 4 (October 1998), p.412.

10 Digby, 'Some Account', p.118.

11 Cometti (ed.), *American Journals*, p.15–16; Digby, 'Some Account', pp.106–107.

12 Horatio Rogers (ed.), *Hadden's Journal and Orderly Books* (Albany, NY: J. Munsell's sons, 1884), pp.197–198, General orders, 29 June 1776.

13 Rogers (ed.), *Hadden's Journal and Orderly Books*, p.205, general orders, 3 July 1776.

14 Rogers (ed.), *Hadden's Journal and Orderly Books*, pp.244–245, 263, general orders, 8 and 29 August 1776.

15 Rogers (ed.), *Hadden's Journal and Orderly Books*, p.224, general orders, 16 July 1776.

their fire broadside.' Soldiers on benches at each end of the boat were prepared to 'give their fire fore and aft.'[16]

On 14 August Fraser's advance corps boarded bateaux and made their way up the Richelieu to Ile aux Noix, just north of the Canada-New York border, beyond which the river opened into Lake Champlain. They set about converting the wooded, one mile by half-mile island into a fortified post, clearing land for an encampment and converting dilapidated works from the previous war into serviceable fortifications. Swampy ground, snakes, heat, lightning, and persistent rain rendered the work tedious. Lieutenant Digby wrote:

> The idea of service to those who have not had an opportunity of seeing any, may induce them to believe the only hardship a soldier endures on a campaign is the danger attending an action, but there are many others, perhaps not so dangerous, yet, in my opinion, very near as disagreeable – remaining out whole nights under rain and almost frozen with cold, with very little covering, perhaps without being able to light a fire; fearing the enemy's discovering the post, and not knowing the moment of attack, but always in expectation of one.[17]

On the night of 3 September intelligence came that an attack on the unfinished post was imminent. Brigadier General Fraser gave orders for the brigade of around 1,400 men to strike tents and leave them on the ground if an alarm was raised, and immediately 'to get under arms without the beating of drums or making the least noise.' The grenadiers were to detach an officer and 40 men to assist gunners handing the 12-pounder cannons on the west side of the island, while the light infantry sent two officers and 60 men to the four-gun battery on the east side. Men were to remain covered from gunfire of hostile ships, and 'be particularly careful not to throw away their ammunition by firing at too great a distance.' An orderly from each battalion would attend Fraser at the four-gun battery. With these preparations in place, the army rested on their arms all night, but no attack came.[18]

In September troops in Montreal, Chambly and other locations prepared to move south 'in order to go in quest of the Rebels.'[19] The hope was to reach Fort Ticonderoga, but Lieutenant John Row of the 9th Regiment's grenadier company presciently penned that they would 'more probable (from the advancement of the season) be obliged to return to Canada.'[20] Each regiment, and the two flank battalions, took 'no more than 304 Rank and File,'[21] presumably so enough men remained behind to sustain operations between Quebec at the advancing army. For the regiments, each with eight companies because flank companies were detached, this meant 38 corporals and private men in each company – presumably three corporals and 35 privates – plus three sergeants and two drummers if the full complement of each was present. The 10-company grenadier and light infantry battalions

16 Rogers (ed.), *Hadden's Journal and Orderly Books*, pp.258–259, general orders, 20 August 1776.
17 Digby, 'Some Account', pp.134–139.
18 Digby, 'Some Account', pp.140–142.
19 Huntington Library, San Marino, CA (HL): mssHM 66: Journal of an Officer of the 47th Regiment of Foot, general orders, 8 September 1776.
20 NRS: GD113/5/73a: John Row to Jane Innes, 26 September 1776.
21 HL: mssHM 66: general orders, 8 September 1776.

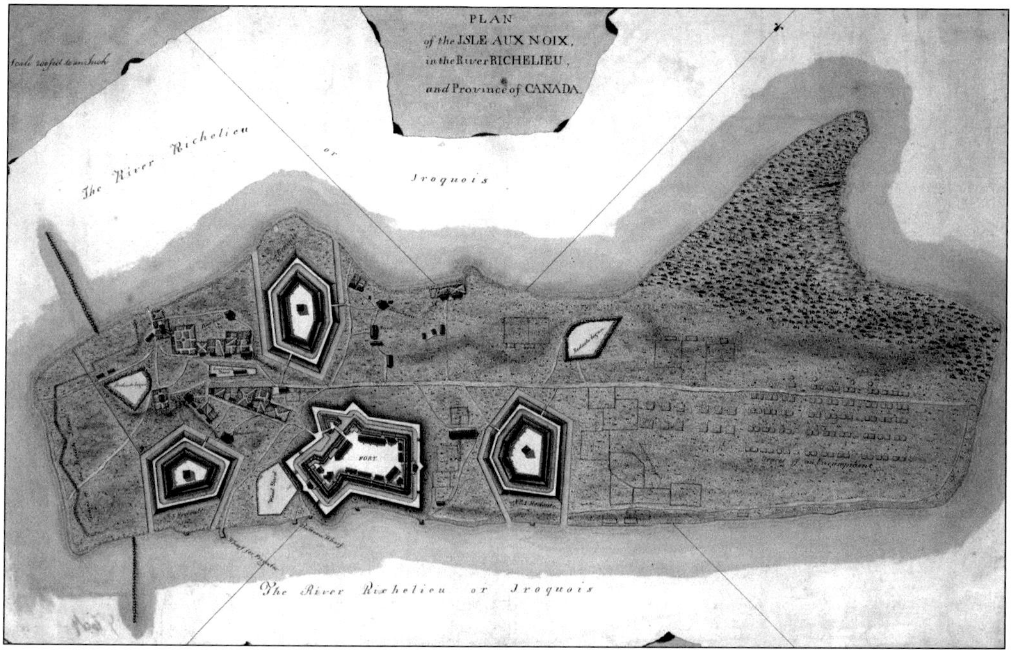

Ile aux Noix, occupied by the British advanced corps in 1776. (Library of Congress)

were left with 30 corporals and privates per company. A company of riflemen, or marksmen, commanded by Captain Alexander Fraser of the 20th Regiment, consisting of men drawn from battalion companies of British regiments, supplemented the advanced corps.[22]

It was not until October that the flotilla was ready to sail, vessels of various sizes carrying soldiers and sailors southward up the lake. Armed vessels with soldiers and sailors went ahead to find and fight the rebel lake navy. Fraser's and one other brigade embarked on the 6th, the grenadiers in flat-bottomed boats, the light infantry in bateaux, laden with tents, ammunition and 14 days' provisions.[23] The waterborne soldiers had learned to change formation from ranks of eight boats abreast to a single line and back again in response to gun signals, which 'had a pretty effect, as our men were all expert at rowing, having been ordered to practice frequently.'[24] They stopped at Point au Fer, just south of the New York border where Lake Champlain narrows into the Richelieu River, landed, encamped, and awaited news from the armed fleet. On the 12th, nebulous accounts trickled in of a naval victory, and on the 14th an aide-de-camp arrived to confirm the British victory at the Battle of Valcour Island. [25] With the lake clear of hostile naval forces, the troops embarked and rowed south, camping without tents on the lake shore each night, 'warm enough in the woods, making large fires ... when it rained, it was not so pleasant, but use reconciled all

22 Cometti (ed.), *Hadden's Journal and Orderly Books*, pp.474–475.

23 Cometti (ed.), *Hadden's Journal and Orderly Books*, p.302, general orders, 5 October 1776; Digby, 'Some Account', p.153

24 Digby, 'Some Account', p.153.

25 Digby, 'Some Account', pp.158–160.

that soon to us, and we slept as sound under the canopy of the heavens as in the best feather bed.' Facing the lake's 'great swells in many parts, but none that did our small fleet any damage,' they proceeded to Chimney Point, opposite Crown Point, and encamped for three days before crossing to Crown Point.[26]

The two brigades landed and stayed for the rest of October at Crown Point, 'a remarkable fine plain, an uncommon sight to us after being so long buried in such boundless woods, where our camp formed a grand appearance.'[27] In spite of the remote location, British troops exhibited the same disciplinary issues that plagued Howe's army. On 17 October the commander in chief gave strict orders not to 'molest any of the Inhabitants at Crown Point or on either side of the Lake in their Persons or property,' noting that 'they are to be considered as British Subjects who have already suffer'd much by the residence of a lawless Banditti among them.' Goods could be purchased for 'ready money.' The orders did not explicitly mention plunder but implied it.[28] Just three days later Brigadier General Fraser admonished his brigade for violating these 'strict orders,' telling them he was 'exceedingly mortified to find the soldiers have presumed to transgress it.' Besides the risk of alienating inhabitants, Fraser warned of 'some Rebel Scouts lurking about in order to make prisoners and pick up stragglers.' He ordered the brigade to send a regular patrol along the east side of the lake to apprehend straggling soldiers and inquire of inhabitants 'if any injury has been done to them in their property, as scandalous outrages have been committed.' The provost marshal, the military officer charged with arresting and confining perpetrators, was directed to 'hang immediately such soldiers as are found marauding' or more than a half-mile from the camp's outposts.[29] The grenadier battalion held a court martial on 21 October, as did the brigade on the 26th, but no records of the crimes or sentences are known to survive, nor any details of 'scandalous outrages,' or whether any summary executions occurred.[30]

The intention was to proceed further and seize Fort Ticonderoga, but 'the severity of the approaching season' persuaded General Carleton that further advance was impractical 'without endangering the health of the troops.'[31] The army embarked on 1 November, this time voyaging northward down Lake Champlain, passing through the season's first snow squall and a patch of fog so thick that General Fraser ordered drummers in his boat to beat so that others could find him.[32] They took winter quarters in well-supplied posts along the Richelieu River; Fraser's brigade, with the grenadiers and light infantry, went to Montreal area and took quarters in the various Quebec villages along the east bank of the Richelieu.

* * *

26 Digby, 'Some Account', pp.164–165.
27 Digby, 'Some Account', p.165.
28 Society of the Cincinnati, Washington, DC (SC): orderly book, Major Acland's Grenadier Battalion, general orders, 17 October 1776,.
29 SC: orderly book, Major Acland's Grenadier Battalion, brigade orders, 20 October 1776.
30 SC: orderly book, Major Acland's Grenadier Battalion, brigade orders, 21 October 1776, and battalion orders, 26 October 1776.
31 SC: orderly book, Major Acland's Grenadier Battalion, general orders, 31 October 1776.
32 Digby, 'Some Account', pp.177–178.

The flank companies had been embodied into battalions since June, campaigning and encamping together, separated only when distributed in boats or strung along a route of march. Winter quarters introduced a different set of challenges for the battalion commanders, in charge of companies each acclimated to their own regiments' standing orders and procedures. Complicating matters, each company still relied on its parent regiment for clothing, pay, and the myriad administrative matters necessary for maintaining a military organization. And, the companies of each battalion were dispersed among several villages, the soldiers '2 or 3 in each house.'[33]

The grenadier companies of the 20th and 24th Regiments were in Varennes, the 21st's on Île Sainte-Thérèse, those of the 29th, 34th, 47th, 53rd and 62nd at Verchères, the 31st's at Contrecœur and the 9th's on the other side of the St. Lawrence River.[34] Orders from the battalion commander, Major Acland, highlight the management difficulties caused by this distribution. On 16 November he directed officers to send him a state of their companies – the number of men fit for service, on duty, sick, etc. – each Saturday, and prescribed a method of distributing orders from his headquarters at Verchères, in the centre of the battalion, to the companies extending out towards each flank. A sergeant from each of the two companies nearest headquarters was to carry a written order to the next company to the right or left; the commanding officer of that company was to sign the order, including the time he received it, and have a sergeant of his company carry it on to the next company. When the order reached the last company and was signed, it was to be sent back to headquarters 'through the same channel' so Major Acland could see that it had been received by all companies. Although this seemed straightforward, just three days later Acland received orders from the left half of the battalion with neither signatures nor time of receipt recorded; the following day he reminded company officers of the procedures, and also pointed out that half of the companies had not yet sent in weekly states. Those orders came back unsigned by two companies, and were not delivered at all to a third; he sent another copy the next day, with additional directions that if no officer was available to sign a sergeant should do so.[35] When preparing semi-annual muster rolls in late February, Acland found that companies completed them for different time periods, some for an entire year, some for the time since their last muster, some for two separate periods.[36]

On 1 December Acland responded to complaints that some inhabitants were quartering more soldiers than they had agreed to, prompting him to prohibit soldiers from changing billets without permission and directing officers to 'immediately rectify any such disorders.' He was also 'sorry to hear that some of the men exchange their rations for rum' obtained from inhabitants, and warned that he would 'show no mercy to a man convicted of a crime so detrimental to the service of good order and the men's health.'[37] Discipline within the battalion was sufficiently good that there were only five battalion courts martial between November and early March, trying six men for minor crimes such as selling personal

33 Digby, 'Some Account', p.179.

34 SC: orderly book, Major Acland's Grenadier Battalion, battalion orders, 15 and 18 November 1776. SC: orderly book, Major Acland's Grenadier Battalion, general orders, 17 October 1776

35 SC: orderly book, Major Acland's Grenadier Battalion, battalion orders, 16, 20 and 21 November 1776.

36 SC: orderly book, Major Acland's Grenadier Battalion, battalion orders, 8 February and 2 March 1777.

37 SC: orderly book, Major Acland's Grenadier Battalion, battalion orders, 1 December 1776.

clothing, embezzling company funds, letting a prisoner escape, and being drunk on duty.[38] In normal circumstances regiments paraded to witness corporal punishments to discourage bad behaviour, but when a soldier of the 53rd's grenadier company was sentenced in December to receive 200 lashes for selling some of his clothing, Acland allowed company commander Captain John Wight to administer the punishment at the time and place of his choosing and directed company commanders to 'communicate this sentence to their men.'[39]

A series of orders addressed the difficulties of procuring and distributing provisions – what could and could not be purchased from inhabitants, which carts were available for moving goods, and other considerations.[40] The usual method of each company sending a number of men for guard duty each day, so that the guard detachment consisted of men from each company in the battalion, was impractical; instead, companies alone in villages provided their own guards, and in Verchères, where five companies were quartered, a different company provided the guard each day. As the weather got colder, sentries were relieved every hour. With the entire brigade dispersed just like the grenadier battalion, Brigadier General Fraser directed orders to be carried from place to place on foot, unless expedience required hiring a horse and buggy. Troops assisted local inhabitants in procuring and cutting firewood. Companies that did not already have blanket coats for their men procured them.[41]

Of particular importance was maintaining operational readiness in spite of worsening weather. Fraser directed ammunition to be examined and reported on, and for each company to parade 'in the most centrical place to their several cantonments' twice weekly for inspection of arms and equipment. Anticipating no new camp equipage – tents, kettles, canteens and haversacks – before the next campaign, existing supplies were to be carefully preserved. The troops were ordered to 'hold themselves in readiness to march on the shortest notice,' to frequently assemble at alarm posts when weather permitted, and to practice with snowshoes. The grenadier battalion mustered at the church in Verchères on 25 February 1777 wearing leggings, mittens and winter caps, with blanket coats if the weather was severe, 'arms and accoutrements will be in high order and their hair well powder'd.'[42] Company commanders were keenly aware that 'the discipline and appearance of the Battalion' depended upon their 'vigilance and activity,' and Major Acland reminded them early in the winter to 'most effectually exert themselves to put their companies in such a situation that they may open the ensuing campaign with credit to themselves and advantage to their country.'[43] By May the army was 'in remarkable high Health and Spirits,' and some regiments were 'amazingly com'd on in point of Discipline and drill.'[44]

38 SC: orderly book, Major Acland's Grenadier Battalion, battalion orders, 30 November, 4 and 28 December 1776, 28 January and 4 March 1777. Not all of the charges are recorded in the orderly book.

39 SC: orderly book, Major Acland's Grenadier Battalion, battalion orders, 1 December 1776.

40 SC: orderly book, Major Acland's Grenadier Battalion. For example, brigade orders, and battalion orders, 21 and 28 November 1776.

41 SC: orderly book, Major Acland's Grenadier Battalion, general orders, 11 November 1776, battalion orders, 20 November 1776, brigade orders, 1 December 1776.

42 SC: orderly book, Major Acland's Grenadier Battalion, brigade orders, 1 December 1776, general orders, 2 December 1776, battalion orders, 8 February 1777.

43 SC: orderly book, Major Acland's Grenadier Battalion, battalion orders, 16 November 1776.

44 Clarke, 'Letters to Lord Polwarth,' p.416.

Boats carrying British light infantry to the attack on Fort Washington, 16 November 1778. Detail from 'A View of the Attack against Fort Washington and Rebel Redoubts near New York.' (New York Public Library)

British troops scaling the cliffs on the New Jersey side of the Hudson River, 20 November 1776. (New York Public Library)

Soldier of the 24th Regiment of Foot on General Burgoyne's 1777 campaign. Grenadier and light infantry companies were probably clothed almost identically, except for wings on the shoulders and red waistcoats for the light infantry. (New York Public Library)

Order of battle of the British grenadier battalion (labeled D) at the end of the Battle of Freeman's Farm, 19 September 1777. Each company is represented by a square; half of the square is filled with the regiment's facing color – from right to left, the 9th Regiment's company in yellow, the 21st in blue, 29th in yellow, 34th in yellow, 53rd in red, 62nd in buff, 47th in white, 31st in yellow, 24th in green, and 20th in yellow. Detail from map *The encampment & position of the army under His Excy. Lt. Gl: Burgoyne at Swords's and Freeman's Farms on Hudsons River near Stillwater, 1777.*

Order of battle of the British light infantry (top) and grenadiers (bottom) in the early stages of the Battle of Bemis Heights, 7 October 1777. Each company is represented by a square; half of the square is filled with the regiment's facing color – yellow for the 9th Regiment on the right of each battalion, blue for the 21st Regiment next to it, and so forth. Detail from map *The encampment & position of the army under His Excy. Lt. Gl: Burgoyne at Swords's and Freeman's Farms on Hudsons River near Stillwater, 1777.* (Library of Congress)

Lieutenant Richard St George Mansergh St George's sketch *Myself on Piquet in a Tempest disdaining a Cloak* shows him wearing a jacket with a wing on the shoulder, trousers with spatterdashes, and a hat with a plume. (Harlan Crow Library)

Lieutenant Richard St George Mansergh St George's sketch *My triumphant entry into Philadelphia* shows Captain John West of the 4th Regiment's grenadiers greeting the wounded St George after the battle of Germantown. West wears a jacket with blue cuffs and linen trousers tucked into spatterdashes. A bedraggled flank company soldier, identifiable by the prominent wing on his shoulder, carries another soldier's firelock and hat. (Harlan Crow Library)

Modern impression of a light infantry company in 1777 or 1778. The soldiers wear single-breasted jackets with wings on the shoulders, linen trousers that button around the ankle and over the shoe (making spatterdashes unnecessary), round hats with the brim cocked up on the left side and decorated with bearskin crests and green feathers. (Photo: Gary Vorwald)

By 1777 and 1778 the accoutrements worn by light infantry soldiers included shoulder belts holding a bayonet and tomahawk on the left side, and a cartridge pouch on the right side, and a tin canteen. Powder horns, known to have been used in 1776, may have been laid aside by this time, but shot pouches or shot bags affixed to one of the belts were often used to hold extra ammunition. (Photo: Gary Vorwald)

Undated image of an officer wearing a short coat and cap hat typical of the light infantry in the 1770s and 1780s. (Yale Center for British Art)

* * *

Casualties had been light since leaving Great Britain – no grenadiers deserted from the beginning of the campaign through February 1777, and only one light infantryman, James Maxwell of the 34th Regiment, who absconded on 6 August at Chambly. Fewer than 10 men of the light infantry battalion died between March 1776 and the end of February 1777, and the grenadiers lost 16 dead over the same period.[45] Causes are not known, except for grenadier John Yeaton of the 53rd who, when his transport collided with another at sea, fell between the two ships and was crushed to death.[46] Scant losses meant that mostly veterans of the 1776 campaign would march out for the 1777 campaign, men now experienced at marching in the wilderness, sleeping in the open, handling boats on the lake, and serving side by side with officers and men in their battalions. Suitable men moved from each regiment's battalion companies into the flank companies to bring them to full strength.[47]

Normally, each regiment would have received new coats, waistcoats and breeches for each soldier in the fall, and the regiment's tailors would spend the winter fitting them to each man use during the next campaign. One transport bearing 1776 clothing for the army in Canada was captured at sea, and the other was severely delayed, preventing regiments in Quebec and Montreal from receiving new clothing. On 12 February Major General William Phillips, commanding the army in the region during the winter, ordered 'battalions to accommodate the present cloathing as shall be most convenient for the men, and it is to be repaired so as to serve the campaign.'[48] 'The Army have cut their Skirts to light Infantry measure in order to repair the remainder of the Coat,' wrote an aide-de-camp, referring to the tails of the soldiers' coats that normally reached almost to the knee, but for light infantry were about three inches shorter; 'the old Hats cut up into light Infantry Caps, which I think gives them a lively smart appearance.'[49] Unlike the grenadier battalion in General Howe's army, grenadier companies with Burgoyne did not standardize on a single type of firelock.[50]

By the end of May the army was ready to move out of winter quarters. General Burgoyne reviewed the advanced corps on 27 May, and they began their march south to the northern end of Lake Champlain on 2 June.[51] Unlike the previous year, boats, stores and other necessities were ready. The advanced corps under Brigadier General Fraser still consisted of the light infantry, grenadiers, the 24th Regiment and Captain Fraser's company of marksmen;

45 TNA: WO 12: muster rolls of the various regiments.

46 Digby, 'Some Account', p.97. Digby recorded the date as 20 May; the muster rolls give the date as 17 May.

47 No muster rolls survive after February 1777, but lists of prisoners of war for the flank companies of the 29th, 31st and 34th Regiments, prepared after their surrender in October 1777, include a few men who were not in those companies before February 1777.

48 SC: orderly book, Major Acland's Grenadier Battalion, general orders, 12 February 1777, orderly book.

49 Clarke, 'Letters to Lord Polwarth,' p.416.

50 Two short land (1769) pattern firelocks from the 34th Regiment's grenadier company are known to survive in private collections, both with provenance to having been surrendered at Saratoga in October 1777.

51 S. Sydney Bradford, 'Lord Francis Napier's Journal of the Burgoyne Campaign,' *Maryland Historical Magazine* Vol. 57 No. 1 (December 1962), p.294.

the flank battalions each consisted of the same 10 companies as the previous year, even though the 29th, 31st and 34th Regiments remained behind in Canada. Six British regiments on the expedition each left detachments of 50 men behind in Canada, but the advanced corps did not – the companies of the flank battalions and 24th Regiment were at, or close to, established strength.[52] By 6 June the advanced corps was encamped at Point au Fer, where they received two days' worth of provisions, inspected weapons and ammunition, made last-minute repairs to boats and bateaux, and loaded heavy baggage. At 4:00 a.m. on the 7th drummers beat the Grenadiers March, tents were struck and loaded, soldiers boarded boats, and the flotilla pushed off together on the signal of a gun at five o'clock, the grenadiers leading in flat boats followed by the light infantry, the 24th Regiment, and a gun boat. The light infantry, grenadiers and 24th each contributed a sergeant, a corporal and 15 men 'to navigate the gun boat,' commanded by an artillery officer, and each sent 'two of their very best oars men' to row Brigadier General Fraser's boat. Four men each from the light infantry and grenadiers handled the commissary's bateau. [53] 'Soldiers are always in good spirits when taking the field,' wrote Lieutenant Row of the 9th's grenadiers.[54]

They covered some 30 miles that first day, getting to the Ausable River where they encamped. Boats were arranged on the shore, gun boats on the right, then those of the grenadiers, the 24th Regiment, and the light infantry on the left, and tents were pitched in the same order, 'in double rows, with eighteen yards between the bell tents and thirty yards between each battalion, fronting the wood and as near the lake as the land will permit for the benefit of the air, the whole being nearly in a line. Quarter guards to be well advanced into the wood. Cooking places in the rear, and necessary houses in the front beyond the quarter guards, with centrys over them from each of those guards.' Five flints per man were delivered to each flank battalion. Major Acland, noting 'a great deal of firing in the grenadier encampment,' directed company commanders to ensure that no ammunition was 'improperly used,' and Brigadier General Fraser gave orders to the advance corps for 'no person under the rank of a commission officer to fire at pidgeons or any other birds.'[55]

The army sailed again on 11 June, 'the five Right hand Companys of the Light Infantry to lead, the five left hand Companys next, the 24th Regiment to follow them, then the Grenadier Battalion,' one bateau carrying 'intrenching tools for two hundred men.'[56] The advance corps landed at the mouth of Bouquet River and encamped again. The four companies on the left of the light infantry battalion's line, the 20th, 24th, 31st and 47th, moved three miles up the river and established a post, protecting their camp with works constructed of logs and earth; the other six light infantry companies joined them five days later.[57] Men

52 Douglas Cubbison, *Burgoyne and the Saratoga Campaign: His Papers* (Norman, OK: University of Oklahoma Press, 2012), pp.232–233. The last surviving muster rolls are from February 1777, making it impossible to know the exact strength of the flank companies.
53 New York Historical Society (NYHS): orderly book, Major Acland's Grenadier Battalion, brigade orders, 6 and 7 June 1777.
54 NRS: GD113/5/73a: John Row to Jane Innes, 30 May 1777.
55 NYHS: orderly book, Major Acland's Grenadier Battalion, brigade orders, 8–10 June 1777, battalion orders, 9 June 1777.
56 NYHS: orderly book, Major Acland's Grenadier Battalion, brigade orders, 10 June 1777.
57 Bradford, 'Lord Francis Napier's Journal,' p.294.

were detached to make musket cartridges and to butcher cattle for provisions.[58] General Burgoyne, encamped with the rest of the army some miles behind the advance corps, issued orders for operations in the wilderness:

> Officers of all ranks commanding out posts and detachments are constantly to fortify, in the best manner the circumstances of the place and the implements at hand will permit felling trees with their points outwards, barricading churches and houses; breast works of earth & timber, are generally to be effected in a short time, and the science of engineering is not necessary to find and apply such resources. The practice of fortifying which is usefull in all services is particularly so in this, where the enemy, infinitely inferior to the kings troops in open space and hardy combat, is well fitted by disposition and practice for the stratagems and enterprizes of little war. And neither the distance of camps, nor the interference of forests and rivers are to be looked upon as security against his attempts.
>
> Upon the same principle it must be a constant rule in or near woods to place advance centries where they may have a tree or some other defence to prevent their being taken off by single marksmen.
>
> Together with these precautions officers will ever bear in mind how much the publick honour & their own are concerned in maintaining a post, and that to justify a retreat in the present war the number of the enemy must be much superior to that which would make their justification when acting against brave and disciplined forces.
>
> The officers will take all proper opportunities and especially at the beginning of the campaign to inculcate in the mens mind, a reliance upon the bayonet men of half their bodily strength and even cowards may be their match in firing, but the onset of bayonets in the hands of the valiant is irresistable. The enemy convinced of this truth, place their whole dependence in entrenchment and rifle pieces.
>
> It will be our glory and preservation to storm where possible. The attention of every officer in action is to be employed upon his men. To make use of a fusil except in very extraordinary cases of immediate personal defence, would betray an ignorance of his importance and of his duty.
>
> No occasion can make it necessary to keep the arms loaded in the bell tents: nor are the battalions of the line ever to be loaded upon the march till very near the time when they may be expected to engage.[59]

The orders detailed aspects of encampment in wooded country with limited space:

> The camp will always be extended as widely as the ground will admit for the sake of cleanliness and of health, but as it must often happen that the extent will be insufficient for the line to form in the front of the encampment according to the present established rule of open files and two deep, the quarter master general will

58 NYHS: orderly book, Major Acland's Grenadier Battalion, brigade orders, 13 and 15 June 1777.

59 NYHS: orderly book, Major Acland's Grenadier Battalion, general orders, 20 June 1777, recorded by the advanced corps on 22 June.

> therefore mark at every new camp the portion of ground each battalion is to clear, over and above its own front in order to make the work equal. To clear this ground must be the immediate business after arriving in camp and in this country, it may often be necessary to have an alarm post cleared in the rear as well as in the front. By clearing is meant the removal of such obstructions as might prevent the ready forming of the troops to receive or advance upon the enemy. It is not necessary to cut the large trees for that purpose, except where they may afford shelter for the enemy.
>
> Quarter Guards are always to face outwards, and at the distance of a hundred yards from the bells of arms, and to have a fleche of earth or timber thrown up before them.
>
> When the encampment of the line is with the front to the water & too near to admit of this regulation the quarter guards are to be posted in the rear or those of the flank regiment occasionally upon the flanks.
>
> Though the ground will seldom admit a strict regularity in pitching the officers tents, they are never to be placed so, as to interfere with the line of defence.

Burgoyne directed the Articles of War to be read to every regiment, and dispensed with the formality of soldiers at outposts saluting him.[60]

On 22 June the light infantry struck tents and rejoined the advanced corps at the mouth of the Bouquet River.[61] On the 24th they set off southward up the lake again, this time in a column three bateaux wide with the grenadiers in the lead, followed by the 24th Regiment, and finally the light infantry, gun boats bringing up the rear. Captain Richard England of the 47th's grenadiers went 100 yards ahead with one bateau, carrying a pilot. Over the next several days they hopped down the lake, arriving on 30 June at Three Mile Point, named for the distance from the campaign's first major objective, Fort Ticonderoga.[62] The trek up the lake took longer than the previous year because the army brought heavy artillery to besiege this fortress that had bedevilled British troops two decades before, but finally the grenadiers and light infantry 'had a full view from our post of their works lines &c and their flag of Liberty displayed on the summit of the Fort.'[63] Here, with the enemy near, the advance corps was 'very particular in posting experienced soldiers with the young ones' as sentries.[64]

At 1:00 p.m. on 2 July Brigadier General Fraser led a detachment of 20 'very best marchers' from each company in the flank battalions and the 24th Regiment, 480 private soldiers, plus a proportion of non-commissioned officers, led by six captains and lieutenants from each flank battalion and four of each from the 24th, to 'take possession of an eminence, said to command the Fort.'[65] They met and drove back 'a large party of the enemy' with the loss of one Indian killed and a few wounded, including Lieutenant Richard Houghton of the 53rd's

60 NYHS: orderly book, Major Acland's Grenadier Battalion, general orders, 20 June 1777.
61 Bradford, 'Lord Francis Napier's Journal,' p.295.
62 NYHS: orderly book, Major Acland's Grenadier Battalion, brigade orders, 21, 23 and 30 June 1777.
63 Digby, 'Some Account', pp.200–201.
64 NYHS: orderly book, Major Acland's Grenadier Battalion, brigade orders, 30 June 1777.
65 NYHS: orderly book, Major Acland's Grenadier Battalion, brigade orders, 2 July 1777; Digby, 'Some Account', p.203.

grenadiers and two of Fraser's marksmen; one marksmen was captured. The detachment took position 'very near' enemy sentries and spent the night alert; 'sleep was a stranger to us' recalled Lieutenant Digby.[66]

With the new position secure, the army moved heavy artillery into range of the fort and opened roads through the woods to surround it. Cannon fire from the fort menaced the camp – on the 3rd a cannon ball 'went through two tents of the 62 L.I.' and on the 4th 'another passed thro' two tents of the 31st L.I.,' but the only casualty was a man of the Royal Artillery.[67] By 5 July the investment was sufficient to force the fort's understrength garrison into a hasty retreat, those in Ticonderoga fleeing over the footbridge to Mount Independence on the lake's eastern shore. While those unable to march were loaded into boats along with whatever military stores could be salvaged and sent south up the lake, most of the American garrison set off on the only overland escape route, a crude military road cut inland to the southeast towards Castleton, passing through the hamlet of Hubbardton.

Brigadier General Fraser learned in the early hours of 6 July that the American posts were abandoned. After initial caution in case of a ruse, he sent troops to occupy Fort Ticonderoga. Part of the advance corps crossed the bridge to Mount Independence, a walkway supported by boats which, because of damage by the retreating rebels, had to be crossed single-file; Lieutenant Digby of the grenadiers was surprised that no rear guard was left with cannon to rake the defenceless British soldiers off the precarious bridge, but no such opposition occurred.[68]

After securing Mount Independence, Fraser set off at about 5:00 a.m. with a detachment of the advance corps in a rapid pursuit. Part of each flank company and six of the 24th Regiment's eight battalion companies took routine duties in the captured fortifications, leaving Fraser a total of 850 men consisting of 50 or so scouts and marksmen, two companies of the 24th, and probably about 350 men from each flank battalion, half to two-thirds of each company. After covering about 13 miles, slowed by minor skirmishing, they stopped to butcher and cook two cows they found, 'which, without bread, was next to nothing among so many.'[69] During this halt the advance elements of an 1,100-man reinforcement joined them, German jägers and grenadiers. Fraser agreed with the German commander that the British advance corps would continue forward about three more miles, stop for the night, and continue early the next morning, hoping to catch the fleeing enemy.[70]

After lying on their arms for the night the advanced corps set out before dawn, Fraser leading his two companies of the 24th followed by the light infantry and then the grenadiers. As the road approached Hubbardton it went down a slope to a creek, then through a broad low forested area with a steep hill to the left, rising above the east side of the road. Just over the crest of the hill was another north-south road, with a stout log fence along the east side, and beyond the enclosure bounded by the fence, even further east, was a steep-sloped ridge. Fraser had wisely sent out scouts – Native Americans and soldiers from the corps of

66 Bradford, 'Lord Francis Napier's Journal,' p.298; Digby, 'Some Account', pp.202–203.
67 Bradford, 'Lord Francis Napier's Journal,' p.299.
68 Digby, 'Some Account', pp.208–209.
69 Digby, 'Some Account', p.209.
70 Bruce M. Venter, *The Battle of Hubbardton: the Rearguard Action that Saved America* (Charleston, SC: History Press, 2015), pp.38–58.

marksmen – who reported a substantial American encampment in the low area beyond the creek, and more troops formed on the road beyond the crest of the adjacent hill. Although the scouts estimated the enemy to be more than twice his own number, Fraser opted for a swift attack. As the companies of the 24th approached the creek they formed a line and fired on their alarmed opponents. The obstruction of the creek afforded some time for the Americans to mount a hasty defence and the 24th suffered casualties but pushed on. This allowed the light infantry to move in column to their left, extending along the base of the hill. They went to the right of the 24th, into the woods on the western side of the road, and with the 24th's companies pushed south.[71]

Aware of American regiments beyond the crest of the hill, Fraser halted the light infantry column, faced left, and they rushed in line up the steep, wooded slope. American troops on the other side of the hill, already formed to march out that morning, heard firing in the encampment. They faced to the right, the west, and crested the hill, meeting the British light infantry near the top of the opposite slope. As little as 30 yards separated the opposing forces when they first met. Fierce fighting ensued, at a distance of perhaps 60 yards, and the light infantry may have recoiled initially. But training and zeal were on their side, and they soon pushed their opponents back, perhaps relying on bayonets. American forces withdrew across the road, where the log fence afforded a strong position into which they retreated and rallied; the fence was strong enough that British officers took it to be a prepared fortification. A severe firefight ensued. The light infantry, trained to rely on speed and movement, faced a force at least twice their size in a fixed position.[72]

The few British accounts of the ensuing battle differ in some key areas, leading to different understandings of the path the grenadiers took during the fray; the description given here is based on the most recently published histories. Having driven resistance out of the low-lying region, the grenadiers were now past the slope that the light infantry had climbed. Learning that the lights were facing stiff resistance, the grenadiers looped to their left and made their way up the hill's southern slope. One, possibly embellished, account says, 'the grenadiers scrambled up an ascent which appeared almost inaccessible ... the men were obliged to sling their firelocks and climb up the side, sometimes resting their feet upon the branch of a tree, and sometimes on a piece of rock; had any been so unfortunate as to have missed this hold, he must inevitably been dashed to pieces.' In spite of 'showers of balls mixed with buck shot, which they plentifully bestowed among us,' the grenadiers formed on the right of the light infantry and pushed forwards on the American left flank. But the rail fence that sheltered the Americans formed three sides of a rectangle – the long side faced the light infantry to the west, and a shorter side on the south provided protection against the grenadiers who now faced north. A ridge formed the eastern side of the enclosure, preventing the grenadiers from continuing around the American flank.[73]

---

71 Venter, *The Battle of Hubbardton*, pp.61–67.

72 Joshua Pell, 'Diary of Joshua Pell Junior an Officer of the British Army in America,' *The Magazine of American History with Notes and Queries*, Vol.2 (1878), p.108; Venter, *The Battle of Hubbardton*, pp.60–76.

73 Thomas Anbury, *Travels through the Interior Parts of North America* (Boston: Houghton Mifflin, 1923), Vol.1, p.195; Venter, *The Battle of Hubbardton*, pp.83–88.

Significant resistance over an hour or two weakened the light infantry's left flank, and they may have run low on ammunition as well as endurance. The best avenue of retreat for the Americans was now to the north, past that same flank, making it ripe for an American counterattack. It materialized, but German jägers joined the fight, ascending the slope and strengthening the British left flank just in time. At about 10:00 a.m., three hours after the battle began, American troops abandoned their protective fence line and retreated eastward, over the ridge and into the wilderness. Whether British and German troops pursued them to the top of the ridge is not clear. After the fighting ended Captain John Shrimpton of the 62nd's grenadiers was shot and wounded by a sniper.[74]

The Battle of Hubbardton was the first pitched battle for the flank battalions formed in Canada the previous year. Perhaps many of the soldiers felt the momentary trepidation that Lieutenant Digby described: 'when we received orders to prime and load, which we had barely time to do before we received a heavy fire, the idea of perhaps a few moments conveying me before the presence of my Creator had its force; but a moment's thought partly reconciled it.'[75] The battalions fought well, remaining cohesive in wooded terrain and rapidly ascending steep inclines. They also incurred significant casualties – those killed in the light infantry included Lieutenant James Douglas of the 29th Regiment, two sergeants and 17 soldiers; five officers, two sergeants and 70 men were wounded, putting about a quarter of their strength out of action. The battalion's commander, the Earl of Balcarres, 'had many escapes, no less than five Balls went through his Cloathes,' wrote an aide-de-camp who was not in the battle, adding, 'you know that the light Infantry Uniform does not hang very loose about a Man's Body; unfortunately however one Ball passed through the outside of his thigh'; Balcarres was able to continue on the campaign.[76] Three wounded men from the 34th's light infantry can be identified: Samuel Hopkins, born in 1751 in Kidderminster, Worcestershire, in the army only two years; John Chambers of Herefordshire, three years older than Hopkins but with 10 years in the army; 31-year-old Belfast native John McConnell, who joined the army in 1770 and 'received two wounds in his head.'[77]

Thirteen grenadiers were killed and seven officers, four sergeants and 37 soldiers were wounded – including Lieutenant Row of the 9th, who returned to England to recover from the 'unlucky wound I received in my right knee.' Also killed was Major Robert Grant of the 24th Regiment, and Lieutenant James Haggart of the Marines who was serving with the 9th's grenadier company.[78] Each battalion had gone into the battle with only about two-thirds of their total strength. So great was Fraser's haste to pursue his fleeing quarry that he had no medical personnel with him, nor provisions, although extensive quantities of captured materials somewhat rectified the latter deficiency. Now, exhausted from the previous day's march and this day's march and battle, the advance corps built bark shelters and had prisoners fell trees for makeshift breastworks in case of a counterattack. Rain began, making the

74 Eric H. Schnitzer and Don Troiani, *Don Troiani's Campaign to Saratoga – 1777: The Turning Point of the Revolutionary War in Paintings, Artifacts, and Historical Narrative* (Mechanicsburg, PA: Stackpole Books, 2019), p.55; Anbury, *Travels*, p.197; Venter, *The Battle of Hubbardton*, p.105.

75 Digby, 'Some Account', p.27.

76 Clarke, 'Letters to Lord Polwarth,' pp.420–421.

77 TNA: WO 121/3/39, WO 121/3/40 and WO 121/15/211: discharges of Samuel Hopkins, John Chambers, and John McConnell respectively.

78 Bradford, 'Lord Francis Napier's Journal,' pp.301–302; NRS: GD113/5/73a: John Row to Jane Innes, 12 November 1777.

wounded miserable, and continued throughout the next day. On 9 July the 600 or so able-bodied men of the advanced corps marched south to join the rest of General Burgoyne's army at Skenesboro at the southern end of Lake Champlain, leaving their wounded behind in the care of a doctor who had arrived from Ticonderoga the previous day.[79]

Table 5.1: Light Infantry Battalion casualties, Battle of Hubbardton, 7 June 1777

Company	Killed			Wounded			Total
	Officers	Sergeants	Rank & File	Officers	Sergeants	Rank & File	
9th		1	1			5	7
21st			6			10	16
29th	1		1		1	14	17
34th		1	2	1		22	26
53rd			1	2		2	5
62nd			3	1	1	4	11
47th			3	1		2	6
31st						1	1
24th						8	8
20th						2	2
Total	1	2	17	5	2	70	97

Source: Napier 'Lord Francis Napier's Journal,' p.301.

Table 5.2: Grenadier Battalion casualties, Battle of Hubbardton, 7 June 1777

Company	Killed			Wounded			Total
	Officers	Sergeants	Rank & File	Officers	Sergeants	Rank & File	
9th			1	2	1	6	10
21st			1		1	5	7
29th			3	1	2	11	17
34th			3	2		8	13
53rd			2			2	4
62nd				1		1	2
47th			1			1	2
31st			1			1	2
24th						2	2
20th			1	1			2
Total			13	7	4	37	61

Source: Napier, 'Lord Francis Napier's Journal,' p.302.

79 Bradford, 'Lord Francis Napier's Journal,' pp.301–302; Digby, 'Some Account,' pp.217–219. Some authors incorrectly state that Roger Lamb, a soldier of the 9th Regiment, tended the wounded; Lamb tended the wounded of the 9th Regiment after the battle at Fort Anne on 8 July. Don N. Hagist (ed.), *A British Soldier's Story: Roger Lamb's Narrative of the American Revolution* (Baraboo, WI: Ballindalloch Press, 2004), pp.40–41.

The path from Hubbardton to Skenesboro was about 30 miles 'thro rivers, swamps and a desolate wilderness.' With ammunition depleted, the troops proceeded 'in such a form as to sustain an action with as little loss as possible,' but no fighting occurred on the fatiguing trek.[80] On 10 July General Burgoyne summarized the army's several successes of the previous week, including 'particular distinction' to Brigadier General Fraser and the advanced corps for their 'exploit of material Service to the King, and of signal honour to the Profession of Arms' – with the added note, 'This Corps have the further Merit of having supported fatigue and bad weather, without bread and without murmur.' A *feu de joi* on Sunday 13 July at sunset at each British post celebrated the successes; each regiment formed in a long line and commenced a 'running fire,' the soldier at one end of the line firing a blank round, followed by the next man, and so on down the line. Preparations began for the next phase of the campaign: the advanced corps obtained powder, ball and paper to prepare 100 cartridges per man, and was reminded to be sparing with ammunition because further supplies would need to come from Ticonderoga, a journey that would get ever longer as the campaign progressed.[81]

Progress, though, became difficult. The army that had expected to spend weeks besieging Fort Ticonderoga was instead much further south and far ahead of schedule, outpacing much of the supply infrastructure needed to support it. Ahead, the overland route from Lake Champlain to the Hudson River, only two dozen miles, had been rendered nearly impassable by the retreating rebel forces. The road and the stream that ran parallel to it for part of the way were already inadequate for military purposes, and now were both obstructed by felled trees and large rocks. Although the advance corps travelled light – Lieutenant Digby recalled leaving behind bedding and 'making use of a Buffalo skin, with a cloak to cover me at nights,' it took from 24 to 30 July for the advanced corps to get from Skenesboro past Fort Anne to Fort Edward on the Hudson, after 'great fatigue and labour' moving obstructions and cutting a road where needed. They encamped 'on a beautiful situation from whence you saw the most romantic prospect of the Hudson's river; intersperced with many small islands,' according to Digby. The rest of the army encamped a couple of miles behind.[82]

Resistance was almost non-existent – Native American allies had struck such fear into their foes that none dared approach.[83] Food, on the other hand, was a major issue. Moving provisions from Quebec to Fort Edward was a slow process, and the relative wilderness was too sparse in produce to feed a formidable fighting force. German troops augmented by Fraser's marksmen pushed eastward into New England where stocks of cattle were believed to be, but were completely defeated at the Battle of Bennington. The advanced corps nonetheless pushed on, nine miles to Fort Miller on 9 August, three more miles to Batten Kill on the 13th, where they 'crossed the river with a good deal of trouble, and encamped about two miles west of it. The troops crossed in battows, which was very tedious, as we had but few,' Lieutenant Digby remembered. For two nights, the light infantry lay in a barracks in

80 Digby, 'Some Account', p.220
81 E. B. O'Callaghan (ed.), *Orderly Book of Lieut. Gen. John Burgoyne* (Albany, NY: J. Munsell, 1860), pp.35–36.
82 Digby, 'Some Account', pp.227, 233–240.
83 Schnitzer and Troiani, *Don Troiani's Campaign to Saratoga*, pp.81–87.

Route taken by the Advanced Corps from Fort Ticonderoga to Hubbardton, Skenesboro, Fort Anne and Fort Edward. Detail from 'A map of the country in which the army under Lt. General Burgoyne acted in the campaign of 1777, shewing the marches of the army & the places of the principal actions.' (Library of Congress)

Saratoga before encamping nearby. [84] Sickness, in the form of 'fevers & agues so common to the climate' afflicted many of the grenadiers and light infantry, their discomfort aggravated by hot days and frequent torrential rains. At 2:00 a.m. on 17 August, 'the Corps were ordered to accouter & be in readiness to turn out at a moments warning,' wrote Lieutenant Francis Napier of the 31st's light infantry. The light infantry struck their tents and lay on their arms during the next night, but no attack came.[85]

While the advanced corps was posted on the west side of the Hudson, the main army built a bridge of boats below Batten Kill to bring the remainder of the troops and stores across, but on the 18th it was carried away by rain-swelled river. The advanced corps was now cut off, forcing them to re-cross the Hudson using only a few bateaux; 'it was a most tedious piece of work, and late at night before everything was over – when we lay on our arms – not as yet being exact as to the motions of the enemy,' wrote Digby.[86] Although many of Fraser's marksmen escaped the debacle at Bennington, the corps was rendered ineffective for the time being. A new company of marksmen was formed entirely from men of the advance corps, led by Captain George Petrie of the 21st's light infantry, Lieutenant Arthur French of the 47th's light infantry, and Lieutenant Conolly Coane of the 62nd's grenadiers, but according to Lieutenant Napier, 'they never were made use of upon any occasion.'[87]

The setback at Bennington did more than just deprive the army of fresh beef. Combined with slow progress, sickness and rain, it changed the mood. The Native American allies who had done so much to keep foes at bay departed, returning to their homelands and harvests. Loyalists flocked to the army from the verdant Hudson River Valley to escape rebel persecution, and although many took up arms, they proved less reliable and skilful than the Native Americans; some even left the army and their loyalties behind after hearing of the Bennington defeat. Discontent crept even into the ranks of British regulars. The army that celebrated great victories in early July was now trying men by court martial for desertion. Two trials were held on 24 August, and one offender was executed.[88] Walter Harris of the 53rd's light infantry was tried for advising two fellow light infantrymen, William Bell of the 24th and Joseph Brooks of the 53rd, to desert; Harris was acquitted, 'the charge against him not having been sufficiently supported,' and released.[89] 'Conductors and others, followers of the army' were tried for committing 'great irregularities.'[90] News came on 28 August that another expedition had failed, a move from the west towards Albany that stalled at Fort Stanwix the Mohawk River.[91]

The army foraged extensively around Fort Miller, denuding the area of produce. They entrenched, wary of attack from the rear as well as the front. Detachments of light infantry

84 Napier, 'Lord Francis Napier's Journal,' p.308.
85 Napier, 'Lord Francis Napier's Journal,' pp.308–309.
86 Digby, 'Some Account', pp.244–252.
87 Napier, 'Lord Francis Napier's Journal,' pp.309–310.
88 TNA: WO 71/84: trial of William McDonald, 47th Regiment, and Georg Hundertmark, 9th Regiment, pp.178–181; O'Callaghan (ed.), *Orderly Book of Lieut. Gen. John Burgoyne*, p.81.
89 O'Callaghan (ed.), *Orderly Book of Lieut. Gen. John Burgoyne*, p.90; Napier, 'Lord Francis Napier's Journal,' p.313.
90 O'Callaghan (ed.), *Orderly Book of Lieut. Gen. John Burgoyne*, p.84, General orders, 27 August 1777.
91 Digby, 'Some Account,' p.256.

and grenadiers occasionally went out to drive off rebel patrols.[92] It was early September before sufficient stores and provisions were amassed to recommence the campaign. Reinforcements arrived from Canada; recruits from Great Britain who strengthened British regiments. Burgoyne ordered 'Such Regiments as have Supernumeraries' to 'compleat their Grenadier and Light Infantry Companies.' Some wounded from Hubbardton and others with fevers recovered sufficiently to rejoin their companies, restoring some losses in officers and men. Captain Fraser's marksmen were augmented from British regiments, not including flank companies, to make up for losses at Bennington.[93] The army was ready to move on 10 September, but torrential rains delayed the advance until the 13th.

The army, led as usual by the advanced corps, crossed to the west side of the Hudson on a new bridge of boats and encamped at Saratoga. Albany, their objective, was only about 35 miles away, a two-day march for flank battalions on good roads. The road along the river was sufficient, but the delays in August and early September had allowed American forces, ever-increasing in strength after the victory at Bennington emboldened militias from all over the northeast, to carefully choose a defensive position. A dozen miles south of Saratoga was Bemis Heights, a plateau that rose some 200 feet and commanded the road and river. The land was heavily wooded, dotted with farms and interspersed with crude roads and pathways, offering no room for easy movement of brigades or battalions. Keenly aware of well-emplaced opposition, General Burgoyne's army had no choice but to find a way through. He led the army forward with caution in three columns, the advanced corps on the critical right flank, farthest inland and, with the left anchored by the river, covering the army's only vulnerable flank. Burgoyne ordered his troops 'to move in such a state as to be fit for instant action.'[94]

Between 15 and 18 September the army moved slowly forward, sleeping with accoutrements on and getting under arms an hour before daybreak. Fog cloaked the early hours. Foraging parties attempted to supplement waning provision stores. Soldiers took it upon themselves to forage, many straying too far and falling into enemy hands. A group of men, and possibly some soldiers' wives as well, foraging in front of British lines were attacked by the enemy on 18 September and several were killed; knowing that each man was irreplaceable, Burgoyne to asserted that he would 'no longer bear to lose his men for the pitiful consideration of potatoes or forage.'[95]

The army moved forward at 9:00 a.m. on 19 September, attempting to push through the enemy on Bemis Heights, each man with 60 rounds of ammunition and expecting a fight. The advanced corps, now augmented by a battalion of German grenadiers, first went a mile or so on a road that led west, then turned south into woods and clearings. Three British regiments formed a centre column between the advanced corps and the river, and Burgoyne's German regiments proceeded along the Hudson, holding the army's left. In the early

92 Napier, 'Lord Francis Napier's Journal,' pp.312, 314.

93 O'Callaghan (ed.), *Orderly Book of Lieut. Gen. John Burgoyne*, p.93, general orders, 2 and 5 September 1777; Digby, 'Some Account', pp.265–266.

94 O'Callaghan (ed.), *Orderly Book of Lieut. Gen. John Burgoyne*, p.105, general orders, 14 September 1777.

95 Napier, 'Lord Francis Napier's Journal,' p.315; O'Callaghan (ed.), *Orderly Book of Lieut. Gen. John Burgoyne*, p.113, general orders, 18 September 1777.

afternoon the centre and right columns encountered stiff resistance, the weight of it falling on the centre as it attempted to advance through the open fields of Freeman's Farm and into the woods beyond. Brigadier General Fraser used the British and German grenadiers to protect the right flank by deploying them in a line facing west, the German grenadiers to the extreme northern end of this line. The British grenadiers deployed in their usual formation of companies by seniority from the outside towards the middle, the 9th's company on the right, the 20th's on the left, the 21st's next to the 9th's, and so on.[96] Near the other flank, the light infantry got into an hour-long firefight in the woods. Fraser's column did well but did not attempt to advance far due to the tenuous situation of the centre column, but could not directly assist due to 'the situation of the ground.' It became a slugging match, both sides pushing but unable to advance far, woods and ravines and rivulets preventing Burgoyne from putting sufficient pressure on any part of American lines.[97] 'Such an explosion of fire I never had any idea of before,' remembered Lieutenant Digby, 'and the heavy artillery joining in concert like great peals of thunder, assisted by the echoes of the woods, almost deafened us with the noise.' As daylight faded, the British grenadiers came 'near firing on a body of our Germans, mistaking their dark clothing for that of the enemy.' Darkness saw Burgoyne's troops masters of the field, but at a cost too great to bear; 'during the night we remained in our ranks, and tho we heard the groans of our wounded and dying at a small distance, yet could not assist them till morning, not knowing the position of the enemy … sleep was a stranger to us,' wrote Digby, 'but we were all in good spirits and ready to obey with cheerfulness any orders the general might issue before morning dawned.'[98] The numbers of killed and wounded were not recorded. Among the latter were Dubliner John Stewart of the 34th's light infantry, a 28-year-old veteran of seven years, wounded in the back, and Isaac Johnston of the 29th's light infantry, born in Ipswich, Suffolk in 1748 and enlisted in 1772, who had been wounded in his right arm at Hubbardton and received another wound in his left foot at Freeman's Farm.[99]

Dawn brought the prospect of a push by the entire army on the right flank where the advanced corps had met with some success the previous day. The British grenadiers were on the right flank; Burgoyne now ordered the other British regiments to form on their right so 'the British Line will extend to the right.'[100] But the fighting on the 19th had exhausted the men. There were wounded to recover. Brigadier General Fraser convinced Burgoyne to wait one day to rest and regroup. Then a message came from the New York that convinced Burgoyne another British force was moving up the Hudson to cooperate with his beleaguered army. Burgoyne chose to encamp, dig in and wait.[101]

---

96 LOC: map gm71000664: 'Position of the Detachment &c &c in the Action of the 7th Octr 1777,' detail from map *The encampment & position of the army under His Excy. Lt. Gl: Burgoyne at Swords's and Freeman's Farms on Hudsons River near Stillwater, 1777* by William Cumberland Wilkinson.

97 Schnitzer and Troiani, *Don Troiani's Campaign to Saratoga*, pp.180–182; Napier, 'Lord Francis Napier's Journal,' pp.316–317.

98 Digby, 'Some Account', pp.271–274.

99 TNA: WO 121/15/217 and WO 121/8/96: discharges of John Stewart and Isaac Johnston, respectively.

100 O'Callaghan (ed.), *Orderly Book of Lieut. Gen. John Burgoyne*, p.114, general orders, 20 September 1777.

101 Digby, 'Some Account', p.275; James Wilkinson, *Memoirs of My Own Times*, Vol.1 (Philadelphia: Abraham Small, 1816), p.251.

The opposing armies remained encamped strangely close to each other, within easy hearing of each other's drums. Occasional skirmishing and frequent sniping occurred, British soldiers deserted or were captured, and every lost man was irreplaceable. Stocks of food and forage decreased. Foraging parties required substantial numbers of troops to protect them, so great was the risk of capture; a foraging party on 27 September was covered by four officers and 150 men of the advance corps along with three officers and 100 men from other British regiments. Frequent forages fed horses but not men; on 3 October, Burgoyne was obliged to reduce rations by a third, from a pound and a half of bread or flour per day to one pound – offsetting this this news with assurance that the men would not be required to pay for rations for the time being. The army grew steadily weaker.[102]

A detachment of 1,200 British and 300 German troops supported by artillery moved off in the early afternoon of 7 October to reconnoitre American positions. Included were about 20 men from each grenadier and light infantry company, formed in the same order that they used as a complete battalion, the men of the senior companies on the flanks and the junior companies in the centre. As the force pushed forward into two adjacent wheat fields separated and flanked by woods, the light infantry took positions on the western side of the clearing, protecting the right flank; the 9th's company on the extreme right end of the line with those of the 21st, 29th and 34th facing west along the crest of a ridge that formed the edge of one wheat field. The other six companies – the 53rd on the right, and the 62nd, 47th, 31st, 24th and 20th progressing to the left, extended across the field facing south, with a pair of field cannon on the corner between the 34th and 53rd companies. The grenadiers were on the opposite flank – eight companies facing east in woods covering the left side of a field, the 20th's company on the extreme left and the 31st's on the right; next to the 31st's, the companies of the 21st and 9th Regiments faced south. The rest of the troops formed a line in line in between the grenadiers and light infantry, spanning the left-hand field and the woods between the two fields. Seeing the opportunity to forage, carts came to gather the wheat, but the enemy soon began to push hard on British lines.[103]

The light infantry had an advantageous position that initially allowed them to hold off attacks, but the grenadiers on the left flank were closest to the American encampment and fell back in the face of superior numbers, some breaking ranks, but ultimately maintaining order when supported by the 24th Regiment. The centre of the line was less stable and began to crumble. Faced with another determined assault, Major Balcarres ordered his light infantry to withdraw. Seeing the impossibility of his situation, Burgoyne ordered the entire British force to retire to their fortified positions, but the retreat became a rout. Brigadier General Fraser attempted to organize a rear guard of whatever troops he could rally, but

102 O'Callaghan (ed.), *Orderly Book of Lieut. Gen. John Burgoyne*, p.125, general orders, 3 October 1777; Rogers (ed.), *Hadden's Journal and Orderly Books*, p.326. The order mentions only bread, but presumably the ration of meat, also typically a pound and half per day on campaign, was also cut to a pound.

103 LOC: map gm71000664: 'Position of the Detachment &c &c in the Action of the 7th Octr 1777,' detail from map *The encampment & position of the army under His Excy. Lt. Gl: Burgoyne at Swords's and Freeman's Farms on Hudsons River near Stillwater, 1777* by William Cumberland Wilkinson.

was shot from his horse. His loyal troops managed to bring him off the field, but his wound was mortal.[104]

The remains of the reconnaissance force scrambled into British lines, primarily into a redoubt manned by the British light infantry that had stayed behind. Eight artillery pieces also defended the redoubt. It was enough to stem the American onslaught. A German-manned redoubt in another part of the line succumbed before darkness ended the fight. The dwindling British army lost about 450 officers and men killed and wounded, and another 180 captured. The grenadier battalion's commander, Major John Dyke Acland, was wounded and captured, as were Captain Malcom Ramsay and Lieutenant William Featherstone of the 21st's grenadiers; the 24th grenadiers' Captain William Agnew was wounded. The 53rd grenadiers had sent out 20 men and lost 16; their captain, John Wight, who had been wounded near Ticonderoga and felled by sickness in August, was mortally wounded, captured, and died the next day.[105]

The campaign was effectively over for Burgoyne's army. They withdrew to Saratoga and capitulated on 17 October. 'Thus ended a campaign, which at the beginning was attended with every Appearance of Success,' remembered Lieutenant Napier; 'the facility with which we obtained Ticonderoga contributed in a great measure to bring us into our disagreeable situation ... We had conceived the Idea of our being irresistible.'[106] The flank battalions were disbanded, and the flank companies of the 9th, 20th, 21st, 24th, 47th and 62nd, which were part of the capitulation, rejoined their regiments in captivity; for administration during their captivity, the companies from the 29th, 31st, 34th and 53rd Regiments were 'formed into a corps under the direction of the Earl of Balcarras.' Those regiments, still in Canada, embodied new flank companies in 1781, but they never had occasion to be formed into battalions.[107]

The grenadier and light infantry battalions had proven to be in their element when fighting where speed and manoeuvre could be used to advantage, regardless of the terrain, fighting effectively in woods and wilderness. They were too few to make the difference needed for success on this campaign – in Lieutenant Napier's words, 'we were not more than Mortals.'[108] The exact losses are not known, but the survivors went into captivity, supposedly to be returned to Great Britain but ultimately to remain captive in America until the end of the war.

104 Schnitzer and Troiani, *Don Troiani's Campaign to Saratoga*, pp.225–239. Decades after the Battle of Saratoga, a story arose of a single American marksman targeting and killing Fraser, but the story has no basis in primary sources and is unlikely given the ferocity and confusion of the battle.

105 Schnitzer and Troiani, *Don Troiani's Campaign to Saratoga*, pp.240–244; Digby, 'Some Account', p.291.

106 Napier, 'Lord Francis Napier's Journal,' p.324

107 Cometti (ed.), *American Journals*, p.53.

108 Napier, 'Lord Francis Napier's Journal,' pp.324–325.

6

'Spirit and determined resolution': Campaign to Philadelphia, 1777

As General Burgoyne's army enjoyed the most successful part of its campaign in July 1777, General Howe pursued a new avenue towards Philadelphia. Having withdrawn his army from New Jersey to Staten Island, he immediately prepared for a new campaign. He ordered regiments to complete their flank companies 'to the same number of the battalions they belong to,' with the rare allowance of including 'Recruits that have some knowledge of their arms.' This was a nod to the fact that some recruits recently arrived in America had enlisted in Great Britain in 1775 and 1776, and had as much as two years of training before embarking for America; there were also 'recruits' who had prior military service, making them suitable candidates for flank companies. Howe instructed that, should both light infantry, or both grenadier battalions, operate together with no general officer present, the senior battalion commander was to take command. He also directed that field pieces would continue to accompany each flank battalion. After only nine days, the entire army was on board transport ships, where they remained for seven weeks, embarking on 8 and 9 July and finally disembarking on 25 August.[1]

Reaching 'the same number of the battalions' did not mean achieving the established strength of 54 private soldiers in each company, but reaching approximately the same number as in each regiment's eight battalion companies, regardless of the regiment's overall strength. As such, no grenadier or light infantry company was at full strength. Numbers varied, from a scant 34 in the grenadier company of the 43rd, to a nearly-complete 53 for the light infantry of the 5th – as reported on muster rolls, which include a few prisoners of war, and probably a few others who did not take the field for one reason or another.[2] For the most part, the companies from lower-numbered regiments were in the 1st Battalion, and those from higher-numbered regiments in the 2nd Battalion. The light infantry battalions varied this by putting one of the double-sized highland companies, that of the 42nd Regiment, into the 1st Battalion, the other, the 71st's, into the 2nd; the 37th's light infantry served in the 2nd Battalion. Lieutenant Colonel Abercromby, with overall command of the light infantry, may have made this choice so that the company from his own regiment, the 37th, would be on the flank of a battalion. The battalions' structure and their estimated strength based on the muster rolls, was as follows:

1 Anon. (ed.), 'British Army Orders,' pp.465–466, 475, general orders, 1, 7 and 8 July, 24 August 1777.
2 TNA: WO 12: muster rolls of the various regiments.

1st Battalion of Grenadiers
Lieutenant Colonel William Meadows, 55th Regiment
5th, 15th, 22nd, 27th, 33rd, 37th, 40th, 38th, 35th, 28th, 23rd, 17th; 10th, 4th
Average 44 private soldiers per company, or about 600, plus six NCOs per company
Estimated total men at arms: approximately 700

2nd Battalion of Grenadiers
Lieutenant Colonel Henry Monckton, 45th Regiment
43rd, 45th, 49th, 52nd, 57th, 64th, 71st, 63rd, 55th, Marines, 46th, 44th, 42nd
Average 44 private soldiers per company (and factoring in larger companies for the 42nd, 71st and Marines), or about 700, plus six NCOs per company
Estimated total men at arms: approximately 800

1st Battalion of Light Infantry
Lieutenant Colonel Robert Abercromby, 37th Regiment
5th, 15th, 22nd, 27th, 33rd, 38th, 42nd, 35th, 28th, 23rd, 17th; 10th, 4th
Average 46 private soldiers per company (plus one double-sized company), or about 640 private soldiers, plus six NCOs per company
Estimated total men at arms: approximately 730

2nd Battalion of Light Infantry
Major John Maitland, Marines
37th, 43rd, 45th, 49th, 55th, 63rd, 71st, 64th, 57th, 52nd, 46th, 44th, 40th
Average 46 private soldiers per company (plus one double-sized company), or about 640 private soldiers, plus six NCOs per company
Estimated total men at arms: approximately 730

The estimates of private soldiers accord reasonably well with an embarkation return recorded by staff officer John André, who listed the total number of grenadiers embarked as 1,271, and the total light infantry as 1,424, without stating whether this included officers. Many of the companies still had only one drummer, and many grenadier fifers were on duty with their regiments.

In almost all companies, well over half of the men, often more than three-quarters, had been there during the campaign that began in August 1776, and were well-acclimated to rapid movement and austere living. Most recently added men, although new to flank companies, were with their regiments during the 1776 campaign and familiar with warfare in America; they had only to adapt to new officers and comrades. Most companies had at least one of the same officers as in the previous campaign; many had two and some had all three. Of the six non-commissioned officers in each company, in most cases at least five if not all six had been in the same company the previous year, albeit in some cases at a lower rank. On the whole, in terms of experience and continuity, the flank battalions were better prepared for this campaign than for any prior action of the war.[3]

3 TNA: WO 12: Muster rolls of the various regiments.

During the previous campaigns the flank battalions refined adaptations to American conditions, including embodying a corps of riflemen from within the light infantry battalions. The War Office sent some 1,000 rifles, patterned after German designs and built by British gun makers; five were provided to each light infantry company, but very little specific information about their use was recorded.[4] Orderly books and other documents occasionally mention the 'corps of riflemen' on the autumn 1777 campaign, but no description of the numbers of men it included have been found. Details will be mentioned in the discussion of the campaign, below. A different rifle company armed with a new type of breech-loading weapon, commanded by Captain Patrick Ferguson of the 70th Regiment, had joined General Howe's army in spring 1777, and Jägers, rifle-armed German troops especially adept at probing and advance-guard actions, had been an integral part of the army since landing on Staten Island in the summer of 1776.

The army had more scouting and skirmish troops than just the flank battalions and rifle corps: the Brigade of Guards included a grenadier and a light infantry company that remained with the brigade; the 16th and 17th Light Dragoons, originally cavalry regiments but now consisting of equal numbers of troopers on horseback and skirmishers on foot; companies of German chasseurs, soldiers selected from German regiments to act as light infantry because those regiments did not have light infantry companies; and the Queen's Rangers, raised in America and consisting of mounted and dismounted soldiers. When the army landed at Head of Elk, Maryland (present-day Elkton), at the northern end of Chesapeake Bay and about 50 miles southwest of Philadelphia, the flank battalions landed first, supported by the Jägers.[5] There was no opposition.

The ensuing campaign was complex; here, only specific aspects of the flank battalions' activities will be discussed. Characteristically, tents and other heavy baggage remained on ships when the flank battalions embarked in boats at 3:00 a.m. and rowed several miles upstream to their landing place.[6] Lieutenant Hale of the 45th's grenadiers wrote that the troops 'passed three most uncomfortable nights in Wigwams, drenched to the skin by those torrents of rain common in this Southern Climate.'[7] They moved to 'Elk Village' on 28 August, quickly driving off some slight opposition and establishing a new encampment.[8] Captain Dansey of the 33rd's light infantry wrote to his mother, 'What a Savage Life ours is, I don't expect to have my Cloths off or see the inside of a House on this Side Christmas.'[9] Rain stymied efforts to move inland quickly; the army expanded its perimeter, but a week passed before the march towards Philadelphia began in earnest. 'We are now encamped, or more properly speaking enwigwamed,' wrote Lieutenant Hale on 30 August, adding of he and his fellow officers, 'for this week past we have lived like beasts, no plates, no dishes, no table cloth, biscuits supply the place of the first but for the others no substitute can be found; my clothes have not been off since we landed … clean straw is as good a bed as I

4 Robbie MacNiven, *British Light Infantry in the American Revolution* (Oxford, UK: Osprey Publishing, 2021), p.21.
5 Anon. (ed.), 'British Army Orders,' p.475, general orders, 24 August 1777.
6 Stirke, 'British Officer's Revolutionary War Journal,' p.167.
7 Wilkin, *Some British Soldiers*, p.227.
8 Stirke, 'British Officer's Revolutionary War Journal,' p.167.
9 Dansey (ed.), *Letters*, p.33.

desire, and if it does not rain I am happy.'[10] During this time some flank battalion soldiers, accustomed to providing for themselves during the harsh winter in New Jersey, saw their position in advance of the army as an opportunity to explore what wealth the countryside had to offer. Despite strict orders against plundering, a general court martial on 29 August tried seven men for plunder or desertion, including two light infantrymen. Another court on 1 September, composed entirely of officers from the flank battalions, tried one man for desertion. Proceedings of these cases give some sense of the activities of these soldiers and their propensity for acquiring anything of material value.

Two days after landing, an officer noticed William Johnstone of the 43rd's light infantry walking away from the army toward an outpost carrying a bundle wrapped in a blue-and-white curtain. He was apprehended, and the bundle found to contain 'a Woman's gown, a small piece of Cloth, of the same colour as the Curtain, and a small white earthen pot, containing butter.' A local resident who had complained of being robbed identified the goods as his (except the gown, about which he was uncertain), but could not identify Johnstone as the thief. Johnstone claimed that a grenadier returning from a foraging party called to him, saying, 'Light Infantry man will you take this,' and that the bundle contained 'something which would be of service to him when he went to Camp.' With no direct evidence that Johnstone was the thief, the court acquitted him.[11] Three soldiers of the 23rd Regiment, including grenadiers William Houston and John Smith, were tried for 'disobedience of orders by straggling beyond the posts of the Army and Plundering Sundry Articles.' They were caught coming into British lines, one on horseback, carrying fowls; one also had a spyglass. They claimed to have caught the horse, a stray, when on duty as advanced pickets, and that the fowls and spyglass came from an abandoned house within British lines. The court found them guilty and sentenced each man to 1,000 lashes.[12] General Howe disagreed with the verdict for Johnstone and considered the sentences for Houston and Smith 'inadequate to their Crimes' – plundering was too prevalent for corporal punishment to deter it. The Articles of War, however, did not allow either a second trial or a change in verdict or sentencing, so the prisoners were released to rejoin their regiments.[13]

Daniel Hollowell, a 34-year-old weaver from Northowram, Yorkshire who had been in the 33rd Regiment for 12 years, was confined by his commanding officer, Captain Dansey of the 33rd's light infantry, for 'irregular behavior' the day after landing. Confinement meant doing normal duty during the day but being held in a tent at the quarter-guard, a short distance from the battalion's encampment where soldiers on guard were armed and alert, during the night. His spare shirts, stockings and shoes were brought to him while he was a prisoner so that he had them available for duty. His routine of daily duty and nightly confinement went on until the night of 31 August – 1 September, when the guard noticed him missing after he was confined at dusk. At around 9:00 p.m. an advanced picket, Thomas Knight of the 15th's light infantry, noticed a man approaching, who fell in the road. Knight, a native of Richmond, Surrey, who had worked as a mason before joining the army at the age of 23 eight years earlier, issued a challenge. It was a drunken Hollowell who got up and

10 Wilkin, *Some British Soldiers*, p.228.
11 TNA: WO 71/84: trial of William Johnstone, pp.197–200.
12 TNA: WO 71/84: trial of Abraham Pike, William Houston and John Smith, pp.200–202.
13 Anon. (ed.), 'British Army Orders,' p.483, general orders, 2 September 1777.

came forth out of the darkness, claiming to be bringing a drink to a comrade who was also a sentry. Knight, not knowing of Hollowell's confinement, pointed him in the right direction, but a little later heard a disturbance in bushes. Receiving no response to his challenges, Knight took aim, but his gun misfired. Advancing to investigate, he found Hollowell, who now claimed to have lost his way back to the encampment. Not having any reason for suspicion, Knight once again pointed him in the right direction and sent him on his way.

Around dawn, two non-commissioned officers were visiting Robert Creed of the 46th's light infantry at his sentry post. Creed was carefully observing an approaching man whom he had twice challenged with no response. The non-commissioned officers stepped out of view to let the man get closer. When the intruder was about 40 yards away, they rushed out and ordered him to stand. It was Hollowell, who this time claimed to be going to wash a shirt (according to one of the non-commissioned officers) or to fill a canteen (according to the other). Not satisfied with these stories, they confined him. He wore a cloak over his clothing, carrying nothing besides a canteen. On trial the next day, Hollowell testified that he was drunk, had no intention of desertion, but had simply lost his way and was making for the campfires of the battalion when he was taken. Because he was never seen going away from the army and never behaved as though attempting to desert, the court found him innocent and released him; oddly enough no one sought an explanation for why he left confinement or how he had gotten liquor.[14]

* * *

On 3 September the flank battalions and several other corps moved northeast to secure Iron Hill, a strong position blocking the route to Philadelphia. The Jägers ran into resistance at a bridge, but the 2nd Battalion of Light Infantry 'dash'd over and drove the Rebels,' according to Lieutenant Peebles of the grenadiers.[15] General Howe wrote that they gave the enemy 'a complete Trimming,' advancing 'with more (I think) than their usual spirit.' 'Their rapidity was so great,' continued Howe, 'that the Grenadiers who were as willing to have had their share in ye business as could be wished, could hardly keep up to support them in a run, their Guns Galloping to get a shot.'[16] The 1st Battalion of Light Infantry attempted to get around the enemy's eastern flank but was 'prevented by an impassable morass, which the guide was not acquainted with.'[17]

The army marched again on 4 September, led by the Jägers followed by the light infantry, the Queen's Rangers and Ferguson's rifle company, then the British and the German grenadier battalions followed by one battalion of the Brigade of Guards. Behind this advanced corps was a substantial corps of field artillery. This arrangement put the most mobile troops in front, battalions that could rapidly deploy extended lines in any direction and delay a threat long enough for the rest of the army to come into position. General Howe consistently ordered the army to march 'by half companies from the right,' which for the flank battalions meant the right half of the rightmost company marched forward, followed by

14 TNA: WO 71/84: trial of Daniel Hollowell, pp.209–214.
15 Gruber (ed.), *Diary*, p.130.
16 BC: James Grant Papers: William Howe to James Grant, 3 September 1777.
17 Stirke, 'British Officer's Revolutionary War Journal,' p.168.

the left half of that company, followed by the next half company, and so on. This put the 4th Regiment's light infantry at the front of the light infantry column, followed by the 10th's, then the 17th's; the companies of the 5th, 15th and so on were at the rear of the 1st Battalion's column. Companies of 40 to 50 rank and file, formed in two ranks, when divided into half-companies, stood 10 to 14 men across. Even at close order, allowing about two feet for each man's width, each half-company spanned some 20 feet or so when formed in line, probably an unwieldy width except on the best roads. A more likely interpretation of Howe's marching orders is that each half-company advanced simultaneously by files from the right, resulting in the two half-companies marching in column, side-by-side, producing a four-man front. Reforming into a line was somewhat more complex, but could be accomplished rapidly by these well-trained soldiers.[18]

On 7 September the order of march was revised, putting the light infantry battalions in the lead accompanied by a dozen mounted jägers; the British grenadiers followed, then the German grenadiers, jäger infantry, the Brigade of Guards, and the rest of the mounted jägers, all under command of Lieutenant General Cornwallis. This was the advance guard when the army, having advanced into Pennsylvania, broke camp and marched at 4:00 a.m. on 11 September. The American army was positioned to make a stand along Brandywine Creek, running from the northwest to the southeast. While a portion of the British army under *Generalleutnant* Wilhelm von Knyphausen approached American positions directly, Cornwallis led the greatest part of it, light infantry in the lead, northwest several miles, crossing two branches of the creek at unguarded fords. Knyphausen's force engaged but deliberately did not cross the waterway, distracting their opponents.

After what Lieutenant Richard St George Mansergh St George of the 52nd's light infantry called 'a rapid march from 4 o'clock in the morning till four in the eve,' covering some 17 miles including wading through two creeks, the flanking force was within striking distance.[19] They were discovered, and Americans hastily but skilfully realigned to defend their northern flank, taking strong ground but lacking prepared positions like the defenders along the creek. Lieutenant Hale wrote that British troops 'came in sight of the Rebels drawn up in four lines on very advantageous ground behind railings.'[20] The British battalions deployed into line, the light infantry battalions on the left, grenadiers in the centre, and the Brigade of Guards on the right closest to Brandywine Creek. An unidentified officer wrote that 'the different Corps doubled up.' No other writer mentioned this detail, which typically meant that the left half of each battalion formed behind the right half. If this was the case it explains, as will be seen, the experience of three companies in the 1st Battalion of Light Infantry as the battle progressed; 'the whole were form'd immediately & without hurry or confusion.'[21]

18 Anon. (ed.), 'British Army Orders,' p.484, general orders, 2 September 1777.

19 Richard St George Mansergh St George, 'The Actions at Brandywine and Paoli, described by a British Officer,' *Pennsylvania Magazine of History and Biography*, Vol. 29 No. 3 (1905), p.368.

20 Wilkin, *Some British Soldiers*, p.231.

21 American Philosophical Society Library (APSL): Sol Feinstone Collection No. 409: Anonymous British Journal, 1776–78. Some sources identify the author as Lieutenant Frederick Augustus Wetherall of the 17th Regiment, who served in one of the regiment's battalion companies.

A troop of mounted Jägers and the light infantry companies of the 17th and 42nd Regiments advanced to reconnoitre enemy positions – no record survives to indicate why these two companies were selected. An officer of the 17th's company wrote that Jägers advanced on a party of American dragoons, while the two light companies, to support them, 'quitted the road for this purpose to gain an orchard on the flank.' Here they 'received a fire from about 200 men in the orchard, which did no execution; companies ran up to the fence and halted.' They advanced no further.[22]

While this was happening, the rest of British troops completed their deployment and surged forward. Although ordered to march 'without beat of drum' since landing two weeks before, now 'the signal to march was drummed everywhere,' remembered a German officer.[23] Lieutenant Hale wrote, 'the Grenadiers put on their Caps and struck up their march,' a phrase implying that they had their bearskin caps with them and donned them for this action, recognizing the significance of it. The march that they struck up was the traditional 'Grenadiers March,' widely used as a signal to advance, probably played by one or two drummers on duty in each battalion.[24]

'We immediately formed, and began the attack,' wrote Hale, the army arrayed on either side of a road.[25] The 1st Battalion of Light Infantry was on the left, or east side, the 2nd Battalion of Light Infantry further left, the Jägers on the far-left flank. 'As soon as the line approached the advanced guard,' wrote the officer of the 17th's light infantry, 'Lt Col Abercromby ordered the 17t light company to form on the right of the battalion, the 42nd, on the left,' resulting in an unconventional order of battle for the 1st Battalion of Light Infantry which showed the adaptability of these seasoned officers and men.[26] Ahead of them, to the left of the road, was a church with a walled yard defended by an American regiment, and beyond that, rising ground atop which was the bulk of American opposition including a battery of field artillery. 'As soon as the line came up to Dilworth Church,' recalled the officer of the 17th lights, 'the enemy opened a fire from five field pieces.' The company commander opted to go along the road in an attempt to flank the church and so close to the artillery that it would be unable to fire down the slope at them: 'the church yard wall being opposite the 17t light company, the captain determined to get over the fence into the road, and calling to the men to follow ran down the road and lodged the men without loss at the foot of the hill on which the guns were firing. the hedge on the left side of the road much cut with the grape shot.'[27]

At the same time, 'The Grenadiers charged and drove them from six successive railings under an exceeding heavy fire,' wrote Lieutenant Hale.[28] A staff officer wrote, 'The English,

22 APSL: Sol Feinstone Collection No. 111: 'Memo battle of Brandiwine. 11t Sepr 1777'. Some sources identify the author as Captain William Scott of the 17th Regiment, but the text refers to 'the captain' in the third person, suggesting the author was one of the company's lieutenants.

23 S. Smith (ed.), *At General Howe's Side, 1776–1778: The Diary of General William Howe's Aide de Camp, Captain Friedrich von Muenchhausen*, (Monmouth Beach, NJ: Philip Freneau, 1974), p.31.

24 Wilkin, *Some British Soldiers*, p.231. For details on the role of drummers in battle, see Hagist, *Noble Volunteers*, pp.209–213.

25 Wilkin, *Some British Soldiers*, p.231.

26 APSL: Sol Feinstone Collection no. 111: 'Memo battle of Brandiwine.'

27 APSL: Sol Feinstone Collection no. 111: 'Memo battle of Brandiwine.'

28 Wilkin, *Some British Soldiers*, p.231.

and especially the English grenadiers, advanced fearlessly and very quickly; fired a volley, and then ran furiously at the rebels with fixed bayonets without firing a shot, in spite of the fact that the rebel fire was heavy.'[29] Although they moved quickly from position to position, overall progress was 'impeded by several rail fences.'[30] The 17th's light infantry, already ahead of the grenadiers, 'had a view of part of the enemys line opposite the grenadiers and opened a fire from about half the company on it; no more being able to form on the space,' recalled their officer. Two more light infantry companies from the 1st Battalion got past the church and joined the 17th lights at the base of the hill; first the 38th's, of whom 'some of their gallant soldiers wanted to ascend the hill immediately; objected as too imprudent,' but then 'the 33rd company joined immediately afterwards, and the men of the three companies calling out up the hill, at their cannon, ascended the hill and had a glimpse of the enemys line as far as the eye could reach to the right and left.'[31] Even though the 'enemys guns too far back on the height to annoy us,' three light infantry companies with no support to their left, and ahead of the grenadiers to their right, were far outnumbered. 'The impatient courage of both officers & men inducing them to ascend the height,' in the words of an anonymous officer that echoed the setbacks light infantry companies had experienced in September and October 1776, 'the whole Rebel Line presented itself to view & so close that those who compos'd this spirited attack had nothing to expect but slaughter.'[32] 'Their line advancing on us,' wrote the17th's officer, 'we were compelled to throw ourselves on our knees and bellies, and keep up a fire from the slope of the hill. Enemy repeatedly attempted to come on, but were always drove back by our fire.'[33]

If the battalion was 'doubled up' as an unidentified officer wrote, it explains why the 17th, 33rd and 38th's companies were able to take the road around the right side of the church while the others stopped at the fence facing the church. In a single line the 33rd and 38th companies were next to each other near the centre of the battalion. With the battalion doubled – the left half of the battalion formed behind the right half – and the 17th and 42nd companies on the flanks after initially being sent forward, the formation looked like this:

42nd, 35th, 28th, 23rd, 10th, 4th, 17th
5th, 15th, 22nd, 27th, 33rd, 38th

Far forward of their own battalion and pinned down on the slope, the three companies sought support from grenadiers behind and to their right, who were having their own difficulties with the enemy on the hill. Major Charles Stuart, who had commanded the 4th Battalion of Grenadiers before it was disbanded and now accompanied the army with no command, happened to come up with the isolated light infantry companies. Recognizing that Stuart was in the 43rd Regiment, and that the 43rd's grenadiers happened to be the nearest company to them on the left end of the 2nd Battalion of Grenadier's line, they 'persuaded Major Stuart to run down the hill and prevail on that company to hasten to

29 S. Smith (ed.), *At General Howe's Side*, p.31A.
30 APSL: Sol Feinstone Collection No. 409: Anonymous British Journal, 1776–78.
31 APSL: Sol Feinstone Collection no. 111: 'Memo battle of Brandiwine.'
32 APSL: Sol Feinstone Collection No. 409: Anonymous British Journal, 1776–78.
33 APSL: Sol Feinstone Collection no. 111: 'Memo battle of Brandiwine.'

our support.'[34] But support was not needed after all – the rest of the 1st Battalion of Light Infantry appeared on their left, providing momentum to rout the enemy on the hill. 'To my inexpressible joy,' remembered the 17th's officer, 'saw Captain Cochrane of the 4t company on my left throw up his cap and cry Victory – and looking round saw the 43d company hastening to our relief; we dashed forward passed the five pieces of cannon which the enemy had abandoned and made some few prisoners, enemy running away from us, with too much speed to be overtaken.'[35]

Further to the left, the 2nd Battalion of Light Infantry moved forward, more or less in parallel with the 1st Battalion, but 'having swampy & broken ground to go over, & besides oppos'd with great numbers retarded their advance.'[36] Lieutenant Hunter of the 52nd's light infantry, who had turned 20 years old four days before, remembered that their opponents were posted behind strong fences; 'they allowed us to advance till within one hundred and fifty yards of their line, when they gave us a volley, which we returned, and immediately charged.'[37] 'There was a most infernal fire of cannon & musketry, most incessant shouting – incline to the right! incline to the left! halt! charge &c.' wrote Lieutenant St George of the 52nd lights, referring to lines shifting laterally as they moved forward, 'The balls ploughing up the ground. The trees cracking over ones heads. The branches riven by the artillery – the leaves falling as in autumn by the grapeshot.'[38] Finally, in the words of Lieutenant Hale of the grenadiers, 'the Light Infantry drove a much superior body out of a wood on our left.'[39]

The enemy was in full flight, but the troops 'were by this time much fatigued,' according to Lieutenant Peebles.[40] Another officer commented that 'the fatigue of the day having been very great & the Men encumbered with their Blankets &c. it soon became necessary to halt.'[41] 'Having marched seventeen miles of very dusty road' before the battle took a toll on the soldiers; 'it growing dark, together with the vast fatigue the first column had gone through, prevented any further pursuits.'[42] A staff officer acknowledged, 'The Rebels were driven back by the superior fire of the Troops, but these were too much exhausted to be able to charge or pursue.'[43]

The flank battalions suffered more casualties in this action than in any single battle since Bunker Hill – five grenadier officers and one light infantry officer killed, nine grenadier and 13 light infantry officers wounded. The grenadiers lost Captain Edward Drury, a 30-year-old Irishman with 15 years in the army; 20-year-old Dutch-born Lieutenant Willem Arnold Falconer of the 15th and Lieutenant Richard Barber of the 40th, both of whom had received their first army commissions in 1775; Lieutenant Hadley D'Oyly, who had made the unusual transfer from the Marines into the 52nd Regiment the previous year, and George Minchin of the 27th, the oldest and most experienced of the deceased lieutenants at 22-years old and

34 APSL: Sol Feinstone Collection no. 111: 'Memo battle of Brandiwine.'
35 APSL: Sol Feinstone Collection no. 111: 'Memo battle of Brandiwine.'
36 APSL: Sol Feinstone Collection No. 409: Anonymous British Journal, 1776–78.
37 Hunter, *Journal*, p.29.
38 St George, 'The Actions at Brandywine and Paoli,' p.368.
39 Wilkin, *Some British Soldiers*, p.231.
40 Gruber (ed.), *Diary*, p.133.
41 APSL: Sol Feinstone Collection No. 409: Anonymous British Journal, 1776–78.
42 Robert Francis Seybolt, 'A Contemporary British Account of General Sir William Howe's Military Operations in 1777,' *Proceedings of the American Antiquarian Society* 40 (April 1930), pp.78–79.
43 C. Willcox (ed.), *Major André's Journal* (Tarrytown, NY: William Abbatt, 1930), p.46.

four years of service. The commander of the 1st Battalion of Grenadiers, Lieutenant Colonel William Meadows, was shot from his horse by a ball that broke his right arm, and his left collar bone broke when he hit the ground. Also wounded were Captains Andrew Cathcart of the 15th, John Graves Simcoe of the 40th, and Benjamin Fish of the 44th. Both the 33rd's grenadier lieutenants, John Hill Harris and Adam Drummond, were wounded, and both of the 37th's, Ligonier Chapman and Stephen Cooke, as well as Thomas Peters of the 64th. [44]

General Howe's report on the battle listed the numbers of soldiers killed and wounded in each battalion but did not delineate them by company. Regimental muster rolls give names of those killed but not wounded, making it impossible to determine whether any companies suffered disproportionately to the others. In the 1st Battalion of Grenadiers, one man was killed in both the 5th and 27th companies, and a sergeant and a private soldier of the 37th; the companies of other six killed have not been determined. The 10 killed in the 2nd Battalion of Grenadiers include a sergeant and a private from the 44th, three from the 46th, two from the 52nd, and one each from the 49th, 55th and 63rd. A few of the 107 wounded grenadier privates can be identified: 28-year-old Andrew Graham, a weaver from the town of Armagh in Ireland who spent five years in the 14th Dragoons before volunteering for serving in America and joining the 33rd Regiment, was wounded in the left breast; Samuel Stratton, a whitesmith from Madeley, Shropshire who joined the 6th Regiment in 1768 and was wounded in the head and neck on the island of St. Vincent during the Carib War of 1773, was drafted into the 37th Regiment in 1776 and then shot through the right arm and right leg at Brandywine; James Gamble from Lisburn, County Antrim, in the 37th for just three years before being wounded in the thigh at Brandywine; writing clerk John Hawkins of Lurgan, County Armagh, who joined the 37th at the age of 24 shortly before they sailed for America, whose head wound received at Brandywine left him suffering from 'melancholy'; 23-year-old Corporal Richard Bradley, a weaver from Colne, Lancashire who had joined the 37th six years before and was wounded in the left thigh; stocking weaver Samuel Featherstone in the 44th's grenadiers, born in Nottingham in 1751, in the army for seven years, wounded in the right knee; and William Butt, a 31-year-old house thatcher from Somerset who had spent eight years in the 50th Regiment before joining the 63rd in 1776, wounded in the left leg.[45]

The sole light infantry officer killed was Lieutenant Francis Johnstone of the 38th Regiment, who had been with the company in the march to Concord in 1775 and was among the officers who had boldly suggested charging uphill with only three companies. The wounded officers in the light infantry were Captains James Douglas of the 15th, Thomas Mecan of the 23rd, William Dansey of the 33rd, Nicholas Wade of the 49th, Henry Downing of the 55th, and James Murray of the 57th, all veteran officers in the army since the 1760s; the considerably-younger Captain James De Courcy of the 40th, 22 years old with barely

44 'Return of the killed, wounded, and missing … Sept. 11, 1777,' in John Almon (ed.), *The Remembrancer, or impartial repository of public events* (London: J. Almon, 1778), Vol.5, pp.415–417; TNA: WO 27/32 and WO 27/35: Inspection returns, 63rd Regiment, and 15th and 27th regiments respectively; Anon. (ed.), 'British Army Orders,' p.418; Wilkin, *Some British Soldiers*, p.194.

45 TNA: WO 12: muster rolls of the various regiments; WO 121/15/122: discharge of Andrew Graham; WO 121/10/51: discharge of Samuel Stratton; WO 121/15/31: discharge of James Gamble; WO 121/1/6: discharge of John Hawkins; WO 121/15/30: discharge of Richard Bradley; WO 121/13/305: discharge of Samuel Featherstone; WO 121/1/375: discharge of William Butt.

five years in the army; and Lieutenants Charles Leigh of the 15th (also wounded at Harlem Heights), John Birch of the 27th, Thomas Nicholl of the 33rd, Samuel Ruxton of the 45th, Thomas Armstrong of the 49th, and Bent Ball of the 63rd. Some wounds were minor – Captain Dansey was shot in the right thumb, 'which did not make me quit the field or my duty afterwards,' and Lieutenant St George was not reported wounded even though 'a ball glanced against my ankle & contused it,' requiring him to be 'lifted on horseback in men's arms' for several days afterwards.[46]

One private soldier was killed in each light infantry company of the 4th, 15th, 17th, 22nd, 27th, 33rd, 38th, 44th and 52nd Regiments. A total of 77 were wounded, among them the 10th Regiment's John Booth, a 24-year-old paper maker from Chester who had been in the army for just three years, wounded in the right leg; the 37th's Hugh Holt, a weaver who joined the army at 22 in 1770, wounded in the left arm; Daniel McGraa, born in 1753 in Morayshire, and Thomas Stanton born the previous year in Bolton, Lancashire, both of whom joined the 44th Regiment in 1769, both wounded in New York in 1776, and both wounded again at Brandywine.[47]

Although 107 private soldiers were wounded in the grenadier battalions and 77 in the light infantry, General Howe ordered regiments to replace only the dead in their flank companies.[48] Perhaps most of the wounds were not severe enough to take men entirely out of action, or the regiments, dealing with their own battle losses, could not afford to send men to their flank companies. A small boost in strength occurred because Howe dissolved the rifle company commanded by Captain Ferguson, who was wounded in the battle. The soldiers were dispersed into the light infantry companies; no rolls for Ferguson's company survive, but the rolls of the 43rd and 57th light infantry companies each denote two men from Ferguson's corps joining, suggesting that other companies also received two men each.[49] The commander of the 2nd Battalion ordered them to join the corps of riflemen commanded by Lieutenant Robert Shaw of the 64th's light infantry, apparently embodied since the beginning of the campaign. Lieutenant George Mathews of the 37th's light company also joined the rifle corps at this time, perhaps to accommodate the increase in numbers.[50]

The light infantry captured seven cannon at the Battle of Brandywine, five by the 1st Battalion and two by the 2nd Battalion. They were rewarded at the rate of $100 per cannon. This meant only a small sum for each soldier, perhaps three quarters of a dollar in the 1st Battalion and one quarter in the 2nd Battalion, but at an exchange rate of four shillings eight pence per dollar this was a bonus of one or a few days' pay at the base rate of eight pence per day.[51]

* * *

46 'Return of the killed, wounded, and missing … Sept. 11, 1777,' pp.415–417; Dansey (ed.), *Letters*, p.34; St George, 'The Actions at Brandywine and Paoli,' p.368.

47 TNA: WO 121/23/284, WO 121/7/306, WO 121/13/309 and WO 121/13/307: discharges of John Booth, Hugh Holt, Daniel McGraa, and Thomas Stanton respectively.

48 Anon. (ed.), 'British Army Orders,' p.497.

49 Anon. (ed.), 'British Army Orders,' p.495; TNA: WO 12: muster rolls of the various regiments.

50 LOC: George Washington Papers: orderly book, 2nd Battalion of Light Infantry (64th Regiment's company), battalion orders, 19 September 1777.

51 Stirke, 'British Officer's Revolutionary War Journal,' p.170. Exchange rates are given in Sullivan, *From Redcoat to Rebel*, p.27.

The army stayed in place for a few days. 'Some stupid people are dwelling on the fact that our General does not quickly follow Washington with his whole force,' wrote a staff officer, explaining that it was impossible because the only wagons available to take the sick and wounded to safety were the same ones needed for moving provisions.[52] Opportunistic flank battalion soldiers took the opportunity to procure what they could from the countryside, again ignoring strict orders against plundering. The problem was so severe that General Howe finally followed through with his 29 August order to execute soldiers caught in the act of plundering. Grenadier William Merrit of the 28th Regiment and light infantryman William Harrison of the 5th were executed at eleven o'clock in the morning of 15 September 'in the front of the grenadiers Encampment for plundering in Disobedience of General Orders.' 'It is with the greatest Concern that his Excellency the Commander in Chief is Reduced to the Disagreeable Necessity of ordering the Execution,' Howe announced in general orders, 'but the shocking & Cruel Robberies that have been Committed on the innocent Inhabitants of this Country who have already Suffered much from the Rebels for their Loyalty Renders it absolutely Necessary. It is likewise a Justice due to the good Soldier who in a Land of plenty must be Deprived of every Comfort by the outragious Depredations of a few Desperate Villains.' Three officers and 50 private soldiers from each regiment and battalion witnessed the executions.[53]

Moving again towards Philadelphia, on 16 September the 1st Battalion of Light Infantry 'attack'd a body of 500 rebels,' according to Captain Stirke of the 10th's company, 'posted behind a fence, on a hill.' Upon the light infantry 'advancing very briskly they gave us one fire and run away.' Once again, an aggressive advance won the day; the light infantry had only one man wounded in the affair.[54] A British artillery officer, making a general comment on the flank battalions' success, accurately wrote, 'The rebels fly before us; they run whenever we advance. They say we are mad or drunk or we would never dash in among them as we do. Our light infantry are the finest set of fellows in the world for this mode of fighting.'[55]

Three companies of light infantry and a corps of riflemen moved forward on 18 September to 'take possession of a large store, the Rebels have at Valley Forge.' The next day the 1st Battalion of Light Infantry and both British grenadier battalions supported them when rebels threatened the post.[56]

Two days later Major Turner Straubenzee took three companies of the 2nd Battalion of Light Infantry 'to get all the information they could' about 1,500 Americans posted a few miles west of General Howe's army. 'They returned about four o'clock in the evening,' recalled Lieutenant Hunter of the 52nd's light infantry, 'and as soon as it was dark the whole battalion got under arms.' Major General Charles Grey took the light infantry battalion, the 42nd and 44th Regiments and a party of dragoons on a march that began at 8:00 p.m.

52 S. Smith (ed.), *At General Howe's Side*, p.32.
53 LOC: George Washington Papers: orderly book, 2nd Battalion of Light Infantry, general orders, 15 September 1777. Muster rolls confirm that these executions were carried out. TNA: WO 12, muster rolls of the various regiments.
54 Stirke, 'British Officer's Revolutionary War Journal,' p.171.
55 F. A. Whinyates (ed.), *The Services of Lieut. Colonel Francis Downman, R. A. in France, North American and the West Indies, between the years 1758 and 1784*, ed. (Woolwich: Royal Artillery Institution, 1896), p.35.
56 Stirke, 'British Officer's Revolutionary War Journal,' p.173.

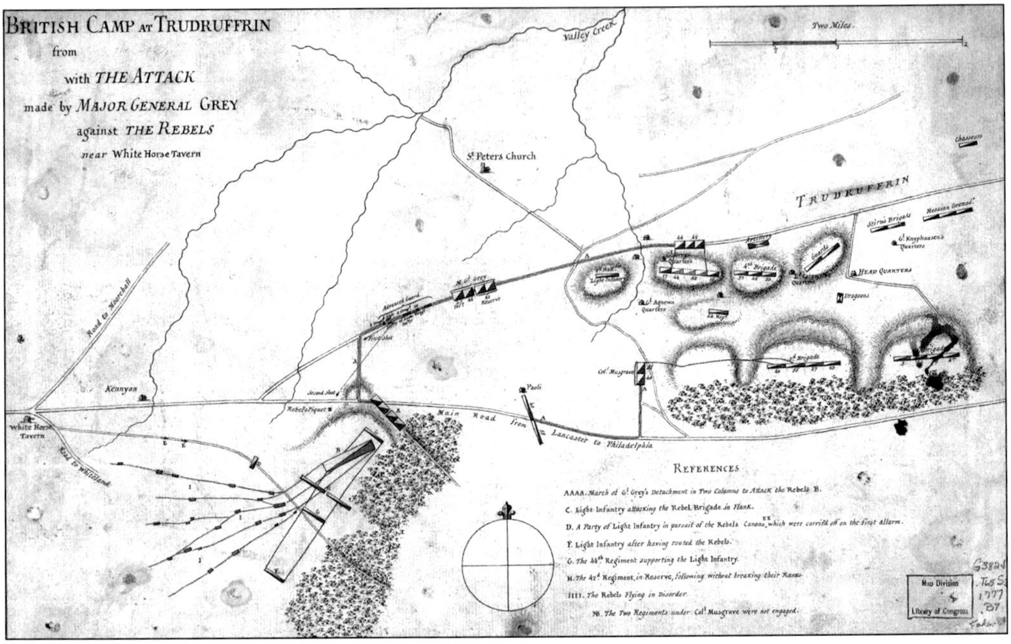

Map showing the British encampment, route of march, and battle that has since been called 'the Paoli Massacre' on the night of 20–21 September 1777. (Library of Congress)

along a road that led north of the American position. Two dragoons led the way, followed by six light infantrymen; a few yards behind was a company of light infantry – apparently of the 52nd Regiment – followed by 10 more dragoons. They were followed by rest of the light infantry battalion and the 44th Regiment, with the 42nd bringing up the rear as a reserve. Grey gave orders not to load, and to draw the rounds out of any firelocks that were loaded; Major Maitland, commanding the light infantry, assured Grey that although 'the whole of the battalion was always loaded,' according to Hunter, 'if he would only allow them to remain so, he would be answerable that they did not fire a shot.' Hunter's fellow lieutenant in the 52nd's light infantry, Richard St George, recalled that 'the men were ordered to unload – on no account to fire.'[57]

A left turn brought Grey's force onto a southbound road along one flank of the enemy encampment. As they closed in at around 1:00 a.m., American sentries challenged and fired, but failed to raise a sufficient alarm. Hunter remembered Grey shouting, 'Dash, Light Infantry!' The battalion pursued the fleeing sentries through woods into the enemy encampment, giving 'such a cheer as made the woods echo.' St George wrote, 'For two miles we drove them now and then firing scatteringly from behind fences Trees &c. The flashes of the pieces had a fine effect in the night – then followed a dreadful scene of Havock.' 'The Light Infantry bayonetted every man they came up with,' recounted Hunter, 'this, with the

57 Hunter, *Journal*, p.30–31; LOC: Map Division: 'British Camp at Trudruffrin with The Attack made by Major General Grey against the Rebels near White Horse Tavern,'; St George, 'The Actions at Brandywine and Paoli,' p.368.

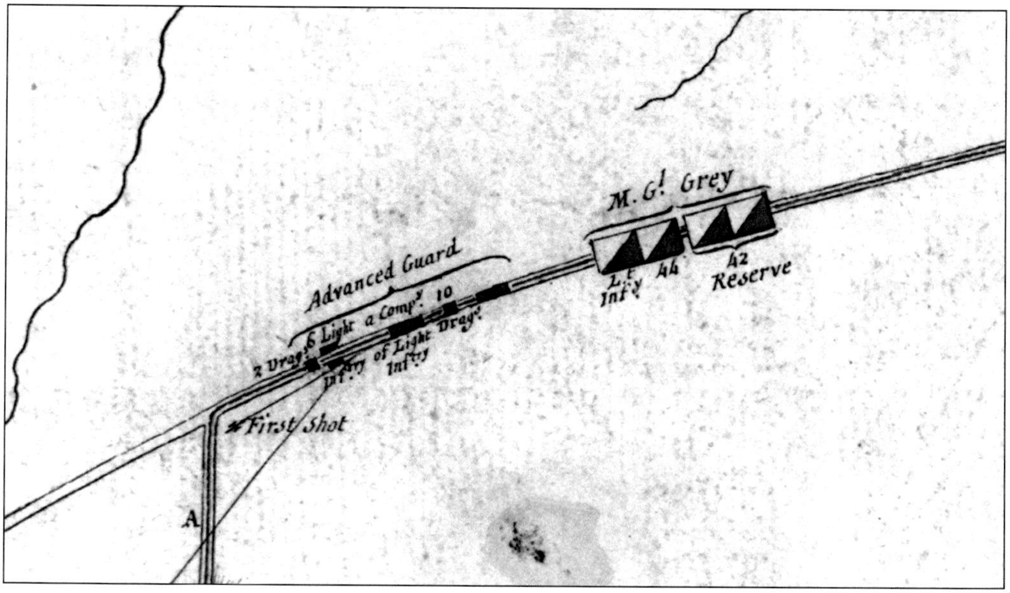

Detail of Major General Charles Grey's order of march on the night of 20–21 September 1777, from the map 'British Camp at Trudruffrin with The Attack made by Major General Grey against the Rebels near White Horse Tavern.' (Library of Congress)

cries of the wounded, formed altogether the most dreadful scene I ever beheld.' The light infantry relied entirely on their bayonets, while their opponents fired only scattered shots.[58]

Grey's triumphal troops returned to camp after a rout that was so complete historians call it the Paoli Massacre. In general orders on 22 September General Howe gave his 'particular thanks to Major General Grey and the officers and men of the Detachment Under his Command, that Yesterday Morning Surprised a part of the Enemy; their Steadiness in Charging With Bayonets without firing a Single Shot not only proves their Spirit and Discipline but Also their Evident Superiority over the Enemy.'[59] Only four British soldiers were killed, among them Captain William Wolfe, commander of the 40th's light company. Four others were wounded including Lieutenant Hunter, shot through the right hand.[60] He remarked, years later, that the surprise night-time bayonet attack caused the Americans to call the 2nd Battalion of Light Infantry 'the Bloodhounds,' and that 'I don't think our battalion slept very soundly after that night for a long time.'[61] His colleague Lieutenant St George wrote 12 days after the affair, 'They threaten retaliation, vow that they will give no quarter to any of our Battalions.'[62] Some writers believe that the battalion adopted red feathers for their caps in response to this reputation, but others ascribe it to a similar action in New Jersey a year later, if it occurred at all.

58 Hunter, *Journal*, p.31; St George, 'The Actions at Brandywine and Paoli,' p.368.
59 Anon. (ed.), 'British Army Orders,' p.501.
60 Almon (ed.), *The Remembrancer*, Vol.5, p.412; Hunter, *Journal*, p.31.
61 Hunter, *Journal*, p.32.
62 St George, 'The Actions at Brandywine and Paoli,' p.369.

Manoeuvring over next week found the army in Germantown, a few miles north of Philadelphia. Lieutenant General Cornwallis led the two British and two German grenadier battalions, two squadrons of dragoons and 10 artillery pieces into the city in the middle of the day on 26 September. 'The streets crowded with Inhabitants who seem to rejoice on the occasion,' wrote grenadier Captain John Peebles, 'tho' by all accounts many of them were publickly on the other side before our arrival.' They took quarters in public buildings, the 1st Battalion of Grenadiers at the south end of town, the 2nd Battalion in an almshouse called the Bettering House.[63] One month after landing, following 'the fatigues of a march exceeding 100 miles, supported with the utmost chearfulness by all ranks, without tents, and with very little baggage,' in the words of General Howe, the army had succeeded in its principle objective.[64] The campaign, however, was far from over.

The next morning several American warships appeared in the Delaware River at the southern end of the city. Four British 12-pounders and two howitzers exchanged fire with the ships for a half hour. The 1st Battalion of Grenadiers turned out in support. One of the largest ships, the frigate *Delaware*, closed within musket shot, and the hail of fire from the grenadiers 'threw her crew into such confusion that they neglected the management of the sails,' according to the British artillery officer commanding a gun battery.[65] The vessel ran aground and surrendered. With the artillery still busily engaging the other warships, 10 grenadiers, appropriately from the Marines' company, went on board and put out a fire, saving captured ship.[66] In November company commanders in the grenadier battalion each received £45 13s prize money for the captured ship to divide among their men; assuming that each soldier got an equal share, this was a reward of roughly one pound, about a month's pay, for most companies.[67]

* * *

Much the army remained in the Germantown area between the city and the enemy, encamped in an east-west line centred on the road that led northward out of Philadelphia, half the army on each side of the road. The 1st Battalion of Light Infantry and the Queen's Rangers occupied wigwams a mile in front of the right wing; the 2nd Battalion of Light Infantry and the 40th Regiment's wigwams were in front of the left wing at the road. Lieutenant St George, in the 2nd Battalion, presciently wrote on 2 October, 'We are always on the advanced Post of the army – our present one is unpleasant – our left too open & unguarded.' He indicated that the battalion consisted of only 300 men by this time, suggesting significant numbers of

63 Gruber (ed.), *Diary*, p.138.
64 Almon (ed.), *The Remembrancer*, Vol.5, p.415.
65 F. A. Whinyates (ed.), *Services*, p.36.
66 F. A. Whinyates (ed.), *Services*, p.37; Almon (ed.), *The Remembrancer*, Vol.5, p.413; Gruber (ed.), *Diary*, p.139. The latter two accounts attribute the boarding to the Marines; another writer said it was the 17th's grenadiers. LOC: George Washington Papers, Series 6, Military Papers, 1755-1798, Subseries 6C, Captured British Orderly Books, 1777-1778: Captured British Officer's Accounts Ledger, 1769-1771, and Diary, 1774; 1777.
67 Gruber (ed.), *Diary*, p.229. Peebles complained that his company from the 42nd Regiment, although twice the size of other companies, received only one and a half shares.

sick in addition to the wounded; Lieutenant Hunter wrote that the battalion 'was very weak … they did not consist of more than three hundred and fifty men.'[68]

At dawn on 4 October enemy forces attacked the pickets of the 2nd Battalion of Light Infantry, and soon after the 1st Battalion came under attack. Breaking daylight did not reveal the extent of the attack because the morning was 'so foggy that their columns cou'd hardly be distinguished at twenty paces distance,' wrote Lieutenant Stirke.[69] Lieutenant Hunter remembered that the 2nd Battalion 'was out and under arms in a minute,' and that 'many of them rushed out of the back part of the huts.' Lieutenant St George saw bullets striking around him as he exited his tent, and noted that another officer would have been 'killed in his tent as he was pulling on his boots had he not been on his back.'[70] Hunter, writing two decades after the event, claimed to have 'heard a loud cry of "Have at the Bloodhounds! Revenge Wayne's affair!",' referring to the 2nd Battalion's night-time bayonet attack at Paoli two weeks before; no one on either side who wrote of the action soon after it occurred made any such claim.[71] Regardless of whether this was their motivation, American troops pushed hard on the light infantry. Thanks partly to thick fog and partly to discipline from 14 months in close proximity to the enemy, they made 'an obstinate defense as could support for an hour and half,' wrote St George. 'We charged them twice, till the battalion was so reduced by killed and wounded that the bugle was sounded to retreat,' remembered Hunter, and the battalion scrambled to the rear just in time to avoid being surrounded.[72] Six companies of the 40th Regiment took refuge in a large stone house from which they repelled repeated assaults and stalled the enemy advance, allowing the light infantry a clean escape.

The 1st Battalion of Light Infantry also came under intense pressure. Although 'entirely surrounded, their wigwams & provision wagon in possession of the enemy,' wrote Lieutenant Stirke, with support from the 4th Regiment of Foot, 'they fought their way thro' and retook them.'[73] Captain Charles Cochrane, commanding the 4th's light company, wrote that his and the 42nd's company were 'separated in the Fog from the rest of the Battalion,' when they discerned an American regiment behind them, 'between us and our own Hutts.' Thinking they might surrender, Cochrane summoned them to lay down their arms but received gunfire in response, upon which the two light infantry companies 'drove them into and through our own Hutts & killed … most of them with our bayonets.' He wrote that the enemy soldiers had been 'in my Companys Wigwams & the 42d. had taken out our Bread and divided it among themselves So certain they then were of carrying the Day.'[74] General Howe wrote that 'the light infantry, being well supported by the 4th regiment, sustained the enemy's attack with such determined bravery, that they could not make the least impression on them.' Daunted by obstinate opposition, delayed by the 40th Regiment's defence of the stone house, confused first by the fog of nature and then by the fog of battle, the American

68 St George, 'The Actions at Brandywine and Paoli,' p.369; Hunter, *Journal*, p.34.
69 Stirke, 'British Officer's Revolutionary War Journal,' p.172.
70 St George, 'The Actions at Brandywine and Paoli,' p.369.
71 Hunter, *Journal*, pp.33–34.
72 St George, 'The Actions at Brandywine and Paoli,' p.369; Hunter, *Journal*, p.34
73 Stirke, 'British Officer's Revolutionary War Journal,' p.172.
74 National Library of Scotland (NLS): MS5375: Correspondence of Andrew Stuart, Charles Cochrane to Andrew Stuart, 19 October 1777, ff. 35–42.

attack faltered then failed. British regiments encamped in Germantown formed, rallied and began to push the enemy back.[75]

Soon after the sounds of battle reached Philadelphia at 6:00 a.m. the British grenadier battalions and other corps in the city 'got an order to march thither in all haste.'[76] They proceeded 'full of ardour' and ran most of the way to Germantown but arrived too late to join the fray. Instead, finding the enemy in full flight, the grenadiers 'pursued them eight miles, but were only able to get near enough to exchange a few cannon shot with them,' according to Lieutenant Hale.[77] Leaving off the pursuit, the grenadier battalions returned to Philadelphia by nightfall, having covered over 30 miles out and back.[78]

Casualties among the light infantry were light considering the fierce fighting. In the 1st Battalion, Lieutenant Marcus Antony Morgan of the 17th Regiment, wounded on Long Island in August 1776, was killed, as were a sergeant and five soldiers; Captain Forbes Champagne of the 4th Regiment, a sergeant and 36 soldiers were wounded. The 2nd Battalion lost two sergeants and seven soldiers killed; wounded were Captain Sir James Baird of the 71st, Lieutenant John Weir of the 43rd (also wounded on Long Island in 1776), Lieutenant Richard St George Mansergh St George of the 52nd ('in the first volley ... badly wounded in the head,' according to Lieutenant Hunter), Lieutenant Campbell of the 71st (his first name not determined because there were several Lieutenant Campbells in the regiment), as well as three sergeants, a drummer, and 51 soldiers. Captain Edward Speke of the 37th and four soldiers were taken prisoner.[79] Muster rolls show one man each killed from the 15th, 17th, 37th, 38th, 44th, 46th, 49th, 52nd and 57th companies.[80] A few of the wounded are known: John Davis, 27 years old from St. James, London with seven years in the 15th Regiment, shot in the ankle; Thomas Swift, a framework knitter born in 1748 in Thurcaston, Leicestershire who joined the 37th at the age of 20, wounded in the left arm; 33-year old William Bragg, a weaver from Darlington, Durham who enlisted in the 63rd in 1766, wounded in the left thigh; and fellow 63rd soldier Thomas Witherill, a clothier born in Bedale, Yorkshire in 1751 with just four years in the regiment, who lost part of a finger on his left hand.[81] Thomas Knight, the soldier of the 15th's light infantry who had stopped a man of the 33rd when on picket back on 31 August, was wounded in the left side.[82] All of these men recovered from their wounds and continued to serve in the war.

Many wounded Americans were left behind. One was an ensign in the 1st New Jersey Regiment named Martin Hurley, struck down in an assault on the stone house defended by the 40th Regiment. As British regiments pushed forward past the stone house, soldiers recognized Hurley – he deserted from the 44th Regiment's grenadier company in Boston

75 Almon (ed.), *The Remembrancer*, Vol. 5 p.414.
76 Gruber (ed.), *Diary*, p.140; *The Remembrancer*, Vol.5, p.414.
77 Wilkin, *Some British Soldiers*, p.232.
78 Gruber (ed.), *Diary*, p.140.
79 Almon (ed.), *The Remembrancer*, Vol.5, p.418; Hunter, *Journal*, p.34.
80 TNA: WO 12: muster rolls of the various regiments. The two battalions lost three sergeants and 12 private soldiers, of whom one sergeant and eight soldiers have been identified. Several men died within the next few days, and some of these may be among those reported as killed in the battle.
81 TNA: WO 121/10/190, WO 121/10/45, WO 121/1/160, and WO 121/1/166: discharges of John Davis, Thomas Swift, William Bragg, and Thomas Witherill, respectively.
82 TNA: WO 121/10/183: discharge of Thomas Knight.

back in November 1775. His eight years of British training were invaluable to the nascent American army, and he quickly became a sergeant, then an officer. Two days after the Battle of Germantown, he was tried by a general court martial for 'desertion and bearing arms in the Rebel Army.' With no viable defence – he was, after all, caught on the battlefield in an officer's uniform with a commission in his pocket – Hurley told the court 'that he had nothing to offer in his defence, but that he never had been guilty of such crimes before.' He was found guilty and executed on 8 October.[83]

The same court heard the case surrounding the death of John Wilkins of the 4th Regiment's light infantry. Wilkins was found dead the morning after the battle, shot through the chest at close range, but he was not a casualty of war. During the night he tried to steal a horse belonging to the 16th Light Dragoons. When a dragoon standing sentry summoned him, Wilkins responded, 'Kiss my arse, you bougre,' and led the animal way. The sentry and another dragoon pursued him in the darkness, suspecting him to be a rebel prisoner attempting escape. After catching up to and scuffling with Wilkins one of the dragoons, still not realizing he was a British soldier, shot him with a pistol. The dragoon was tried for murder but acquitted when the circumstances became clear. The 4th Regiment's muster rolls record the date of Wilkins' death as 5 October, which would lead to the assumption that he died of wounds were it not for the trial record.[84]

* * *

'We have been very quiet since the 4th,' wrote Captain Cochrane two weeks after the battle, for the light infantry battalions had, except for an inconsequential 17-mile reconnaissance on 18 October, largely remained in their Germantown wigwams.[85] The grenadier battalions quartered in the city had hard work to do. To sustain the army in Philadelphia for the winter, navigation up the Delaware River was essential. Knowing this, the rebels had built two forts on opposite sides of the river south of the city, one on aptly named Mud Island and the other on the New Jersey shore. The defenders were proving difficult to dislodge. On 7 October, four companies of the 1st Battalion of Grenadiers went to Province Island to work on an artillery battery directed against adjacent Mud Island. Throughout the next month detachments of grenadiers laboured with other soldiers in this battery. Rain fell heavily, flooding the works and the roads to them, forcing men to wade up to their waists 'for miles' according to Lieutenant Peebles of the 42nd's grenadiers, just to arrive at the batteries where they toiled in knee-deep water. When not working at the lines, the grenadiers and other troops made fascines, bound bundles of saplings nine feet long, and sent them to the batteries to reinforce earthen walls. Various plans were made to storm the rebel fort, some of which called for the participation of the British grenadiers, but it was the German

83 TNA: WO 12: muster rolls, 44th Regiment; Francis B. Heitman, *Historical Register of Officers of the Continental Army during the War of the Revolution* (Washington, DC: Rare Book Shop Publishing, 1914), p.311; TNA: WO 71/84: trial of Martin Hurley, pp.337–342.

84 TNA: WO 12: muster rolls, 4th Regiment; TNA: WO 71/84: trial of Roger Thorne, pp.337–342.

85 NLS: MS5375: Correspondence of Andrew Stuart, Charles Cochrane to Andrew Stuart, 19 October 1777; Stirke, 'British Officer's Revolutionary War Journal,' p.173.

grenadiers that made the attempt and were repulsed with heavy losses. The defenders finally gave up the forts in mid-November due to attrition rather than direct assault.[86]

The 2nd Battalion of Grenadiers 'went to the North end of the Town & encamp'd in huts' on 8 October, returning to campaign-like discomfort.[87] Two weeks later, Lieutenant Hale of the 45th's grenadiers wrote, 'a tent begins to feel rather cold, and I have no other covering than my cloak, the remainder of my baggage being on board, so that I am almost as ragged as last year.'[88] It had been two months since the army disembarked with no tents for soldiers, soldiers' tents for officers, and minimal baggage.

The 1st Battalion of Light Infantry and the 27th Regiment crossed the Delaware to support the abortive German attack on the rebel fort on 23 October. On 17 November, after the Mud Island fort fell, the 1st Battalions of Light Infantry and Grenadiers, the German grenadiers, a German chasseur company and two British regiments crossed again and joined about 4,000 reinforcements from New York that had landed at Billingsport. For 10 days they worked to secure the eastern bank of the Delaware, making it safe for ships to pass. Rebels had destroyed bridges over creeks feeding into the river, which were duly repaired, sometimes with difficulty. On 22 November, the light infantry of the 4th, 5th, 10th, 15th and 17th Regiments took boats across Timber Creek to provide cover while the bridge was repaired. Late in the day 'small party's of the Rebels appear'd and begun to be troublesome firing on us from a railing on the other side of a small swamp,' recalled Lieutenant Stirke. The light infantry drove them off, but not without the loss of John Key and Stephen Sutton of the 5th's company killed, and a man of the 4th's wounded. An attack on the 25th was repelled by German chasseurs, and when the last of the light infantry were embarking in flat boats for Philadelphia on the 27th, 'a large body of the Rebels threw themselves into a Wood, near the beech, and were very troublesome,' wrote Stirke; 'We had one officer and several men slightly wounded.'[89]

Philadelphia and the waterway were secure. Fortifications protected the landward approach to the city from the north, but enemy troops remained nearby. Late at night on 4 December General Howe took a large force north in one final attempt to defeat the rebel army before winter weather halted campaigning. Just as they had done since August, they took no baggage.[90] The light infantry battalions took post on Chestnut Hill and were attacked by about 1,000 enemy troops. 'Upon the first onset of the 2d battalion of light infantry, and part of the 1st,' wrote General Howe, 'they were instantly defeated.'[91] During the 'very cold' night the soldiers slept in improvised huts, 'accoutered & their arms by them.'[92] They stayed for a day, then moved at 1:00 a.m. on 7 December. At midday the 1st Battalion of Light Infantry and 33rd Regiment attacked and defeated a strong enemy force posted on a hill. 'The thickness of the wood where the rebels were posted, concealing them from the view of the light infantry,' wrote General Howe, 'occasioned the loss of one officer killed, three wounded, and between 20 and 30 men killed and wounded, from

86 Anon. (ed.), 'British Army Orders,' pp.518, 524–525; Peebles, *Diary*, pp.141–146.
87 Gruber (ed.), *Diary*, p.141.
88 Wilkin, *Some British Soldiers*, p.238.
89 Stirke, 'British Officer's Revolutionary War Journal,' p.175; TNA: WO 12: muster rolls, 5th Regiment.
90 Gruber (ed.), *Diary*, p.152.
91 Almon (ed.), *The Remembrancer*, Vol.5, p.504.
92 Gruber (ed.), *Diary*, p.153.

their first fire.'[93] 'The troops no provision today,' commented an officer of the 42nd Regiment, testifying to the intensity of the day's activities.[94] The next day General Howe opted to retire to Philadelphia, having found the enemy too strongly posted to attack. The flank battalion casualties were all in the 1st Battalion of Light Infantry. Lieutenant Kingsmill Penefather of the 15th Regiment was killed; Lieutenants Arthur French of the 22nd and Matthew Ankertel of the 17th were wounded. Howe reported two sergeants and 11 soldiers killed in the battalion, of whom muster rolls identify Sergeant Murdoch McPherson of the 17th and Sergeant Joseph Palmer of the 33rd, two men each from the 10th, 17th and 35th Regiments, and one each from the 15th and 38th killed on 7 December; the losses in the 10th's and 17th's companies, next to each other on the right wing, suggest the weight of the action fell on them. In addition, the 37th's company had one killed on the 6th, and the 22nd's lost a man on the 8th. Sergeant James Reed of the 10th died of wounds on the 11th; 25 private soldiers were also wounded, their companies not identified.[95] Lieutenant Colonel Christopher French of the 52nd Regiment, who had commanded the 22nd Regiment's light infantry before the war, recorded in his journal, 'Heard that my Son Arthur had been wounded in the Leg, but that no Bone was broke, & that he had behaved so well that the whole Army ring with his praise, & Genl Howe had thank'd him in the Field & conver's with him a long Time at the head of the Corps of Rifle Men which he commands.'[96]

There would be no more pursuit of the enemy for the time being, but there was still work to do to prepare for winter. The army needed substantial amounts of forage for horses, and looked to the countryside to obtain it. The flank battalions and other troops went out early in the morning of 12 December, returning in the evening. The next day, they crossed the Schuylkill River on the west side of the city on a pontoon bridge, each time returning with 'a good hawl of forage.' On the 22nd they went out one final time, this time remaining in the country west of the city for a week, covering parties that loaded wagons with hay and sent them into the city each day, in weather that began mild but ended 'exceeding cold … not a bit of shelter for the men' until they finally returned to the city on the 28th.[97] Captain Dansey of the 33rd's light infantry wrote home that on Christmas day the men of his company 'had Musket Balls flying about our Ears for a Minuit as thick as anytime during the War, a drole Way of keeping Christmas but thank God neither Officers or Men were hurt,' adding whimsically, 'I like it prodigiously, it is better than a Fox Chace.'[98] The light infantry settled in the city's barracks, and the grenadiers quartered in the almshouse, their best accommodations since leaving Boston almost two years earlier. The flank battalions had been on the front lines continuously since the end of August 1776, 16 months, 'our best habitations wigwams, through which the heavy rains of this climate whenever they fell easily penetrated,' recalled Lieutenant Hale, adding, 'Notwithstanding the lateness of the year … the 31st of Dec. where we went into winter quarters, till which time I constantly slept in my cloths from the first landing, I never enjoyed a greater share of health.'[99] Now, with winter setting in, they had a well-deserved respite.

93 Almon (ed.), *The Remembrancer*, Vol.5, p.504.
94 Gruber (ed.), *Diary*, p.153.
95 Almon (ed.), *The Remembrancer*, Vol.5, p.504.
96 LOC: Journal of Christopher French: 23 December 1777.
97 Gruber (ed.), *Diary*, pp.154, 156–157.
98 HSD: William Dansey Letters: Dansey to his mother, 19 January 1778.
99 Wilkin, *Some British Soldiers*, pp.246–247.

7

'Anxious for their Country's Honor': New Jersey and Rhode Island, 1778

During the winter in Philadelphia changes occurred in the flank battalions. The 7th and 26th Regiments, which had been captured piecemeal at posts between Lake Champlain and Quebec in late 1775 then exchanged in the middle of 1777, arrived in Philadelphia in December. The flank companies of the 7th joined the 1st Battalions of Grenadiers and Light Infantry, and those of the 26th joined the 2nd Battalions.[1] The 71st Regiment left Philadelphia to join the army in New York, taking its flank companies with it. Officers and men recovered from wounds and illness. A few officers retired or were promoted out of their companies; for the most part, officers from the same regiment replaced them, but here and there officers moved from one regiment to a flank company in another. Soldiers no longer fit for service were discharged; those still fit but no longer suited for flank companies joined their regiments, and replacements transferred in.[2]

Captain Dansey described attrition in the 33rd's light infantry company over the previous two years. On 1 January 1776, his company was at the peacetime strength of two sergeants, two corporals, a drummer and 36 private soldiers. From then until the end of 1777, three sergeants had been wounded, four corporals died, killed, were wounded or captured, and two drummers were wounded; of the private soldiers, eight died, five were killed in battle, 20 were wounded, and four taken prisoner, for a total of 37. He did not mention that many of these wounded recovered, and the overall strength of the company increased, so that 'fresh men for those kill'd and disabled' did not mean that it was an entirely new company. Muster rolls prepared semi-annually show that all three sergeants serving at the end of 1777 had been in the company since January 1776, one as a sergeant and two as corporals. All three corporals present at the end of 1777 had also been in the company since January 1776, two originally as privates and one as a drummer; a private present in January 1776 replaced the drummer appointed corporal. Of the 40 private soldiers present at the end of 1777, 23 were in the company since January 1776. Only one corporal and 17 private soldiers were new to the company. Of the three officers, Captain Dansey and Lieutenant James Ingram were present for the entire two-year period.

1 WLC: William Howe orderly book, 1776–1778, general orders, 15 December 1777.

2 TNA: WO 12: muster rolls of the various regiments.

Dansey's dire tabulation of casualties did not reflect the actual state of his company, now mostly seasoned veterans.[3]

In March 1778 General Howe gave orders to complete flank companies with men fit for a new campaign; as usual flank companies were to have the same numbers as other companies in each regiment, rather than the full strength of 54 private soldiers.[4] For Dansey's company, this meant transferring seven soldiers to the regiment, six of whom had been in the company for the previous two years. Ten new men came into the company, only one of whom had been in the light infantry before; four had joined the regiment within the last three years, but all had the benefit of at least one campaign in America.[5]

And so it was for the flank companies in general. Most changes were complete by the end of April. Most grenadier and light infantry companies had between 45 and 50 men. Some required no replacements at all, most took in two or three new men; only a few needed more than 10 replacements. With only three officers in each company, the impact among them was proportionately more significant, but among grenadiers fewer than a quarter of the officers were new to their companies for the 1778 campaign. The light infantry had more attrition among officers, with about a third of them new; some companies had the same three officers they had had since the previous August, and all had at least one. Most replacement officers came from within the same regiments, and although lieutenants were often only in their late teens or early twenties with only a year or two in the army, they at least had the benefit of a very active campaign under their belts. Captains commanding flank companies varied in age from veterans of the Seven Years War in their forties, to those in their early twenties, none without at least six years in the army.[6]

Not all officers were present with their companies. Captain John Graves Simcoe, commander of the 40th's grenadiers, took command of the Queen's Rangers on 15 October 1777; he nonetheless retained his position as commander of the grenadier company, leaving the actual management of it to the senior lieutenant, Alexander Philip Forbes, who had only four years' experience in the army. Lieutenant Arthur Ross of the 35th's grenadiers was appointed captain in the Queen's Rangers the following month while also retaining his rank in the 35th.[7] In early 1778 Captain Alexander Ross of the 45th's grenadiers was appointed aide-de-camp to Lieutenant General Cornwallis, leaving command of the company to 22-year-old South-Carolina-born Lieutenant William Hale, who had joined the company in late 1776 and was 'now wishing for a Continuance or rather the opening a campaign, in the course of which I might at the head of a Company of Grenadiers' to gain recognition for promotion.[8]

In spite of the visibility of service in flank battalions, some officers began to see being detached from their regiments as an obstacle to promotion. 'I find there is nothing to be

3 HSD: William Dansey Letters: Dansey to his mother, 19 January 1778; TNA: WO 12, muster rolls, 33rd Regiment.
4 Anon. (ed.), 'British Army Orders,' p.556, general orders, 17 March 1778.
5 TNA: WO 12: muster rolls, 33rd Regiment.
6 TNA: WO 27/32 and WO 27/35: Inspection returns for the various regiments. Ages are based on reports of annual inspections in Great Britain before the war, corrected to 1778.
7 Anon. (ed.), 'British Army Orders,' pp.519, 544.
8 Wilkin, *Some British Soldiers*, pp.214, 255.

Table 7.1: Age and experience of grenadier company commanding officers, April 1778

Regiment	Grenadier company captain	Age	Years service
15th	Andrew Cathcart	37	22
17th	William Brereton	28	9
22nd	Henry Elves	38	24
27th	Samuel Waring	25	12
28th	Thomas Coppinger Moyle	34	13
33rd	Hildebrand Oakes	24	10
35th	Hugh Massey	29	16
37th	Francis Graham	36	20
42nd	Charles Graham	28	19
44th	Colin Campbell	42	20
45th	Alexander Ross	36	18
55th	Colin Lindsay	23	7
57th	Charles Brownlow	21	6

Table 7.2: Age and experience of light infantry company commanding officers, April 1778

Regiment	Light Infantry company captain	Age	Years service
15th	James Douglas	35	18
17th	William Scott	26	9
22nd	Andrew Grant	44	16
27th	Nicholas Parker	27	14
33rd	William Dansey	33	18
35th	Archibald McAlister	36	21
37th	Edward Speke	24	15
42nd	George McKenzie	34	18
44th	George Benson	27	8
49th	Nicholas Wade	34	18
55th	Henry Downing	37	16
57th	Matthew Anketell	21	4

gained by fighting with Light Infantry but Lord knows broken Bones, and as to the honor of it if it was not for self satisfaction it is all a farce. Merit goes by Favor, and we are only tools for the favorites to work with,' wrote Captain Dansey on 20 March, 'an Officer of the Light Infantry's Character is always at Stake and if he does ever so well the merit becomes other peoples, whose Impudence or Sycophancy gains them the Ears of People in power, but I'll persevere.'[9] Lieutenant Hale expressed similar feelings three days later, lamenting the situation of 'flank companies who have all the danger and fatigues to themselves without the chance of raising by the fortune of war.'[10]

9 Historical Society of Delaware, Wilmington (HSD): William Dansey Letters: Dansey to his mother, 20 March 1778.

10 Wilkin, *Some British Soldiers*, p.241.

From January through May the light infantry covered a few foraging expeditions, but nothing of consequence occurred. 'These foraging parties are very peaceable,' wrote Lieutenant Hale, 'quite different from our Jersey executions last year, when we were generally sure of fighting twice a week.'[11] On 7 May the 2nd Battalion of Light Infantry embarked in flat boats and accompanied a fleet of armed vessels up the Delaware River to Burlington, New Jersey, where they burned two enemy frigates and a number of smaller craft undergoing maintenance; they returned on the 10th.[12] On 20 May the flank battalions led a substantial portion of the army north in an attempt to surprise an American force commanded by the Marquis de Lafayette, but failure to seize a critical ford allowed their quarry to escape. 'We marched from ten at night till eight in the morning at what is called the Grenadier step without halting ten minutes, and after a tour of 47 miles returned that night to Philadelphia,' wrote Hale; 'some men died on the road from the heat and excessive fatigue. Having no horse I walked the whole way except the last five miles, when my strength being nearly exhausted I accepted a horse.'[13]

* * *

The next campaign was not what Lieutenant Hale probably hoped for. General Howe resigned command of the British army in North America and was replaced by General Henry Clinton. Of greater importance was the entry of France into the war, vastly expanding the scope of the conflict. The loss of General Burgoyne's army had strengthened rebel resolve and diminished British military strength; with the added French threat to economically valuable British colonies in the West Indies, holding Philadelphia was no longer a priority. General Clinton immediately initiated plans to evacuate the city and take the troops back to New York. Heavy baggage would make the journey by sea, but the foot soldiers who had marched nearly 100 miles from the Elk River to reach Philadelphia in 1777 now had a similar distance to walk across New Jersey to Sandy Hook, where small craft would take them to Staten Island. Even when slowed by a substantial wagon train, the journey should take no more than two weeks.

'After procuring a Horse,' wrote Captain Dansey of his preparations to go on campaign again, 'I have been this Month past contriving what things to carry on him that will be most comfortable and convenient and not overload him.' He took a small tent of his own design, and furniture that he carefully described to relatives back home:

> First a Floor cloth, which serves as Bedstead as also to cover my Baggage when loaded. A Paillasse, weight about two pounds, to stuff either with leaves, Straw or Grass for a Bed. Two Blankets, my Portugee Cloak, my Bed Cloths. A small Portmanteau holding a change of Necessaries is my Pillow. A pair of Canteens holding my Liquor and Provisions and a small writing Trunk holding Paper and some Nick Nacks. This the whole of my Baggage that I expect to see before Christmas next

11 Wilkin, *Some British Soldiers*, pp.238–239.
12 Gruber (ed.), *Diary*, pp.179–180.
13 Wilkin, *Some British Soldiers*, p.258.

> and these are great Conveniences and Comforts compared with what I had last Campaign.[14]

The army crossed from Philadelphia into New Jersey on 16 and 17 June, and camped at Haddonfield, 'in the usual manner, viz. Wigwams,' according to John Peebles, now a captain in the 42nd Regiment.[15] They proceeded in stages of 13 or 14 miles a day for the next three days.[16]

British light infantry soldier on campaign near Philadelphia, late 1777. This detail from a cartoon published by Matthew Darley was almost certainly based on a sketch by Lieutenant Richard St George Mansergh St George of the 52nd Regiment, and shows the utilitarian adaptations often made to uniforms for this and other campaigns. (*A View in America*, Matthew Darly, 1778)

Approaching Mount Holly, New Jersey on 19 June, a party of Jägers was fired upon by enemy troops sheltered in a clump of woods. The Jägers rushed into the woods and scattered some skulking militia men, most of whom fled, but one was on the ground wounded, wearing a bayonet and cartridge box but with no musket. They brought him to the British column where he was recognized as John Fisher, a drummer from the 28th Regiment's light infantry who had deserted on 11 April 1777 when quartered in Piscataway, New Jersey. When the army stopped at Mount Holly to rest and distribute provisions, General Clinton convened a court martial to try Fisher for desertion and bearing arms with the enemy. Fisher claimed not to have deserted, 'but was cut off from his Quarters by a party which came between him and them'; after some time as a fugitive he joined the rebel army as a way of getting close to the front lines so he could rejoin the British army. But another British soldier who had been a prisoner of war and was now back in Clinton's army testified that, while a prisoner, he had met Fisher and 'heard him acknowledge that he had Deserted.' Fisher was found guilty and sentenced to death on 21 June; the next morning he was hanged from a tree by the road so that, as the army marched past, his lifeless body would deter desertion.[17]

14 Anon., 'The "Dansey" Letters', part IV, *The Iron Duke: The Regimental Magazine of the Duke of Wellington's Regiment*, no. 84 (January 1952), p.64.
15 Gruber (ed.), *Diary*, p.189.
16 Anon. (ed.), 'British Army Orders,' pp.594–596.
17 TNA: WO 71/87: trial of John Fisher, pp.202–208.

It did not.

Desertion in the 28 grenadier and 29 light infantry companies in Philadelphia was relatively infrequent. The grenadiers lost two per month from January through April, except for three in March; the light infantry, which ranged into the countryside more often, lost four in January, six in March, seven in April. In May, when they learned they would leave the city, desertion increased among the grenadiers, to 10 that month and nine more in the first three weeks of June before Fisher's execution. The light infantry lost only four in May and one in early June; perhaps those inclined to desert had already done so. Between the execution on 21 June and landing on Staten Island in the first week of July, 22 grenadiers and 11 light infantrymen absconded. The problem was not isolated to the flank battalions; British regiments in General Clinton's army lost over 130 men to desertion in June alone, and others deserted from the army's German and loyalist regiments.[18]

* * *

The next two-day halt was at Freehold. The army was about two-thirds of the way to Sandy Hook. For the last few days, enemy troops had been sighted on the flanks and rear, causing General Clinton concern about his valuable, but vulnerable, baggage train. He sent the baggage off at dawn on 28 June, covered by a division that included the 2nd Battalion of Light Infantry. The rest of the army waited until 8:00 a.m. to march, the Queen's Rangers and 1st Battalion of Light Infantry forming a rear guard, on a northeast-bound road that descended from high ground at Freehold into what Clinton called 'a plain near three miles in length, and about one mile in breadth.'[19]

As the column moved slowly northeast, the Queen's Rangers skirmished with probing enemy troops, and before long the light infantry supported them. They easily deflected these skirmishers but soon, according to General Clinton, 'several columns of the enemy appeared likewise descending into the plain.' By ten o'clock that morning the rear guard was under attack, and other forces were circling around both flanks. Clinton opted for a sudden counterattack on the enemy behind him, 'pressing it so hard, as to oblige the detachments to return from our flanks to its assistance.'[20] He led this assault with the British grenadier battalions and the Brigade of Guards who, in the words of Lieutenant Hale with the 2nd Battalion of Grenadiers, 'were ordered to the right about and march to the heights of which the Rebels were already possessed.'[21]

By now both the battle and the day were heating up. The enemy on the plain was quickly routed, but Hale wrote about the push towards Freehold:

> … such a march may I never again experience. We proceeded five miles in a road composed of nothing but sand which scorched through our shoes with intolerable heat; the sun beating on our heads with a force scarcely to be conceived in

18 TNA: WO 12: muster rolls of the various regiments.
19 John Almon (ed.), *The Remembrancer, or impartial repository of public events* (London: J. Almon, 1778), Vol.6, pp.348.
20 Almon (ed.), *The Remembrancer*, Vol.6, p.349.
21 Wilkin, *Some British Soldiers*, p.258.

> Europe, and not a drop of water to assuage our parching thirst; is it to be wondered that in these circumstances a number of the soldiers were unable to support the fatigue, and died on the spot. A Corporal of the 43rd Grenadiers, who had by some means procured water, drank to such excess as to burst and expired in the utmost torments. Two became raving mad, and the whole road, strewed with miserable wretches wishing for death, exhibited the most shocking scene I ever saw.[22]

'The heat of the weather was intense, and our men already suffered severely from fatigue,' wrote General Clinton, 'but our circumstances obliged us to make a vigorous exertion.' The 1st Battalion of Grenadiers in the centre, the 2nd Battalion on the left and the Guards on the right, 'began the attack with such spirit, that the enemy gave way immediately.'[23] That soon changed. A large enemy force poured fire from woods on the right; the Guards and the 1st Battalion's right hand grenadier companies immediately charged upon them. The remainder of the 1st Battalion and the 2nd Battalion continued forward on enemy and 'when within a short distance ... pour'd in their fire & dashing forwards drove the foe before them for some considerable time, killing many with their Bayonets.'[24] Once again the enemy was 'completely routed,' but fell back to the support of another line, this one on high ground beyond 'a marshy hollow' passable only by two small bridges.[25]

Lieutenant Hale, writing just six days after the battle, vividly described how the 2nd Battalion of Grenadiers struck at an enemy where Clinton himself later wrote 'it would have been scarcely possible to have attacked them':[26]

> We rose on a small hill commanded by that on which they were posted in excellent order notwithstanding a heavy fire of Grape, when judge of my inexpressible surprise, Gen. Clinton himself appeared at the head of our left wing accompanied by Lord Cornwallis, and crying out 'Charge, Grenadiers, never heed forming'; we rushed on amidst the heaviest fire I have yet felt. It was no longer a contest for bringing up our respective companies in the best order, but all officers as well as soldiers strove who could be foremost, to my shame I speak it. I had the fortune to find myself after crossing the swamp with three officers only, in the midst of a large body of Rebels who had been driven out of the wood by the 1st Battalion of Grenadiers, accompanied by not more than a dozen men who had been able to keep up with us; luckily the Rebels were too intent on their own safety to regard our destruction. Lt. Bunbury of the 49th killed one of them with his sword, as we all might have done, but seeing a battalion running away with their Colours, I pushed for them with the few fellows I had, but to my unutterable disappointment they out ran us in a second.[27]

22 Wilkin, *Some British Soldiers*, p.258.
23 Almon (ed.), *The Remembrancer*, Vol.6, p.349.
24 Gruber (ed.), *Diary*, p.193.
25 Almon (ed.), *The Remembrancer*, Vol.6, p.349.
26 Almon (ed.), *The Remembrancer*, Vol.6, p.349.
27 Wilkin, *Some British Soldiers*, pp.258–259.

Lieutenant Colonel Henry Monckton, the 36-year-old commander of the 2nd Battalion of Grenadiers from Lieutenant Hale's own regiment, the 45th, who had been wounded at the Battle of Brooklyn in August 1776, 'was shot through the heart at the first charge, to the unspeakable loss of the Regiment,' wrote Hale, not to mention to the grenadier battalion that he had commanded for two years. Also killed was Lieutenant Archibald Kennedy of the 44th's grenadiers, a distant relative of Hale.[28]

Other regiments came to support the grenadiers who were unable to advance further, from exhaustion as much as disarray caused by losses. As this portion of the battle became an artillery duel across the morass, 'The shattered remains of our Battalion, and part of the 1st who had joined us, being under cover of our hill suffered little,' Hale related, 'but from thirst and heat of which several died, except some who preferred the shade of some trees in the direct range of shot to the more horrid tortures of thirst.' One officer who preferred the shade, Captain John Powell of the 52nd's grenadiers, was hit by a cannon round that shattered his arm, a wound to which he succumbed within a few days. Hale remembered the day as one of 'the Rebel's cannon playing Grape and Case upon us at the distance of 40 yards and the small arms within little more than half that space; followed by a most incessant and terrible cannonade for near three hours' continuance.'[29]

The 1st Battalion of Light Infantry and the Queen's Rangers had circled to the northwest when the grenadiers' attack began, hoping to turn the enemy flank; they were thwarted by 'swamps & much impediment in the woods.'[30] Captain Dansey of the 33rd's lights wrote of 'a very narrow Escape from being taken Prisoner with my whole Company. We were obliged to run up to our middles in a Bog to get away from the Rebel Light Horse and I had only one man taken.'[31] They returned before the end of the day, exhausted from their long march, having not a single officer or soldier killed that day. The 22nd Regiment's light infantry recorded one desertion, Israel Schroder, a Dutch-born veteran of service in the Prussian army who had come into British service in 1776 and joined the light infantry just before the 1778 campaign began.[32] The 2nd Battalion of Light Infantry was not involved in the fighting. The grenadier battalions, spearheading Clinton's counterattack, had suffered much. General Clinton did not enumerate the casualties of each battalion, but did list the officers killed and wounded. In the 1st Battalion, Captain John Gore of the 5th Regiment was killed, and Captains Andrew Cathcart of the 15th, William Brereton of the 17th and Thomas Wills of the 23rd were wounded. Muster rolls show 20 private soldiers died: six in the 22nd Regiment's company, three each in the 23rd's and 37th's, two each in the 5th's, 33rd's and 40th's, and one each in the 7th's and 35th's.[33]

28 Wilkin, *Some British Soldiers*, p.259.

29 Wilkin, *Some British Soldiers*, pp.260, 262.

30 Gruber (ed.), *Diary*, p.193.

31 HSD: William Dansey Letters: Dansey to his mother, 28 July 1778.

32 TNA: WO 12: muster rolls of the various regiments; Don N. Hagist, 'Forty German Recruits: The Service of the von Scheither Recruits in the 22nd Regiment of Foot, 1776–1783,' *Journal of the Johannes Schwalm Historical Association*, Vol.6, no. 1 (1997), p.66.

33 Almon (ed.), *The Remembrancer*, Vol.6, pp.350–351; TNA: WO 12: muster rolls of the various regiments.

The 2nd Battalion of Grenadiers fared worse. Lieutenant Hale wrote that 11 officers were killed and wounded, and that 'our battalion lost 98,' without saying whether that included the officers.[34] According to General Clinton's report, Lieutenant Colonel Monckton and Lieutenant Kennedy were the only officers killed; wounded were the battalion's major, William Gardner of the 10th Regiment (the 10th's grenadier company was in the 1st Battalion); Captains Baldwin Leighton of the 46th and John Powell of the 52nd; and Lieutenants Harry Gilchrist of the 42nd (who died of wounds on 26 August), George Kelly of the 44th, Mungo Paumier of the 46th, Francis Grosse of the 52nd, and Laurence Desborough of the Marines, for a total of 10 officers in the battalion.[35] Muster rolls list 33 soldiers died: six in the 46th's grenadiers, four each in the 42nd's, 44th's, 49th's and 63rd's, three each in the 45th's, 57th's and 64th's, and one each in the 43rd's and 55th's; no rolls are available for the Marines' grenadier company.[36] Lieutenant Hale corroborated the loss of three killed in the 45th's grenadiers, and wrote that one soldier was wounded; he also mentioned 'his brother officer' having 'received a painful but not dangerous wound in the neck,' apparently referring to his fellow lieutenant James Gage who was not included in General Clinton's list of wounded officers.[37]

General Clinton reported total British casualties that included 56 soldiers killed and 45 'died with fatigue,' as well as 137 wounded.[38] Muster rolls do not give cause of death, leaving no way of knowing how many grenadiers succumbed to fatigue rather than hostile fire. Lieutenant Hale wrote of a corporal dying from drinking water too quickly, but no corporal of any grenadier company died that day; Hale may have misstated the man's rank, or the one private soldier of the 43rd's grenadiers who died may have been serving as a corporal without being indicated as such on the muster rolls.

Among the wounded grenadiers were 28-year-old Scotsman James Darran of the 7th Regiment, a native of Wick, Caithness, who joined the army in 1768 and was wounded in the right shoulder; Henry Jarvis, a blacksmith born in Crossmolina, County Mayo in 1745 who enlisted in the 22nd Regiment in 1770 and 'lost the use of his right hand in the action'; Bedfordshire wool comber Thomas Partridge, 34 years old, who joined the 63rd Regiment in 1767 and was wounded in the right side; and Morris Buddy of the same regiment, a tailor from County Donegal born in 1742 who enlisted at the age of 31 and was 'wounded in his right foot & lost two toes at Monmouth North America.'[39] William Tate of the 44th, a weaver born in County Cavan in 1748 who enlisted in 1775, received his third wound, having been 'wounded twice in the left shoulder and once in right thigh at the battles of Bedford Heights & Brandy Wine & Monmouth.'[40]

* * *

34 Wilkin, *Some British Soldiers*, p.260.
35 Almon (ed.), *The Remembrancer*, Vol.6, pp.350–351.
36 TNA: WO 12: muster rolls of the various regiments.
37 Wilkin, *Some British Soldiers*, pp.261, 263.
38 Almon (ed.), *The Remembrancer*, Vol.6, p.350.
39 TNA: WO 121/6/35, WO 119/4/257, WO 121/1/373, WO 121/2/75: discharges of James Darran, Henry Jarvis, Thomas Partridge, and Morris Buddy, respectively.
40 TNA: WO 121/8/107: discharge of William Tate.

The army continued across New Jersey without incident, to Navasink, into boats to Sandy Hook, then by larger vessels to Staten Island. On Sandy Hook on 5 July General Clinton gave orders that began, 'The march being now completed, the Commander in chief desires to return his thanks to the army for the cheerfulness with which they have supported the fatigues of the duty.' He complimented the 'the noble ardour shown by that part of the army who repulsed so superior a number of the enemy on the 28th of June.' He followed with the surprisingly terse direction that 'the flank companies of all the British regiments in this division of the army are to join their respective corps until further orders, to settle their accounts, &c.'; the remaining three companies, those of the 22nd, 43rd, and the Marines grenadiers, remained 'embodied under the eldest officer' because their parent corps were not in the New York area.[41]

This abrupt order was taken to be an unceremonious disbanding of the flank battalions, composed largely of companies and men that had served together since May 1776, men who had performed with great distinction during almost continuous campaigning. The order 'was not relish'd,' wrote Captain Peebles, and 'gave no small disgust' to officers and men alike, according to Lieutenant Hale. The next day Lieutenant Colonel Francis, Lord Rawdon, an aide-de-camp to Clinton and former grenadier officer, sent a letter to each flank company commander assuring them that 'your Battalions are by no means to be considered from the Order of yesterday as broken up, but are liable as soon as their accounts are settled, or upon the first prospect of movement, to be called together again'; the battalion staff were still intact, and it was 'merely private economy of the Army which has occasioned their being ordered to join their Regiments for a time.' Whether Clinton himself directed this letter to be sent, or Rawdon did so at his own initiative, is not clear, but the letter included assurance that 'the Commander in Chief has too just a sence of the very meritorious services of those Corps to suffer them to pass unacknowledged.' Lieutenant Hale considered this 'a decent apology for an affront that was never meant,' but others, including Lieutenant Colonels Meadows and Abercromby, took issue with the wording 'liable to be called together' as 'implying our re-embodying to be the object of our dread rather than of our most sanguine wishes.'[42]

Regardless, the respite was short. A powerful French fleet loomed off the coast, threatening to blockade New York and rendering the small garrison in Rhode Island vulnerable. Clinton quickly sent reinforcements to Rhode Island including the 38th Regiment along with their two flank companies.

The Royal Navy also needed reinforcements. Ships in New York harbour were outnumbered and outgunned by the French fleet, and were also undermanned. The Marine grenadier company, on land since 1775 with the army's grenadiers, went on the warship *Eagle*, never to return the army.[43] In addition, '300 Light Infantry and Grenadiers volunteer'd to serve as Marines on board the Fleet,' wrote Captain Dansey from on board the 50-gun ship *Experiment*. In his words, 'The Army not forgetful of the many Services it had experienced from the Fleet embraced with Ardor this Opportunity of shewing their sense of it and anzious for their Country's Honor and to share the Glory of its Defence offer'd their

41 Anon. (ed.), 'British Army Orders,' pp.602–603.
42 Gruber (ed.), *Diary*, p.196; Wilkin, *Some British Soldiers*, pp.263, 267–268.
43 Gruber (ed.), *Diary*, p.200.

Service.' Adjutant General John André recorded that eight companies were chosen by lot from the flank battalions, but rather than a totally random selection, both companies from each of four regiments were chosen – those of the 17th, 33rd, 37th and 64th Regiments. Captain Dansey was proud that his own company was among those chosen from 'the distinguished Corps of Light Infantry and Grenadiers.'[44] Muster books of *Experiment* reveal that his detachment on board was far from a full-strength company; three officers, one sergeant, two corporals and 30 private soldiers. But this was all the men he had available; the company's muster roll indicates only 35 private soldiers in the company, plus three others prisoners of war; presumably the five not on ship were indisposed for some reason. Of the company's three sergeants, one was a prisoner of war and another was 'sick'. One corporal and the company's only drummer also stayed ashore.[45]

Numbers were similar for the other companies on ships, suggesting that the eight companies chosen yielded a little less than 300 men. The 17th Regiment's grenadiers put three officers, three sergeants, three corporals, two drummers, a fifer, 35 soldiers and one volunteer on board the 50-gun *Isis*.[46] The 64th's grenadiers put two officers, a sergeant, two corporals, two drummers and 33 men on the 64-gun *Nonsuch*.[47] The 17th's light infantry put two sergeants, three corporals, one drummer and 28 men on the frigate *Venus*; the company's muster roll indicates 38 private men. Curiously, no officers are recorded in the ship's muster book. In a nuance showing that muster rolls are not always reliable indicators of a company's composition, the man listed as the 17th light company's drummer on *Venus*, Anthony Hite, appears on the muster rolls as a private soldier in a battalion company.[48]

These men from the distinguished corps stayed on board barely long enough to get their sea legs, from 14 and 15 July to the first week of August. Lord Rawdon's 7 July letter said the flank battalions were 'upon the first prospect of movement, to be called together again,' and that prospect had arrived. The French fleet turned from New York towards Rhode Island, and General Clinton ordered the battalions to encamp on Long Island in preparation for operations against whatever threat materialized. The need for Marines remained; to replace the grenadier and light infantry companies, the entire 23rd Regiment went on board warships. The 23rd's light infantry, led by Captain Lionel Smythe, was at its full strength of 56 private men; they were divided between two ships, Lieutenant John Campbell taking a sergeant and 24 men to replace Dansey's company on *Experiment*, while Captain Smythe took a lieutenant, a sergeant, two corporals and 30 to relieve the 17th's grenadiers on *Isis*.[49] The British fleet put to sea and caught up with the French off Rhode Island, but as the two fleets manoeuvred to do battle a violent storm scattered them. On 14 August, *Isis*, alone, encountered the French 74-gun *Zele*. The captain of *Isis* waited until the enemy vessel was within musket shot before delivering a broadside, and a fierce battle ensued. Thanks in part to the light infantry's skilled musketry, the French ship was bested and bore away, much

44 Willcox (ed.), *Journal*, p.82; Archives of Ontario (AO): Peter Russell Fonds, F 46: Peter Russell to his father, 26 September 1778; HSD: William Dansey Letters: Dansey to his mother, 28 July 1778.
45 TNA: ADM 36/7920: muster book, HMS *Experiment*; WO 12: muster rolls, 33rd Regiment.
46 TNA: ADM 36/7913, muster book, HMS *Isis*.
47 TNA: ADM 36/7960: muster book, HMS *Nonsuch*.
48 TNA: ADM 36/10281: muster book, HMS *Venus*; WO 12: muster rolls, 17th Regiment.
49 TNA: ADM 36/7920: Muster book, HMS *Experiment*; ADM 36/7913: muster book, HMS *Isis*.

worse for the encounter with a much smaller ship. Grenadier Lieutenant Hale wrote that the 23rd's men 'fixed their bayonets and wanted to board,' and when the French vessel broke off the engagement, they 'gave the Indian War hoop.'[50] The victory was not without loss; Corporal John Hunt, who had been in the regiment over 14 years, was killed in the action.[51]

At the end of July the flank companies that had unceremoniously rejoined their regiments on the 6th received orders to assemble as battalions, and by 2 August were together again on Long Island.[52]

* * *

The flank companies of the 54th Regiment had been in Rhode Island since the first landing there in December 1776. The garrison consisted of a British brigade of three regiments (including the 54th) and a German brigade of four regiments; from the latter, picked men were assembled into a chasseur company, effectively the same as light infantry. Throughout 1777 and the first half of 1778, the 54th's flank companies operated together as a little flank battalion, often working with the chasseurs. Several times they supported incursions on the mainland, screening and protecting troops that foraged or attacked posts. In late May 1778 they covered two expeditions, one to the towns of Bristol and Warren, the other to Fall River, each time covering key bridges and roadways while soldiers from British regiments destroyed military vessels and stores. The regiments took these expeditions in turn, but the flank companies participated in all of them.[53] Compared to the flank battalions in General Howe's army, life in Rhode Island was comfortable – tents in the summer and vacant town buildings in the winter – but the flank companies were still the most active troops in the garrison.

When the 38th Regiment arrived, their two flank companies joined those of the 54th under command of Captain Thomas Coore of the 54th's grenadiers – a flank battalion composed of two grenadier and two light infantry companies. A return dated 10 August gives the battalion's composition as two captains, eight lieutenants, 12 sergeants, 10 corporals, four drummers and 194 private soldiers.[54] The situation in Rhode Island allowed for no offensive operations – at the beginning of August the French fleet blockaded the seaward approaches, and then an American army invaded the island from the mainland, forcing the British garrison into defensive lines around the town of Newport. A three-week siege ensued, which the soldiers of the garrison spent mostly at hard labour improving defences and on tense duty awaiting an imminent attack. On 19 August Perthshire native William Musket of the 54th's light infantry, a 27-year-old who had joined the army at the age of 17 after learning the trade of shoemaking, was in his tent with his wife and children, mending shoes, when an 18-pound cannonball crashed through and took off one of his

50 Wilkin, *Some British Soldiers*, p.270.
51 TNA: WO 12: muster rolls, 23rd Regiment.
52 Gruber (ed.), *Diary*, p.205.
53 For details on operations in Rhode Island see Mackenzie, *Diary*, pp.135–437, and Christian M. McBurney, *The Rhode Island Campaign: The First French and American Operation in the Revolutionary War* (Yardley, PA: Westholme, 2011).
54 Mackenzie, *Diary*, p.346.

legs.[55] At 4:00 a.m. on 25 August an exploding 13-inch mortar shell killed James McCauley of the 38th's light infantry; a splinter 'struck him just under the eye & mortally wounded him, so that he died soon after.' McCauley had joined the light infantry in December 1775 and fought with the 1st Battalion of Light Infantry from its formation until his company was sent to Rhode Island.[56]

The opportunity to use the flank battalion to advantage came on 29 August. The French fleet had abandoned the operation after the storm previously mentioned. This and other factors led the American army to give up the siege and withdraw during the night of 28–29 August, retiring to the northern end of the island. Knowing they would be vulnerable while ferrying troops off the island, the British commander ordered a sally to disrupt their retreat. On the morning of the 29th, German troops marched up the west side of the island, a British column up the right, hoping to overtake and engage the enemy. Brigadier General Francis Smith, who led the expedition to Concord on 19 April 1775, commanded the British column consisting of the 22nd and 43rd Regiments and the flank battalion. Now, after three years of war, he unaccountably took his column up the road 'without having flanking parties out, or taking the usual precautions.' The ground sloped gently up to their left towards the centre of the island, and a parallel road ran along the highest ground, but in spite of having spent almost two years on the island and no doubt being familiar with the ground, he kept his flank battalion in the column, apparently behind the two regiments. As the column approached a crossroad, several hundred enemy troops arose from behind a stone wall and opened fire. 'The Flank Companies immediately turned out of the road and attacked the Enemy,' wrote a staff officer. The 22nd Regiment pushed on ahead rather than attempting to form a line while under fire, and the 43rd formed for battle. The rebels were driven from this position and consolidated on high ground on the north end of the island where they were too numerous and well-positioned to dislodge; by nightfall the battle degenerated into an exchange of artillery fire across low ground between the two armies.[57]

Smith's handling of his flank battalion was perhaps the worst of the entire war, and the toll was clear. In the flank battalions, a sergeant was killed, and one officer, one sergeant, one drummer and 19 soldiers wounded. The 43rd Regiment lost three killed and an officer and 14 wounded. The 22nd Regiment, at the head of the column without support of flankers or skirmishers, suffered four officers wounded (two of whom later died), 11 private soldiers killed (another died of wounds a few days later), and two sergeants and 48 soldiers wounded, a 16 percent casualty rate among the private soldiers.[58] Captain Coore prepared a detailed return of the flank battalion's losses. Lieutenant John Thomas Layard of the 54th's light

55 Anon. (ed.), 'Journal of Rev. Joshua Wingate Weeks,' *Historical Collections of the Essex Institute*, Vol. LII, No. 1 (1916), p.15; Mackenzie, *Diary*, p.361 (which incorrectly gives the regiment as the 45th); WLC: Frederick Mackenzie Papers: Box 1 Folder 8, Return of the Killed wounded and Missing of the Four Flank Companies under the Command of Captain Coore 29th August 1778; TNA: WO 116/7: Pension Admission Book, 'Examinations of Invalid Soldiers,' 21 June 1780.

56 Anon. (ed.)., 'Journal of Rev. Joshua Wingate Weeks,' p.15; Mackenzie, *Diary*, pp.371–372; TNA: WO 12, muster rolls, 38th Regiment.

57 Mackenzie, *Diary*, pp.382, 392.

58 John Almon (ed.), *The Remembrancer, or impartial repository of public events* (London: J. Almon, 1779), Vol.7, p.35; the percentage is based on 348 privates reported on 10 August; Mackenzie, *Diary*, p.346.

infantry was wounded; Lieutenant Shapland Swiney of the 38th's grenadiers was wounded, captured, and then exchanged days later. Long-serving Sergeant John Brown of the 54th's grenadiers was killed; Thomas Bower, who had arrived in America as a recruit for the 38th in the summer of 1776 and joined the light infantry only a month before the battle, died of wounds soon after. Eight soldiers in the 38th's two companies were wounded – Captain Coore did not enumerate them by company – as were a sergeant, a drummer and 10 men in the 54th, including grenadier Sergeant Samuel McCardy. Three men who were taken prisoner or got lost during the battle rejoined within the next few days.[59]

The four flank companies of the 38th and 54th Regiments remained in Rhode Island until the following summer, when they returned to New York and joined the flank battalions there. While in Rhode Island, the grenadier companies occasionally received replacement 1756 pattern muskets from the garrison's stores, which kept them armed to the standard that General Howe had set in May 1776.[60] They undertook no further offensive operations during their time in Rhode Island.

* * *

Two days after the 29 August battle, a British fleet arrived at Rhode Island with a strong relief force commanded by General Clinton, which included the 1st Battalions of Grenadiers and Light Infantry. They had embarked on the 27th and sailed with orders for the light infantry and grenadiers, with 70 rounds of ammunition per man, to land first on Rhode Island, the light infantry 'to immediately possess themselves of the Houses & Commanding Grounds on landing & there wait untill supported & ordered to advance,' and to 'join the Enemy with points of Bayonets.'[61] But their quarry had already fled.

Seeking alternative benefits for the expedition, General Clinton sent the fleet further eastward to New Bedford, Massachusetts. The two flank battalions were ferried ashore late in the afternoon of 5 September on the west side of the Acushnet River, and held the landing place while boats returned to transports for the remaining troops. They proceeded north along the river, destroying military stores and vessels in several towns, marching through the night for several miles. They crossed to the east side of the river methodically, the flank battalions taking high ground that covered a bridge, keeping the area secure while the others crossed. After a march of about 20 miles during which they 'met with only a few popping shots' from the enemy, they embarked again by noon the next day. One light infantryman was killed, two light infantrymen and one grenadier wounded, and three men of each flank battalion went missing during the march. On the 7th, Captain William Baillie of the 7th Regiment led his own and three other light infantry companies ashore to destroy a ship under construction. During the next two weeks the fleet seized sheep from the island of Martha's Vineyard,

59 WLC: Frederick Mackenzie Papers: Box 1 Folder 8, Return of the Killed wounded and Missing of the Four Flank Companies under the Command of Captain Coore 29th August 1778; TNA: WO 12: muster rolls, 38th Regiment and 54th Regiments.

60 WLC: George Wray Papers: Commissary account book.

61 AO: Peter Russell Fonds, F 46: Peter Russell to his father, 26 September 1778; Gruber (ed.), *Diary*, p.211.

but the flank battalions stayed on board ship during this operation. They sailed back to New York and disembarked on Long Island on 19 September, encamping once again.[62]

Three days later they were on the move, leaving encampments and crossing to Staten Island, then to Paulus Hook in New Jersey. They pushed north into Bergen County, along with the Brigade of Guards, troops of dragoons and several British regiments, part of a series of operations throughout the region to gather forage to last the garrison through the winter. For the flank battalions, the time was spent mostly covering foraging parties and sharing the labour of building two redoubts near New Bridge.[63] The exception came a week into the operation when Major General Charles Grey took one of three columns into the night on 27 September, hoping to capture American troops that were themselves looking for opportunities to disrupt the foragers. Grey's column, headed by the 2nd Battalion of Light Infantry and including the 2nd Battalion of Grenadiers, two British regiments, and about 100 cavalry, headed towards a group of houses and barns along the west side of a northbound road near Tappan. They were guided by local citizens who knew that six troops of American dragoons were quartered there, the officers in a house and the troopers in three barns.

The composition of the 2nd Battalion of Light Infantry on this expedition is not clear. Captain Peter Russell, with the 64th Regiment that was part of the column, wrote that four light infantry companies were not on the expedition but did not specify which ones.[64] Other accounts suggest a total of 12 light companies, too many for four to have been left behind.[65] Lieutenant Hunter recalled years later, 'The greatest part of the Light Infantry were mounted behind Dragoons, and marched after it was dark, but the Light Infantry soon tired of riding' and continued on foot since they 'preferred marching,' a detail not corroborated by any other account; with only 50 to 100 dragoons in the column, only a small portion of the light infantry could have ridden in this way.[66] Regardless, they approached the enemy quarters at about 3:00 a.m. with perfect secrecy and detailed intelligence. Major Turner Straubenzee led six companies into the fields to the west of the road, where they deployed to advance on the barns in unison. The remaining light infantry companies under Lieutenant Colonel John Maitland, still commanding the battalion after his promotion from the Marines into the 71st Regiment, continued north on the road, sealing off any escape from the barns.

With the barns surrounded, the light infantry descended upon the unsuspecting enemy in the predawn darkness. An American officer later wrote that the light infantry's 'charges were drawn from their firelocks & the flints taken out that the men might be constrained to use their bayonets only: This has occasioned the general to be nicknamed … the no flint general.'[67] They used bayonets, and musket butts too, 'beating even those they thought were mortally wounded, not excepting any of the officers, and stripping every man, in a very cold night, of almost all their cloaths,' wrote an American general. Several American dragoons

62 Gruber (ed.), *Diary*, pp.215–220; Willcox (ed.), *Journal*, pp.87–96.

63 Gruber (ed.), *Diary*, pp.221–222. For a full discussion of these operations, see Todd W. Braisted, *Grand Forage 1778: The Battleground around New York City* (Yardley, PA: Westholme, 2016).

64 AO: Peter Russell Fonds, F 46: Peter Russell to his father, 26 September 1778.

65 MacNiven, *British Light Infantry in the American Revolution*, p.54.

66 Hunter, *Journal*, p.43.

67 Braisted, *Grand Forage 1778*, p.103.

interviewed after the action gave similar accounts. Many received over a dozen bayonet wounds in their breasts, midriffs and arms. Some had fractured skulls from musket butts. They talked of surrendering, but of an officer – Captain Bent Ball of the 63rd was identified by name – ordered prisoners and wounded men to be killed. They heard light infantry soldiers saying phrases like 'skiver them, and give no quarters,' 'There is no quarter for you,' 'run him through,' 'kill them! kill them!' A few heard their assailants saying they could give no quarter as it was against their orders, one even saying that British soldiers 'muttered about it' when ordered to club wounded men. In spite of the viciousness of the attack, only one or two dozen dragoons were killed (accounts vary from 14 to 22), anywhere from 13 to 33 wounded, and 33 taken prisoner.[68]

After 'laying on their arms till break of day,' the column moved on, taking the horses of the hapless dragoons they had slaughtered. 'In a very thick wood and swamp' the light infantry, still at the head of the column, was fired on by a company of militia. Captain William Montgomery's light infantry of the 40th Regiment returned fire, killing some and driving the rest off. Some fleeing militia came in the way of a grenadier company that killed three. 'The light infantry,' according to a newspaper account by an anonymous light infantry officer, 'in pursing them ... they were intirely dispersed, took five prisoners, all of them wounded.'[69] They then linked up with the other British columns operating that night, which included the other grenadier and light infantry battalions; those columns did not succeed in their planned attacks because their opponents were warned and fled. The British columns returned to their camps, arriving at nightfall 'pretty much fatigued, marching & halting far above 20 hours & little to eat or drink.'[70] Lieutenant Hunter recalled that the light infantry 'all returned to our camp on horseback, mounted on the horses that had been taken, and some most laughable figures these were.'[71]

The flank battalions continued to operate with the army in New Jersey until the middle of October. No other significant clashes occurred. On 29 September a few hundred enemy troops fired from a distance on British works at New Bridge 'for above an hour when a party of Light Infantry dash'd out after them & drove them off,' but nothing else came of it. The foraging expedition wound down as collected crops and stores were sent into the New York garrison, and finally the troops followed unmolested. The closing weeks of October saw the flank companies once again joining their regiments, but this time big changes were afoot.[72]

68 Almon (ed.), *The Remembrancer*, Vol.7, pp.292–299; Braisted, *Grand Forage 1778*, p.109.
69 *New York Gazette and Weekly Mercury*, 5 October 1778.
70 Gruber (ed.), *Diary*, pp.222–223.
71 Hunter, *Journal*, p.43.
72 Gruber (ed.), *Diary*, p.223.

8

Green and White Feathers: New York, 1778–1779

In July 1777, after the rigorous winter and spring in New Jersey, light infantry Captain William Dansey sent a song to his mother in Great Britain which he said 'will flatter you that your Son and his Company are very well known in the Corps of Light Infantry.' It was, he said, written by 'a Highlander' who he did not know. The song has not been found, but in December 1778 a series of other songs about the British light infantry appeared in New York newspapers. All of them consisted of lyrics set to popular tunes, a popular way to relate current events.

The first one was written by 'a Soldier' who, according to his introduction, thought the light infantry deserved their own song to complement the navy's *Hearts of Oak* and the army's *British Grenadiers*. His song, fittingly set to the tune 'Hark! hark! the joy-inspiring Horn,' mentioned 'the bugle's lofty sound,' 'nodding plumes,' 'feather'd caps and wings,' and the dramatic night-time actions at Paoli in 1777 and Tappan in 1778.[1] A week later appeared a song submitted by 'Loyal American Refugee' that he assured was 'frequently sung and re-echoed in loyal companies for many months past in this city.' To the tune 'Black Sloven,' it took the light infantry 'Cross the deep gull'd vale, up the mountains steep side, Through the rough foaming rivers impetuous tide,' and called them 'As fierce as the tyger, as swift as the roe.'[2] A final exhaustive musical tribute appeared in early January, 'A Medley for the Light Infantry' consisting of verses set to five different tunes, submitted by 'A Soldier.' Capturing the spirit of American campaigns with passages like 'amid the rattling rain, Some of Britain's light-arm'd troops Sit around their fires in groupes; Some, in wigwams seeking rest,' it had 'the light bobs spring to arms' upon hearing 'the bugle's warlike voice.'[3]

These spirited songs did not foretell the idle winter that approached, the first the flank battalions would spend in the New York garrison. Immediately after foraging operations in the fall of 1778 concluded, major changes began in the organization of the army and the flank battalions. Ten regiments – the 4th, 5th, 15th, 27th, 28th, 35th, 40th, 46th, 49th and 55th – embarked for an expedition to the West Indies led by Major General James Grant. Their flank companies left the grenadier and light infantry battalions and joined their regiments. With them went Lieutenant Colonel William Meadows, turning command of the

1 *Royal Gazette* (New York), 23 December 1778.
2 *Royal Gazette* (New York), 30 December 1778.
3 *Royal Gazette* (New York), 23 January 1779.

1st Battalion of Grenadiers over to Lieutenant Colonel John Yorke of the 22nd Regiment.[4] The 10th, 45th and 52nd Regiments prepared to return to Great Britain – the 10th and 52nd had been in North American since 1767. This meant the loss of three light infantry and three grenadier companies. Their able-bodied men were drafted – transferred – into regiments headed for the West Indies; for the most part, drafted grenadiers went into grenadier companies, and lights into light companies.

With 13 fewer regiments in New York, on 3 November General Clinton reformed the flank companies into one grenadier battalion commanded by Lieutenant Colonel Henry Hope of the 44th Regiment, and one light infantry battalion under Lieutenant Colonel Robert Abercromby of the 37th. Lieutenant Colonel Yorke 'took his leave,' according to Captain Peebles, 'in a verbal message by the Adjutant wishing us much happiness & Glory.' The next morning the companies of the 1st Battalion of Grenadiers struck their tents and loaded them onto wagons, and at 9:00 a.m. 'got under arms & drew up on the right of the parade,' wrote Peebles. When the companies of the 2nd Battalion came from their encampment, marching by half-companies, the 1st Battalion 'presented arms & beat a march.' The 2nd Battalion formed on the left of the 1st, and 'returned the compliment.' Lieutenant Colonel Hope rode onto the parade, took command, and formed them all into one battalion in the typical order, the most senior company on the right, the next on the left, and so forth. The light infantry presumably went through a similar ritual. Both battalions established new encampments at the town of Jamaica on Long Island.[5]

The arrangement of the two battalions was now:

Grenadiers
Right Wing
7th 22nd 26th 37th 43rd 57th 64th
Left Wing
71st 71st 63rd 44th 42nd 33rd 23rd 17th[6]

Light Infantry
Right Wing
7th 22nd 26th 37th 43rd 57th 64th
Left Wing
63rd 44th 42nd 33rd 23rd 17th

Soon after, Lieutenant Colonel Hope opted to return to England for the winter, and Lieutenant Colonel Yorke took over the Grenadier Battalion 'until further orders.' William Dansey, recently promoted to major of the 33rd Regiment, remained assigned to the Light Infantry Battalion as second in command. A pair of field cannons remained attached to each battalion. A Royal Artillery officer, 2nd Lieutenant Francis Laye, 'applied to be attached to'

4 Gruber (ed.), *Diary*, p.226.
5 WLC: Henry Clinton Papers: Vol. 226, general orders, 3 November 1778; Gruber (ed.), *Diary*, pp.229–230.
6 Gruber (ed.), *Diary*, p.230. Peebles described the arrangement of the grenadier battalion; the light infantry is assumed to have been the same.

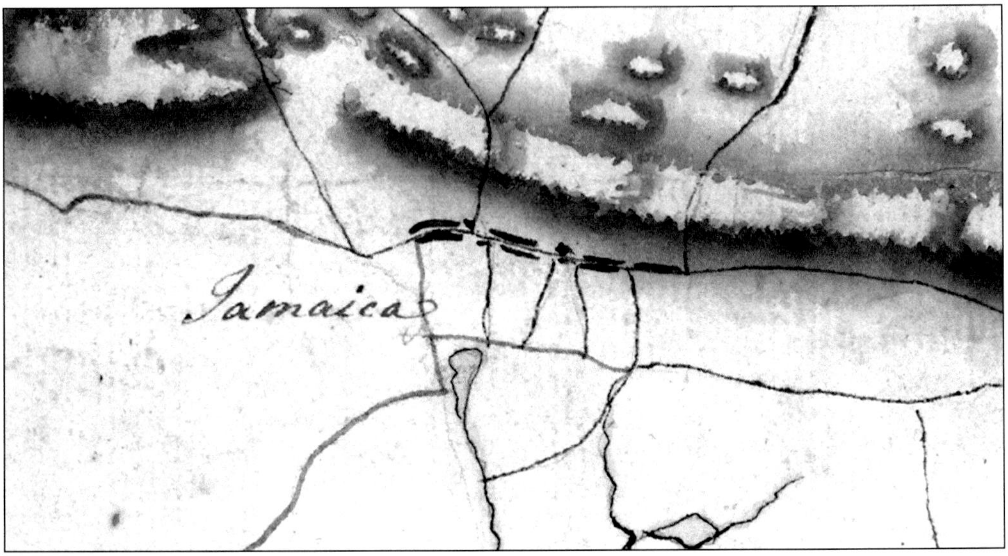

Grenadier battalions' hut camp at Jamaica, Long Island. Detail from 'Plan of New York and Staten Islands with part of Long Island, survey'd in the years 1781, & 82.' (Library of Congress)

the flank battalions because they were 'always the fashion in action,' he wrote in December. The companies, having previously been in separate battalions, had by this time standardized one detail of their dress; Laye wrote that 'The Light Infantry wear a green feather in their Caps & we the Grenadiers a White one in our Hatts.' Captain Eyre Coote, who recently took command of the 37th's light infantry, paid two shillings four pence each for 50 green feathers for his company's caps. Apparently, he had new caps made over the winter of 1778–1779, for he purchased 'moulds for the caps,' 'hair for ditto,' and 'yellow binding.' He paid Robert Watson, a soldier in his company, 'for working the hair for the caps,' and an unnamed hatter 'for dyeing the hair,' but left no details on the design of his company's caps.[7]

In February 1779, the flank companies of the 38th and 54th Regiments left Rhode Island and joined the flank battalions in New York. In March, the flank companies of the 70th and 74th Regiments arrived from Halifax, joining the flank battalions in early May. Those of the 82nd had sailed with them, but their transport ran aground and broke up off the New Jersey coast. 'The people on board were obliged to take to the tops and shrouds,' according to a newspaper account, 'where, for 35 hours, those who were saved bore the severest cold, snow, &c. and while they had light, the survivors were almost every minute shocked with the falling of some of their unhappy ship-mates, who died with the cold, from the tops and other parts of the rigging, where they had endeavoured to secure themselves from the sea, which continually rolled over the ships deck.' Eventually a passing American boat rescued the survivors, 'many of which are much frost bitten in their feet,' and brought them into

7 WLC: Henry Clinton Papers: Vol. 266, general orders, 26 November 1778; NAM: 6807-154: Francis Laye letters; WLC: 6912/14-40: Eyre Coote Orderly Book.

Philadelphia as prisoners of war. Five officers and 30 men were saved, but Lieutenant John Snodgrass and 71 grenadiers, and 41 light infantrymen, died in the disaster.[8]

The Light Infantry Battalion formed a troop of horse soldiers, mounted light infantry. The date of the troop's creation is not known; the first record of its existence is a 5 November 1778 order that 'men of the different Companies who were former mounted are immediately to join the troop,' implying that the mounted troop was already in existence at this time, but this may have been the order to create the troop. The 16th Light Dragoons had just been ordered to return to Great Britain and transferred most of its able-bodied men into the 17th Light Dragoons or into loyalist cavalry regiments, but Sergeant Richard Sperry was appointed quartermaster to the Light Infantry Battalion, and 10 troopers became privates in the 17th Regiment's light infantry company. The 5 November order suggests that all 10 should have joined the mounted troop, but an April 1779 return of the battalion indicates two men from each of the most of the battalion's 15 companies, 35 privates altogether, plus two corporals, two drummers, and 35 privates 'in the Troop.'[9]

The winter of 1778–1779 was the first one that the flank battalions, with the exception of a few companies, spent in the New York garrison, the British army's biggest holding in the colonies. During November they built huts into hillsides in the town of Jamaica, 'each hutt 24 feet by 12 to contain 12 men the wall partly dug in the face of the hill, & the rest made up of sod, the roof to be covered with cedar branches & straw or thin sod,' wrote Captain Peebles. Most of the flank companies still had only 40 to 45 private men, with a few at about 50, plus three sergeants and three corporals; some had the established two drummers, while others had only one, and often the grenadier company's two fifers were 'on duty' with their parent regiments. At these strengths, four huts were sufficient for most companies. Archaeological investigations of hut sites on Manhattan show that huts were arranged in a south-facing row, taking best advantage of the sun, with additional huts, probably for officers and non-commissioned officers, higher up the slope. Similar to encampments, this arrangement allowed battalions to quickly assemble a line in front of the huts. The ranks of British regiments were filled with former tradesmen, many with skills appropriate for building huts – sawyers, carpenters, masons, glaziers, nailers, thatchers, and plenty of laborers. Work proceeded slowly and steadily; the men were out of tents and into huts by early December.[10]

On 3 December the flank battalions were 'roused early,' formed and marched to Brooklyn, then across Manhattan to the Hudson River where they boarded transports. They sailed a few miles upriver, anchored for the night, then proceeded the next day as far as Tarrytown. Other troops were on the move on shore. On the 5th they moved as far north as Verplanck,

8 Gruber (ed.), *Diary*, pp.247, 254, 260; *Edinburgh Advertiser*, 18 June 1779; TNA: CO 5/97: 'Return of the Officers Non Commissioned Officers & Soldiers of the Flank Company's of the 82nd Regt. Lost on Flat Beach 21st March 1779,' p.609.

9 TNA: WO 12: muster rolls, 16th Light Dragoons and 17th Regiment; battalion orders, WLC: 6912/14-40: Eyre Coote Orderly Book, 5 November 1778; LOC: George Washington Papers: ser. 4. F, Present State of the 15 Companys of Light Infantry Commanded by Lieut Colonel Robert Abercromby, 25 April 1779, Southampton, New York.

10 Gruber (ed.), *Diary*, pp.230–234, 237; Reginald Pelham Bolton, 'The Military Hut-Camp of the War of the Revolution on the Dyckman Farm,' *The New-York Historical Society Quarterly Bulletin*, Vol.2, No. 3 (October, 1918), pp.95–97.

the flank battalions staying on board watching some distant gunfire and smoke, but nothing came of it; the next day they headed back down the river, and by 8 December were in their huts again. The little expedition was an attempt to intercept captured soldiers of Burgoyne's army crossing the Hudson; they were being moved from New England to Virginia, and the river crossing was seen as an opportunity to free them, but the relief expedition arrived after the last prisoners crossed.[11]

* * *

On 21 December the Light Infantry Battalion left their huts and endured 'a disagreeable cold march, and a good many men frost bit,' taking up 'plentiful quarters' in Southampton on the east end of Long Island. For both flank battalions, it should have been a comfortable, quiet winter compared the previous three, but the officers faced a new problem. Their active, spirited soldiers were accustomed to foraging and could not be prevented from continuing their exploits even though it was no longer sanctioned or necessary. Already on 24 November a garrison court martial tried three grenadiers from the 71st Regiment for 'marauding and being about two miles from camp without leave,' sentencing each to 300 lashes; the same court tried four men of the 57th's light infantry for 'marauding' but acquitted two 'for want of sufficient proof' and two because no evidence was presented against them. The Light Infantry Battalion held a court martial the same day and another two days later, but no record of the crimes or sentences has been found.[12] On 29 November officers read these orders to their men:

> Lieutenant Colonel Abercromby most Solemnly Declares to the Light Infantry that he is Determined to prosecute with the utmost Rigor at a General Court martial any Solder who Shall be Found Stealing cattle Sheep Hogs &c the property of the Inhabitants. He Expects from the Captains every Exertion Detecting the perpetrators of Such Infamous Crimes. The Different Guards are ordered to make frequent patrols in the Night in order to prevent Irregularities.[13]

No records are known to survive of battalion-level trials during the next several months, making it difficult to gauge the extent these 'infamous crimes.' Several general courts martial, higher-level courts that could sentence capital as well as corporal punishment, tried cases indicative of types of crimes and their severity. One involved a drummer of the 57th's light infantry, John Brayson, and the trial proceedings make it clear that in late March he had been tried and sentenced to lashes for another crime. During his punishment, bearing the pain of the lash, Brayson had a few things to say about his commanding officer, Captain James Graham. He called out, asking for 'Captain Graham, that rascal & Gentleman, that very honorable Gentleman.' He cried, 'Damn you, I know you. I know what you are!' To the soldiers and officers witnessing the punishment, Brayson bellowed, 'his honor is like mine

11 Gruber (ed.), *Diary*, pp.237–239.
12 WLC: 6912/14-40: Eyre Coote Orderly Book, battalion orders, 23 and 26 November 1778.
13 WLC: 6912/14-40: Eyre Coote Orderly Book, battalion orders, 29 November 1778

– damn his honor!' 'He has no more honor than a pig in a potato garden!' 'He is a damn'd Lousey Scoundrel!' 'He is like a pig in a Potato Garden!'[14]

These epithets were repeated throughout the lashing. They brought repercussions. The battalion commander brought Brayson before a general court martial just 11 days after his punishment, this time for mutiny because of the disrespect he voiced towards his company commander. There was no question of what had happened; several witnesses testified of the various expressions Brayson used, over and over again. One indicated that Brayson appeared to have been 'in liquor.' Brayson's only defence was 'that the extreme pain of punishment might have extorted expressions from him which he don't recollect, and denies his having any intention of mutiny.' He called on two officers as witnesses, who both said that 'during a Campaign he served with them, he was remarkable for being a well behaved lad;' Brayson had been in the regiment since before the war. In spite of the amusing nature of his outburst, the court did not deem it benign. They could not allow such behaviour to go unpunished, for it would encourage soldiers to use abusive language towards their officers and perhaps incite other types of insubordination. Brayson was found guilty and sentenced to receive 1,000 lashes, but no record survives to indicate whether the punishment was administered.[15]

Most general courts heard cases that were much more sinister. In early March four light infantrymen of the 43rd were tried for 'being concerned in killing an Ox the property of an Inhabitant,' and a grenadier of the 37th for 'Killing and secreting a Cow.'[16] The same court heard a case where the accused were interested in much more than supplementing their rations. In mid-February 1779, a corporal and five privates of the 71st's grenadiers left their quarters at night, blackened their faces, went to an area home, and asked for water at around midnight. The homeowners directed them to the well, but they forced their way in, the corporal dutifully staying outside to keep watch while the others beat the man of the house and stole an assortment of clothing, bedding, sides of leather, and a gun. They returned to quarters and divvied up their spoils. One later agreed to testify against the others, and an early March general court martial found the perpetrators guilty of absence from quarters and robbery. Allan Boyd, the private soldier who broke down the door, was sentenced to death, the others to 1,500 lashes and to 'make reparation as far as their Abilities will admit.'[17]

While that court was in session in Southampton, another court in Jamaica tried six grenadiers of the 26th and 37th for 'an attempt to maraud the Property of Phillip Platt in the night of 4th instant, and also beating the said Platt in a most inhuman manner.'[18] On 27 February Captain Peebles mentioned 'a long string of punishments & half the prisoners forgiven – a number of the 43rd sold their blankets,' referring to the 43rd Regiment's grenadier company but giving no other details. On 4 April grenadiers from the 7th, 38th and 57th were apprehended and punished for being 'out in the Country with arms no doubt for the purpose of

14 TNA: WO 71/88: trial of John Brayson, pp.428–430. The trial proceedings do not name the crime for which Brayson had been tried by a regimental court.

15 TNA: WO 71/88: trial of John Brayson, pp.428–430.

16 TNA: WO 71/88: trial of Thomas Reedman, pp.324–330; WO 71/88: trial of William Steedman, Donald Monroe and Thomas Martin, pp.330–334; WO 71/88: trial of Michael Farrell, pp.336–338.

17 TNA: WO 71/88: trial of Alexander Cumming, Hugh Mulloy, Allan Boyd, Archibald Campbell, Donald McDonald, and Simon Frazer, pp.346–350.

18 TNA: WO 71/88: trial of Patrick Welsh, Thomas Adams, George Boyce, Walter George, Charles Toyee and Henry Rigby, pp.362–372.

mauroding'; Peebles thought 'some of the rascals deserve to be shot.' Soldiers from other corps were tried for similar crimes on Long Island in the first half of 1779, but the men of the flank battalions were as bad as, if not worse than, any other corps.[19]

In May the Light Infantry Battalion returned from Southampton to join the grenadiers in Jamaica. The disciplinary problems that had plagued the flank battalions came to the attention of the commander in chief, who took the extraordinary measure of singling out one company, the 57th's light infantry, and gave this extraordinary order on 15 May:

> The noncommissioned officers and men of the 57th light company having behaved in a manner which renders them unworthy of the distinction of serving in a flank corps, the Commander in Chief orders them immediately to be sent to their Regiment. His Excellency hopes the Regiment will not be hurt at being directed to receive men stigmatized with much disgrace, it is done with the hope that the character and good behaviour of the battalion may bring back those men to that sense of honour which they now appear to have totally discarded. Should these expectations fail, the Commander in Chief will with signal severity weed out from the Regiment any of those perverse members who might entail disgrace upon it.[20]

The specific behaviour was not described; Captain Peebles called it 'ill behavior & obstinate perseverance in it,' but gave no further details.[21]

The 57th Regiment responded in an extraordinary way. Rather than deprive the Light Infantry Battalion of a company, and rather than retain the light company's elite status within the regiment, the company's three sergeants, two of the corporals, both drummers, and 36 private men were transferred to other companies, and traded for 36 replacements. Only Captain James Graham, Lieutenant James Drury, one corporal who was promoted to sergeant, and 16 private soldiers remained who had been with the company in Southampton (the other lieutenancy was vacant). One transferred sergeant was also reduced to private; he had been tried and acquitted in November, but apparently had further transgressions since. At no other time during the war was there such a drastic turnover of men from a flank company for disciplinary reasons. None of these men were tried by general courts, but they may have been disciplined by the regiment. Drummer Brayson remained in prison due to his sentence for mutiny until 7 September when he was discharged from the army.[22]

* * *

Disciplinary issues did not prevent the flank battalions from preparing for a new campaign. The Light Infantry Battalion, now close to the city, proceeded 'to equip themselves for the

---

19 Gruber (ed.), p.255. For other corps, see, for example, TNA: WO 71/88: trial of Thomas Connoly, British Legion, for highway robbery, pp.324–330, and the trial of John Harris, James Carey and John Williams, Queen's Rangers, for robbery, pp.393–398.

20 WLC: Henry Clinton Papers: Vol. 266, general orders, 15 May 1779.

21 Gruber (ed.), *Diary*, p.260.

22 TNA: WO 12: muster rolls, 57th Regiment.

campaign.'[23] The Grenadier Battalion 'took a walk' for exercise on 11 February and practiced manoeuvres on five other days in February, March and April, including 10 rounds per man of 'firing at marks' – target practice – on 10 April. Captain Peebles penned several diary entries about clothing and equipping his grenadier company – procuring 'stuff' for summer trousers and Russia sheeting (a type of hempen fabric) for summer waistcoats, and setting his company's tailors to work making these garments; obtaining painted knapsacks and tin cartridge boxes; learning that the company's grenadier caps were 'almost all spoiled by putting salt on them' when put into storage in Philadelphia the previous year; taking delivery of the annual issue of regimental clothing, received by the regiment late the previous year but passed on to the grenadier company at the beginning of April, and putting the tailors to work fitting the coats. All of this was effected in March, April and May.[24]

In the closing weeks of May the flank battalions moved out of huts and, with a substantial portion of the army, marched north along the Hudson River in Westchester County, New York. They occupied Stony Point on the west bank and Verplanck Point on the east, fortifying both locations and preparing for further offensive operations. Showing the continued evolution of the army by increasing the numbers of light troops, General Clinton ordered on 5 June that 'The 33d Regiment, having solicited to be employed as a Light Corps, the Commander in Chief grants this request,' and attached a company of German chasseurs to the regiment. The 33rd's grenadier and light infantry companies remained in the flank battalions. At the end of June the bulk of the army moved south again, this time landing just northeast of Manhattan near the town of Eastchester in Westchester County, leaving the 17th Regiment and the 71st's two grenadier companies at Stony Point and the 33rd at Verplanck Point.[25]

The campaign, such as it was, proved inconsequential. On the night of 15–16 July an American surprise attack captured Stony Point and its garrison, taking the 71st's grenadier companies out of the war for the time being. The attackers abandoned the post just days later and it was re-occupied by three British regiments. The army in Westchester County foraged, manoeuvred, probed, patrolled, but no significant fighting occurred during the summer. Rather than ending the disciplinary issues that plagued the battalions during winter, campaigning in the countryside added another dimension to the problem. Desertion was infrequent on Long Island, perhaps because soldiers could not go far undetected. Now soldiers who ventured beyond their own lines, whether to plunder or abscond, could be in the midst of their opponents either by design or by accident. Desertion became the new plague infecting the grenadiers and light infantry.

More than 14 grenadiers and 17 lights deserted in June and July.[26] Among them were William Hudson and William Rowland of the 17th's light infantry, both of whom had joined from the 16th Light Dragoons the previous November and were now in the light infantry's mounted troop. The pair absconded from a foraging party on 16 July and were last seen

23 WLC: Henry Clinton Papers: Vol. 57:26, Archibald Erskine to Clinton, Southampton, 6 May 1779.

24 Gruber (ed.), *Diary*, pp.248 249, 252 256.

25 WLC: Henry Clinton Papers: Vol. 266, general orders, 5 June 1779; Gruber (ed.), *Diary*, pp.272–273.

26 TNA: WO 12: muster rolls of the various regiments. No rolls are available for the 64th and 74th Regiments during this period. Desertions are sometimes not recorded if the men returned within a few days or weeks.

'riding very fast, and enquiring the Road to Horse Neck.'[27] During June, July and August general courts martial sentenced grenadier Benjamin Reynard of the 37th to 1,000 lashes for being 'two miles from camp without leave, and plundering in the country,' and Daniel Davidson of the 54th's light infantry to 1,000 lashes for deserting his sentry post.[28] Henry Smith, James Watson and drummer Robert Mason of the 23rd's light infantry were caught attempting to desert. Smith was killed trying to escape; Watson, who had 'always been a good attentive Soldier,' and 17-year-old Mason, who had 'lately been rather inattentive, owing to an attachment to two Women of the Regiment,' were sentenced to be 'hanged by the Neck, until they are Dead.' Both continued to serve in the regiment, apparently reprieved; perhaps Smith's death was considered enough of a loss.[29] Ralph Brunker of the 33rd's light infantry was caught out of camp and confined; fearing the punishment that he knew was coming, he 'cut his throat & dyed,' recalled Captain Peebles, who wrote that in the typical manner for suicides, he 'was buried in the highway with a stake thro' his body.'[30] Grenadiers George Watkins and Richard Sharp of the 38th were sentenced to death for desertion. On 17 July the army formed to witness the execution and learned that one was to be pardoned by drawing lots. Peebles wrote that Sharp, 'who drew the fatal billet was executed in sight of the Army at Noon,' after which the troops received 'orders not to stir out of Camp.'[31]

The purpose of an execution was to provide a grim example to other soldiers of the fate that might await deserters. Muster rolls of the companies in the flank battalions record only one desertion after 16 July through the end of the month, a grenadier from the 57th who absconded on 22 July, compared to 30 before that date. Some men, like the three light infantrymen from the 23rd and Brunker from the 38th, deserted after Sharp was executed but were captured again. Sharp's execution may have served its purpose in limiting desertion from the flank battalions, but for the rest of the army desertion remained a problem throughout the summer campaign.[32]

* * *

On the last day of July, the flank battalions left Westchester County and encamped on Manhattan several miles north of the city of New York. Some organizational changes took place during this time. A regiment raised in America early in the war, the Royal Highland Emigrants, had been recently redesignated the 84th Regiment. Now part of the regular army, their light infantry company joined the Light Infantry Battalion in the second half of July. At the end of August, the 26th Regiment prepared to return to Great Britain, transferring able-bodied soldiers to other regiments; 11 of their grenadiers joined the grenadiers of

27 TNA: WO 71/94: trial of William Hudson, pp.310–312.
28 TNA: WO 71/88: trial of Benjamin Reynard, pp.524–528; WO 71/90: trial of Daniel Davidson, pp.6–8.
29 TNA: WO 71/90: trial of James Watson and Robert Mason, pp.129–131; WO 12: muster rolls, 23rd Regiment.
30 Gruber (ed.), *Diary*, p.283; TNA: WO 12: muster rolls, 33rd Regiment.
31 TNA: WO 71/88: trial of George Watkins and Richard Sharpe, pp.528–532; Gruber (ed.), *Diary*, p.277; WO 12: muster rolls, 38th Regiment.
32 See, for example, Edward Mathews to Clinton, 29 July 1779, who wrote, 'We continue to have too much Desertion; last Night, three from Light Infantry of 23d, two from 7th Regt, one of whom is brought in by the Legion; & one from Prince Charles.' WLC: Henry Clinton Papers: Vol. 64:29.

the 44th and another five went to the 23rd's grenadiers, while 14 light infantrymen joined the 44th's light infantry. The 44th's flank companies returned to their regiment, which was sent to Canada. On 23 September General Clinton ordered each regiment to bring their flank companies up to the full strength of 56 private soldiers, 'transferring to the Battalion Companies their prisoners of War, & Such men as are unfit for actual Service.'[33] On 11 September the grenadier battalion was divided so that there were once again two battalions of grenadiers. Captain Peebles recorded the arrangement of the two battalions:

1st Battalion of Grenadiers: Lieutenant Colonel Henry Hope, 44th
7th 17th 23rd 33rd 37th 38th 42nd 43rd

2nd Battalion of Grenadiers: Lieutenant Colonel John Yorke, 22nd
22nd 54th 57th 63rd 64th 70th 74th

The companies were assigned numerically, except for the 22nd's which was in the battalion commanded by their regiment's lieutenant colonel.[34]

The summer's active campaigning was over, but a new hardship befell the flank battalions and many other troops in the New York garrison. A fever outbreak in late August caused the Light Infantry Battalion to move to Long Island from 'wet swampy ground' on Manhattan, and grenadiers were 'growing very sickly within these few days, a general complaint over the whole army, they are mostly taken with headache & universal pain a chill & feverishness.'[35] By 6 September some 200 grenadiers, about a quarter of the battalions' total strength, were hospitalised. It wasn't until mid-November that fevers began to abate, and by mid-December most men had recovered. A few of the army's regiments were ravaged, losing some 15 percent of their men to death caused by illness, but the flank battalions fared well. Captain Peebles' grenadier company suffered only three deaths during the time of fever, the same as the companies from the 37th, 54th and 70th; other companies had fewer, and numbers in the light infantry were similar.[36]

At the beginning of November, during the epidemic, the flank battalions moved back into their old huts in Jamaica on Long Island. They, like the rest of the army, received winter clothing and other goods sent from England – mittens, cloth for woollen leggings, linen for shirts, Russia drill for breeches, yarn hose, shoes, extra soles, blankets – to make their stay more comfortable. More companies joined the battalions, from the newly-raised 76th and 80th Regiments that had arrived from Great Britain in August. On 15 December the Light Infantry Battalion was divided into two in an arrangement quite different from the grenadier battalions:[37]

33 WLC: Henry Clinton Papers: Vol. 64:29, general orders, 17 July, 30 August, 8 and 23 September; TNA: WO 12: muster rolls, 23rd and 44th Regiments.
34 Gruber (ed.), *Diary*, p.292.
35 Gruber (ed.), *Diary*, pp.288–289.
36 For more detail on the outbreak, see Hagist, *Noble Volunteers*, pp.141–143.
37 WLC: Henry Clinton Papers: Vol. 266, general orders, 25 October, 2 November, 15 December 1779; Gruber (ed.), *Diary*, p.314.

1st Battalion of Light Infantry: Lieutenant Colonel Robert Abercromby, 37th
7th 22nd 33rd 37th 42nd 54th 63rd 70th 74th

2nd Battalion of Light Infantry: Lieutenant Colonel Thomas Dundas, 80th
17th 23rd 38th 43rd 57th 64th 76th 80th 84th

It looked like it would be another long winter in huts, but that soon changed. Another expedition was in the offing.

9

Acts of Gallantry and Determined Bravery: West Indies, 1778

Lieutenant Colonel William Meadows relinquished his command of the 2nd Battalion of Grenadiers on 17 October 1778.[1] He joined Major General James Grant's expedition to the West Indies, leaving New York on 3 November, sailing first to Barbados, then into Grand Cul de Sac Bay on the west side of St Lucia. In the evening on 13 December Meadows, now a brigadier general, landed with an advanced corps consisting of the army's grenadiers, light infantry and the 5th Regiment of Foot. Meadows had led a grenadier battalion since 1776 and fully understood the employment of flank battalions. His subordinates were equally experienced: Major George Harris, wounded at Bunker Hill leading 5th Regiment's grenadier company but recovered in time for the 1777 and 1778 campaigns, commanded the grenadier battalion; the light infantry battalion was led by Major Sir James Murray, who came to America at the head of the 57th's light infantry company and led it from 1776 through early 1778 when he was appointed major to the 2nd Battalion of Light Infantry.[2]

Each battalion consisted of 10 companies. Muster rolls do not survive to suggest their strength, but presumably they were levelled with other companies in their regiments if not brought to their full strength of 54 private soldiers. Included were drafts from the 10th, 45th and 52nd Regiments. The rolls of the 10th and 45th Regiments indicate which regiments their drafts went to; comparing these to rolls of the 10 West Indies regiments in 1780 suggests that drafted grenadiers remained grenadiers, and drafted light infantry remained light infantry. Nine drafted men from the 10th's grenadier company, and seven from the light infantry, were veterans of the march to Concord on 19 April 1775, and two more of each joined the flank companies after that battle but before Bunker Hill on 17 June. Six light infantrymen and 18 grenadiers who had arrived in America with the 45th Regiment just after the Battle of Bunker Hill were drafted into regiments bound for the West Indies in 1778.[3]

The advanced corps received a spirited but cautionary order from their commander before disembarkation:

1 Gruber (ed.), *Diary*, p.226.
2 BC: James Grant Papers: James Grant to the Secretary at War, 31 December 1778.
3 TNA: WO12: muster rolls, 10th and 45th Regiments.

> Brigadier General Medows is extremely sensible of the high honour conferred upon him in having the command of the flank corps. From the acts of gallantry in the light infantry, the determined bravery of the grenadiers, and the confirmed discipline of the 5th regiment success is to be expected, and he sanguinely hopes the lustre of their actions in the field will not be tarnished by any irregularities out of it. The troops are desired to remember that clemency should ever attend on victory, that an enemy in your power is an enemy no more, that to be cruel and brave are almost incompatible and the glorious characteristic of a British soldier is to conquer and to spare; acting on these principles they never can fail doing honour to their king, their country and themselves.[4]

The advanced corps landed first, each man with only a day's provisions, half a pint of rum and 36 rounds of ammunition. Four 3-pound field pieces accompanied them.[5] Immediately Meadows took them to high ground and 'forced the Heights upon the north side of the Bay,' driving away French troops and local militia, securing the landing of the rest of Grant's troops.[6] 'Our road was remarkably steep and narrow,' recalled the 55th's grenadier Captain Colin Lindsay, 'being cut through thickets which no man could penetrate,' forcing them to advance in single file.[7] The next day they took possession of the principal settlement which included the governor's house, hospital, barracks, and the island's military stores.[8] 'The first object which the advanced guard then saw,' wrote Captain Lindsay, 'was a well-dressed man carrying in his hand a flag of truce.' As he approached, 'a few straggling Frenchmen' fired a volley that wounded several British soldiers. They returned fire, but also shot the man with the flag of truce, a prominent doctor in the town. 'His death was accidental, so say the light infantry,' wrote Captain Francis Downman of the Royal Artillery, 'however, be it as it will, he was pillaged of his watch and a considerable quantity of money.'[9]

While other troops consolidated the area and prepared defences, the advanced corps continued a mile north and took post on the Vigie peninsula, a high point that dominated the entrance to an estuary north of Grand Cul de Sac Bay. A low neck, only 150 yards wide, connected the peninsula to the mainland, and on the south side of the estuary were several batteries of 12- and 18-pounders left operational by the fleeing French garrison, one battery positioned to face the neck leading to Vigie.[10] Captain Lindsay and many others 'were seized with a violent sickness and incessant vomiting' which he later deduced was caused by 'having eaten too freely of the green oranges which grew by the side of the roads along which we had marched … the sickness ceased in a few hours, but left a languor for several days.' The advanced corps settled in on wet, rocky ground, without tents.[11]

---

4 Whinyates (ed.), *Services*, p.92.
5 Whinyates (ed.), *Services*, p.92.
6 BC: James Grant Papers: James Grant to the Secretary at War, 31 December 1778.
7 Colin Lindsay, 'Narrative of the Occupation and Defence of the Island of St. Lucie,' in Alexander William Crawford, Lord Lindsay, *Lives of the Lindsays* (London: John Murray, 1849), Vol.3, p.332.
8 BC: James Grant Papers: James Grant to the Secretary at War, 31 December 1778.
9 Lindsay, 'Narrative,' p.333; Whinyates (ed.), *Services*, p.93.
10 Whinyates (ed.), *Services*, pp.93–94.
11 Lindsay, 'Narrative,' pp.336–337, 341.

The British troops barely had time to take stock of their situation before a large French fleet was sighted on the afternoon of 14 December, bearing towards the island. It closed in the next day, apparently surprised to find it under British control. Soldiers and sailors in town scrambled to prepare a defence. They sent two more days' provisions to the advanced corps on the peninsula. 'Though we were without means to dress our pork,' wrote Captain Lindsay, 'this was not the first time we had eaten it raw, or sliced and broiled upon the end of a bayonet, with yams and plantains.'[12] After probing the fleet and defences, on 16 December some 9,000 French troops landed in a bay just north of the Vigie peninsula. They moved inland, occupying the high ground north of the British forces. Grant ordered the evacuation of a few unimportant advanced posts, giving the French confidence to organize an attack on the advanced corps that was now completely isolated on Vigie peninsula.[13]

Most of the advance corps occupied peninsular high ground that afforded no other cover than elevation, but a battery of three 12-pounders, pointed towards the neck, strengthened the position.[14] The 4th Regiment's grenadier company, led by Captain John West who had been present at the Battle of Bunker Hill and every action since, was in its usual place on the right of the grenadier battalion, the rightmost position in the advanced corps. They took post on a hillock where West 'contrived to find a couple of spades and a pickaxe,' according to Captain Lindsay, and 'told his men that they would probably be attacked in the morning, and that if they wished to have *whole bones* they would work hard.' Five light infantry companies were on the mainland, posted on two hills in front of the neck leading to the peninsula. Captain Henry Downing, a 37-year-old Irishman who had led the 55th's light infantry for the entire war, commanded this detachment. Through the night of 17–18 December it rained, finally abating at 7:00 a.m. The French were active in spite of the weather, taking advantage of thick woods to advance undetected on the light infantry's forward position. Brigadier General Meadows, with Majors Harris and Murray, visited the post just in time to discern a line of French troops, four times the number of the light infantry detachment, advancing towards the two hills. The senior officers retired to the peninsula while the light infantry stood to arms. The troops on the peninsula could plainly see that the five light companies were in danger of being cut off, but Meadows, returning from his visit to the post, assured them that 'the light infantry will take care of themselves.'[15]

The advancing French fired 'two heavy volleys,' which the light infantry returned 'smartly' with a 'straggling fire,' according to Captain Lindsay of the grenadiers. Rather than try to hold a defensive position, the light infantry reverted to the tactic that had served them so well through three years of campaigning, even when under pressure and outnumbered: they 'formed in a body' and charged. Taken completely by surprise, one French regiment broke and ran. The lights turned their attention to another that was still advancing, but it soon became apparent that the entire French army was now closing in on them, advancing in three solid columns. Outnumbered closer to forty-to-one rather than four-to-one, the

12 Lindsay, 'Narrative,' p.339.
13 BC: James Grant Papers: James Grant to the Secretary at War, 31 December 1778.
14 BC: James Grant Papers: James Grant to the Secretary at War, 31 December 1778.
15 Lindsay, 'Narrative,' pp.343–344, 350.

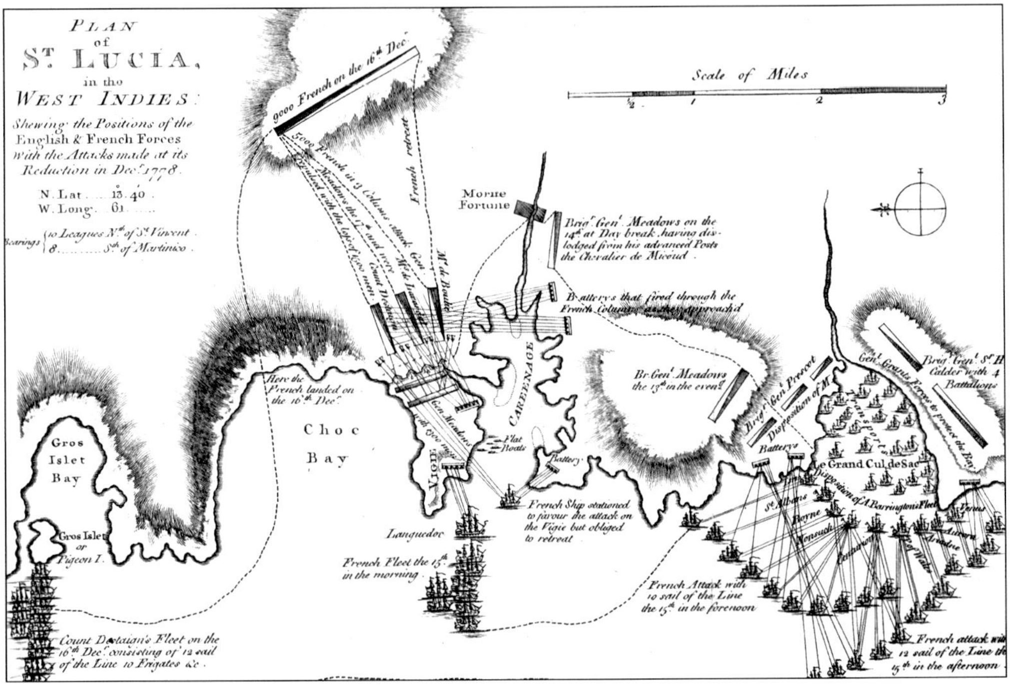

The Vigie Peninsula is just left of centre in this map showing French columns attacking Brigadier General Meadows' advanced corps, 18 December 1778. (Library of Congress)

light infantry took advantage of thick brush and made their escape at the last moment by 'an exertion of their usual agility,' wrote Captain Downman of the artillery.[16]

The ground leading from the hills and onto the neck was choked with underbrush that prevented the French forming the lines and columns that had approached the landward side of hills. Captain Downing took advantage of narrow passages through the brush to cover his detachment's retreat personally, along with fellow 55th officer Lieutenant John Waring, a five-year veteran in spite of being just 20 years old, and three private soldiers, Michael Duffy, John Hargroves and Andrew Rose. According to Captain Lindsay, the little party 'defended a narrow path against the French for a considerable time, till most of the five companies had made good their retreat. These officers and soldiers parried the bayonets of the French grenadiers for some time.' Finally, Lieutenant Waring was 'run through the lungs,' and Captain Downing, seeing the position untenable, surrendered to a French officer who, eschewing needless bloodshed, 'advanced, and slightly touched his sword.'[17]

This was the only hint of French victory that day. Their three columns were now able to cross the neck, but ran afoul of each other on the narrow ground. This brought them to the base of the peninsular hill, where shrubs afforded some cover, but at 300 yards they were just barely within musket range and could approach no further. They brought up three amusettes,

16 Lindsay, 'Narrative,' pp.344–345; Whinyates (ed.), *Services*, p.97.

17 Lindsay, 'Narrative,' p.347; TNA: WO12: muster rolls, 55th Regiment.

light artillery pieces that fired 1-pound solid shot and grape shot up the hill. With no defensive works, the light artillery and musketry took a toll on the advance corps, who returned fire 'with the greatest silence and the least confusion possible,' wrote Captain Lindsay.[18] 'The disposition made by Meadows for the defences of his post was masterly,' lauded Grant, 'He was wounded in the arm early in the day, but remained in the field and gave orders everywhere.'[19] 'Our men dropped fast,' wrote Lindsay, 'Our ammunition could not last long, for we had but thirty rounds at first.'[20] The French pressed the attack for two hours, throughout which the defenders managed to sustain fire, 'the men having collected even what they could from their dead and wounded comrades,' wrote Captain Downman, adding that Brigadier General Meadows had 'prudently reserved to each man three or four rounds' in case French were able to push close, 'and then they were to charge with bayonets.'[21] Lindsay remembered orders 'that we should fire no more until the enemy came close, then to retire to the summit of the hill, to form in a line, to charge and drive them headlong back.'[22]

The grenadiers, light infantry, and men of the 5th Regiment, pinned on the hill, were out of ammunition. 'The firing ceased from us,' wrote Lindsay, 'but the enemy did not advance. Our men sat down and bore the enemy's fire, reserving five rounds each.' A small resupply arrived by boat, allowing them to resume firing.[23] This time the French withdrew, but not because of small-arms fire. What saved Meadows' position was the battery of 12-pounders on the peninsula that 'did amazing execution,' and a battery of 18-pounders perched high on ground adjacent to the peninsula that raked the neck from a distance of 600 yards, ravaging the congested French columns. Some 400 French soldiers were killed, 500 seriously wounded, and a further 600 lightly wounded. The artillery left 'heads, legs, and arms knocked off, and bodies torn to pieces,' wrote Captain Downman, proud to have directed the 18-pounders that staved off the attack.[24]

'Major Harris who commands the grenadiers and Major Sir James Murray who commands the Light Infantry distinguished themselves,' wrote Major General Grant, adding, 'The officers and men were cool and determined – they even surpassed if possible their usual spirit and bravery.'[25] Besides Meadows, who 'never quitted the post and continues to command the reserve to which the surgeons did not think he would have been equal to,' grenadier officers Major George Harris, Captain John Hay of the 28th, Lieutenants Robert Pratt of the 5th, Alexander Philip Forbes of the 40th, and William Gomm of the 46th were wounded, as was Captain Peter Daly of the 28th's light infantry, Lieutenant Waring of the 55th's, and Lieutenant Arthur Ross of the 35th who was serving as brigade major.[26] Grant reported 10 soldiers killed and 130 wounded, including a few from regiments not in the advanced corps; Captain Lindsay wrote, 'The grenadiers had but eighty-seven killed and wounded,' including

18 Whinyates (ed.), *Services*, p.98; Lindsay, 'Narrative,' pp.345, 349.
19 BC: James Grant Papers: James Grant to the Secretary at War, 31 December 1778.
20 Lindsay, 'Narrative,' p.345.
21 Whinyates (ed.), *Services*, p.98.
22 Lindsay, 'Narrative,' p.345.
23 Lindsay, 'Narrative,' p.345.
24 BC: James Grant Papers: James Grant to the Secretary at War, 31 December 1778; Whinyates (ed.), *Services*, p.99.
25 BC: James Grant Papers: James Grant to the Secretary at War, 31 December 1778.
26 Whinyates (ed.), *Services*, p.99.

only a single man from the 4th's company thanks to the breastwork that Captain West had them build. 'The loss of the light infantry,' continued Lindsay, 'in every way was sixty odd; that of the fifth regiment was eighteen,' adding, 'Few of the wounded were disabled.'[27] At the end of the month Grant corroborated this latter point, writing, 'some of them have already joined their corps and our loss upon the whole will be under fifty.'[28] Among those who rejoined their regiments was 29-year-old grenadier Augustus Parsons, a Norfolk weaver who joined the 15th Regiment at the age of 18 and who had been wounded on Long Island in August 1776.[29]

The battle was over by 11:00 a.m. Men of the advance corps now descended the hill and were shocked to see the carnage wrought by the artillery. 'None of us had ever seen so many dead upon so small a spot,' wrote Captain Lindsay, 'The dying were confounded with the dead, and added to the scene their piercing agony and groans, which even by the roughness of the British soldier's nature could not be resisted, nor beheld without concern.' They assisted the wounded and dying in whatever way they could, and began the grim task of burying the dead, but 'this our General was resolved the French should do themselves, and waited for a while before he sent a flag of truce.' At about 4:00 p.m. a light infantry bugler sounded a parley and Captain Conway Courtney of the 15th Regiment's grenadiers went forward with a flag of truce. The French, not recognizing the signal that was traditionally sounded with a drum, fired on him. The mistake was quickly recognized, apologies made, and the two sides went about their business without further incident, the French burying their dead and the advanced corps preparing defensive positions in preparation for another attack.[30]

Major General Grant sent a letter of thanks to Brigadier General Meadows, 'for repulsing with so much spirit and bravery so great a body of the enemy,' making sure to point out that 'it was just what I expected from you and them; and I am sure under your command they will always behave as will do honour to you, themselves, their king, and the country which they serve.' He asked Meadows to pass his thanks to the troops 'in the strongest manner,' which Meadows did, offering 'the officers and men his admiration of their gallantry and good conduct,' and asserting that 'at the head of such a corps, he must be pleased to live or proud to die.' As the French repositioned during the next few days further battle appeared imminent, prompting Meadows to order on 21 December:

> Whenever the picquet is attacked, the drums are to beat to arms, and the lines are immediately to be manned. As soon as our gallant and generous enemy are seen to advance in great numbers, the troops are to receive them with three huzzas, and then to be perfectly silent and obedient to their officers. Whilst they are cool by day and alert by night, they have nothing to fear. If the enemy want our arms, let them come and take them. During the attack, some of the drummers to assemble round the colours of the fifth regiment at the flag-staff, and beat the grenadiers' march.[31]

27 Lindsay, 'Narrative,' pp.345–346, 350.
28 BC: James Grant Papers: James Grant to the Secretary at War, 31 December 1778.
29 TNA: WO 121/148/61: discharge of Augustus Parsons.
30 Lindsay, 'Narrative,' pp.346–347.
31 Lindsay, 'Narrative,' p.352.

No further attack came. The French re-embarked during the night of 28–29 December and sailed away to other ventures in the West Indies.[32] Over the next few years the regiments on St Lucia were shifted to other islands, new regiments from Great Britain joined them, and disease thinned their ranks. In 1780 the 4th, 5th and 49th Regiments were sent back to Britain and the 40th back to New York. The flank companies of the other regiments fought in other actions in the West Indies, some on land and some at sea, notably those of the 15th Regiment at the siege of Brimstone Hill on St. Kitts in early 1782. But the use of flank battalions in the region ended with the spectacularly successful defence of St Lucia in December 1778.

Captain Colin Lindsay of the 55th Regiment's grenadier company wrote his account of the action in January 1779, adding a few annotations in 1793. Twenty-three years old during the battle on 18 December, he had served for the entire American war so far, joining the grenadier battalions as commander of the grenadier company in April 1777. As such, he had seen a great many shots fired, and wrote an important comment not mentioned by other writers. Describing the action on 18 December, he wrote, 'our fire would have been much more destructive, but for a most extraordinary instance of neglect; namely, the badness of our flints. We have always had the same cause of complaint.' 'In the attack, the bayonet is always a remedy for this deficiency,' he wrote, even though the usual reason for relying on the bayonet during the American War was because of how it intimidated unskilled opponents. Referring specifically to the action on St Lucia, Lindsay wrote, 'to find in a defence that one-third of your men are useless from this cause is indeed extraordinary.' In 1793 he added a few lines indicating that the problem continued, and was perhaps exacerbated by the springs on the firelocks being too strong, apparently causing flints to wear quickly or shatter. Explaining that the flints used by their opponents were better, he wrote, 'It was a common saying among the soldiers in America, that a Yankee flint was as good as a glass of grog.'[33]

32 BC: James Grant Papers: James Grant to the Secretary at War, 31 December 1778.
33 Lindsay, 'Narrative,' p.352.

10

Twilight of the Flank Battalions, 1780–1783

Instead of wintering securely in Long Island huts, the flank battalions in New York embarked with much of the army, commanded by General Henry Clinton, in late December 1779. They endured a stormy voyage to Charleston, South Carolina, finally disembarking in the second week of February.

The proportion of skirmishers with General Clinton's army was even greater than it had been for the retreat through New Jersey in 1778. Besides the British flank battalions, Jägers and loyalist legions, the Brigade of Guards and 33rd Regiment acting largely as light infantry, and others, former rifle company commander Patrick Ferguson of the 70th Regiment led a corps of 'Rangers' raised just for this expedition. On the voyage, an officer of this corps wrote down 'Signals for the Dum Bugle or Whistle' issued by Ferguson for use by the corps; they are presented in Appendix IX. This is the only set of bugle or whistle signals known to exist; it may reflect common practice by the flank battalions during previous campaigns – Ferguson campaigned with General Howe's army in 1777 – or be unique to this temporary corps of rangers.

The flank battalions landed first, as usual, on the 'rainy evening' of 11 February.[1] The southwestern end of Johns Island was far enough away from the rebel-held city to ensure an uncontested landing. Troops pushed inland in darkness, 'splashing thro' the mud & rain' before halting at 10:00 p.m. to sleep unsheltered.[2] A medical officer who stayed on board wrote, 'All this day I have been waiting the noise of the Bugle,'[3] but there was no enthusiasm on shore. Two grenadier and four light infantry companies got lost in the darkness, including those escorting General Clinton; the general spent the night with the soldiers, huddled under a tree in the rain. The next morning, they pushed northeast while the rest of the army came ashore. They spent some time in a plantations houses, some in 'wigwams of pine bushes' before tents arrived a few days later.[4]

Charleston was on a neck of land between two rivers where they met the sea. Clinton's army approached from the southwest, first crossing from Johns to James Island adjacent

1 WLC: Henry Clinton Papers: Vol. 266, general orders, 11 February 1780; James Bain, jr. (ed.), 'The Siege of Charleston: Journal of Captain Peter Russell,' *American Historical Review* Vol. IV No. 3 (April 1899), p.483.
2 Gruber (ed.), *Diary*, p.338.
3 WLC: Henry Clinton Papers: Vol. 185:12, John McNamara Hays to John André, 11 February 1780.
4 Gruber (ed.), *Diary*, pp.340–342.

to the city, then moving bit by bit northwest, then northeast above the city, and finally southeast to seal off all approaches. Cavalry and skirmishers ranged ahead to secure key intersections and cut off all approaches by land, while the navy worked close to the city and up the rivers. By 30 March the region was sufficiently secure to begin a formal siege. The army marched towards the city's well-fortified landward side, 'in one Column, by half Companies,' Jägers in front and on the flanks, followed by the two light infantry battalions, the two British grenadier battalions, then the rest. A couple of miles from the city enemy troops fired from some woods. Jägers 'pushed up and spread, and the Light Infantry advanced and formed as fast as they came up,' driving the enemy back without loss. The army encamped in three lines stretching across the neck, 'the light Infantry and Jagers the first, about 1,600 yds. from the Enemys first line,' the grenadiers about 300 yards behind them, the rest still further back.[5]

On the night of 31 March – 1 April the light infantry moved to within 500 yards of enemy lines to cover working parties that built redoubts and dug trenches. The next weeks were spent pushing ever closer to the city's fortifications, the flank battalions taking turns with other corps manning trenches to ward off potential threats, exposed to splinters from exploding mortar and howitzer shells, and eventually within range of enemy musketry. Casualties were few. The town surrendered on 11 May, three months to the day after the first British troops landed. The operation had gone well, but was fatiguing; Lieutenant Colin Campbell of the 74th Regiment's light infantry company gave a vivid description of the difficulties of the campaign, and the pride with which the light infantry endured them:

> traversing the woods of that country for six or eight weeks, without bed, tent, or any other cover than a great-coat against the cold dew and sometimes frosts of the nights, or against the excessive rains or scorching heats of the days in that climate; and for near six weeks more at the siege lying in the open air, except the last fortnight only, at which time we got tents, and then, as well as before, twenty-four hours on duty in the trenches for every forty-eight hours we were off duty, whether cold, hot, wet, or dry, all of which we frequently experienced in the extreme before we were relieved … for ten weeks after landing in South Carolina the 11th February last, I had neither my clothes or side-arms off, except while shifting, or never lay down to sleep without my fuzee stretched alongside of me, or within my arms, ready to start up with it to the first sound of the bugle horn, which the Light Infantry used instead of a drum. It resembled a huntsman's horn, and by different notes, easily distinguished, loudly expresses the different words of command, to be heard at two miles distance; twelve or fifteen of them together make the most lofty warlike music in the world. With these I have known the whole Light infantry roused at one o'clock in the morning on a sudden alarm, formed, and ready for action within the short space of three minutes from the time of their being in a profound sleep after a fatiguing march; and to the honour of these brave fellows be it told, not one man of a company in the whole battalion missing.[6]

5 Russell, 'The Siege of Charleston,' pp.493–494.

6 Colin Campbell to –, 20 November 1780, in Anthony Sterling, *The Story of the Highland Brigade in the Crimea* (London: Remington & Company, 1895), pp.xv–xvi.

The 1st Battalion of Light Infantry lost eight men killed, a sergeant and 17 wounded; the 2nd Battalion had 11 killed, and an officer and 12 wounded. The 1st Battalion of Grenadiers suffered a sergeant and four killed, two officers, a sergeant and 13 wounded, while the 2nd Battalion has 10 killed, and an officer and 11 wounded.[7] They had spent the siege in the camps and trenches, while fast-moving legions and other skirmishing troops worked the countryside, foretelling a new style of warfare in the south characterized by smaller numbers of troops covering larger expanses of territory than they had in the north. When the siege was over, General Clinton returned to New York with much of the army including the British flank battalions. Only a few British light infantry companies operated in the Carolinas and Georgia, often in cooperation with cavalry, never in the flank battalions that had seen such success in the first years of the war.

* * *

June 1780 found the flank battalions back in Long Island encampments. They boarded transports in late July with the intention of attacking a French force that had just arrived in Rhode Island, but the expedition was called off when intelligence reported the enemy too strongly posted; the British troops disembarked again at the beginning of August. None knew it yet, but the grenadiers would see no more fighting in this war. They remained ready – 'we march & manoeuvre through the adjoining fields every evening and morning, when it is not too hot,' wrote Captain Peebles on 22 August. The commander of the 1st Battalion of Grenadiers gave them 'rules for manouvering' to practice, perhaps new, perhaps restatement of past practice (see Appendix VIII). Battalion and general courts tried 'notorious offenders, of which there are a good many in this battalion,' according to Peebles. Winter came, and they moved from tents to huts.[8] The winter of 1780–1781 passed much as the winter of 1778–1779 had passed. The war dragged on.

In the southern colonies war raged and British fortunes changed. Victories through August 1780 gave way to setbacks and the sheer scale of the territory, far too vast for the numbers of soldiers available. In early 1781 General Clinton sent a few regiments into Virginia, operating in the region from Norfolk to Richmond. In late March reinforcements joined them, in the form of the 1st and 2nd Battalions of Light Infantry, together commanded by Lieutenant Colonel Robert Abercromby, and the 76th and 80th Regiments. Leading them was Major General William Phillips, a veteran of Burgoyne's 1777 campaign. There were other veterans of that campaign in the ranks, soldiers who had escaped from captivity, found their way to the British army, and joined other regiments, including Patrick McGreevy of the 62nd Regiment, Duncan Lowdon of the 21st, Alexander Avis and William Rose of the 53rd Regiment, all of whom escaped from prison barracks near Boston and made their way into Rhode Island. McGreevy, Avis and Rose joined the 22nd Regiment, Lowdon the 38th.[9] All were subsequently transferred into the light infantry and now, five years after landing in Canada, they landed in Portsmouth, Virginia at the end of March 1781 for another campaign.

7 Almon (ed.), *The Remembrancer, or impartial repository of public events* (London: J. Almon, 1780), Vol.10, p.44.
8 Gruber (ed.), *Diary*, pp.395–397, 399–400, 417.
9 TNA: WO 12: muster rolls of the various regiments.

Phillips added his troops to British forces already in the region and assumed command. On 5 April he gave instructions that emphasized flexibility, most notably advocating the use – if necessary – of close order formations that had been largely abandoned early in the war. He also recognized that his handful of battalions and regiments might act independently of each other:

> It is the Major Generals Wish that the troops under his Command may Practice forming from two, to three and to four deep, and that they should be accustomed to Charge in all those Orders, in the latter order of 3 & 4 deep the files will of course be closer, so as to render a charge of the greatest force.
>
> The Major General also Recommends to Regiments the practice of Dividing the Battalions by Wings or otherways, so that one line may support the other, when an attack is supposed; and when a Retreat is supposed that the first line may retreat through the intervals of the second, the second Doubling up its Divisions for that purpose, and forming them up again in Order to Check the enemy who may be supposed to have pressed the first line.
>
> The Major General would approve also of one division of a Battalion attacking in the common open order of 2 Deep, to be supported by the other division as a second line, in the charging order of 3 or 4 deep.[10]

The emphasis on charging proved effective on 25 April in a fight at Petersburg when the light infantry drove through lines of American militia with only a few casualties[11] – among them Newcastle native John Thompson of the 22nd Regiment, a 12-year veteran at the age of 20, who had been in the light infantry for the entire war; he was wounded in the head at the siege of Charleston the previous year, and again in the shoulder at Petersburg.[12]

At the end of May Lieutenant General Cornwallis arrived in Virginia with a battered and depleted army that he had led on a vigorous but unsuccessful march through the interior of North Carolina, hoping but failing to subdue rebel resistance in that colony. He joined the British forces already in Virginia and continued the war of manoeuvre that was already in progress, British forces dominant in strength but unable to either isolate and fully defeat their foes or completely eliminate their sources of supply. Operations took a new turn at the end of June when Cornwallis received instructions from General Clinton to establish a defensive post and send part of his force back to New York.

Cornwallis set out towards Portsmouth, which required crossing the James River. On 6 July he arranged his forces deceptively to lure his opponents to attack, placing small parties of skirmishers to give the impression of being a rear guard covering a vulnerable river crossing. Most of Cornwallis's force was arranged to strike back, three regiments in a line anchored on the left by the river, the light infantry to their right ready to circle around an attacker's flank, and a second line of three regiments behind in reserve. During the ensuing Battle of Green Spring an American officer 'saw the British light infantry, distinctly, advancing at

10 WLC: 6912/14-43: Eyre Coote orderly book, general orders, 5 April 1781.

11 For details on operations in Virginia in 1781, see Michael Cecere, *The Invasion of Virginia 1781* (Yardley, PA: Westholme, 2017).

12 TNA: WO 97/425/56: discharge of John Thompson.

arms-length distance, and their second line in close order, with shouldered musket, just in front of their camp.'[13] Another recalled that they, 'advanc'd in open order at arm's length & aiming very low kept up a deadly fire.'[14] As the British line advanced, they made 'a devil of a noise of firing and huzzaing,' according to an American officer.[15] The British were victorious, but once again not decisively so; the onset of darkness and need to move towards Portsmouth prevented pursuit of the defeated enemy. Two days after the battle, Lieutenant Colonel Abercromby expressed in orders that he was 'much pleased with the zeal and spirit of the light infantry on the evening of the 6th,' but added the admonishment that he 'was very sorry to hear shouting from a part of the corps, nothing can be more unmilitary than such practices; it is following the example of savages and undisciplined rebels.'[16]

The move to Portsmouth was countermanded by General Clinton, who insisted Cornwallis take up a position closer to Chesapeake Bay. Cornwallis settled on Yorktown, on the York River, a defensible position that allowed cooperation with the navy. He abandoned the post at Portsmouth, moved to Yorktown in early August, and immediately began preparing defences. Before long, Cornwallis's army was hemmed in and under siege. Over the course of a month the situation worsened as American and French forces, using traditional techniques of trenches and artillery batteries just as the British had done at Charleston the previous year, crept closer; a French fleet blockaded relief or escape by sea. On the night of 15–16 October, the light infantry sallied out into their opponent's trenches to disable cannons and disrupt operations; the attempt was moderately successful but not effective enough to affect the course of events.

Lieutenant General Cornwallis capitulated on 17 October. Between 28 September and 17 October the light infantry lost Lieutenant Colin Campbell of the 74th's light infantry who had written so vividly of the siege of Charleston, three sergeants and 24 soldiers killed; three other lieutenants, two sergeants, a drummer and 51 soldiers were wounded.[17] The dead included William Rose of the 22nd's company, who had been with the 53rd Regiment on Burgoyne's campaign; another was John Cole, who had served the entire war in the 33rd's company and been wounded early in the war; both died on 13 October. Samuel Standering of the 23rd, who march out with the company 19 April 1775 and had been with it the entire war, died on 12 October.[18] At least two of the wounded had also been wounded at Germantown four years earlier – Thomas Swift of the 37th Regiment, 'wounded in the left arm at Germantown 4 October 1777, in the belly at York town 17 October 1781' and 36-year-old clothier Thomas Witherill from Bedale, Yorkshire, who 'lost part of one finger of his left hand at German Town North America and wounded in the left arm at York Town Virginia.'[19]

13 Anon. (ed.), *Military Journal of Major Ebenezer Denny* (Philadelphia: J. B. Lippincott, 1859), p.37.
14 Gaillard Hunt, *Fragments of Revolutionary History. Being hitherto unpublished writings of the men of the American Revolution* (Brooklyn: Historical Printing Club, 1892), p.50.
15 Cecere, *The Invasion of Virginia*, p.142.
16 WLC: 6912/14-43: Eyre Coote orderly book, brigade orders, 8 July 1781.
17 Almon (ed.), *The Remembrancer*, Vol.10, p.45.
18 TNA: WO 12: muster rolls of the various regiments.
19 TNA: WO 121/10/45 and WO 121/1/166: discharges of Thomas Swift and Thomas Witherill, respectively.

Over 7,000 officers and men were surrendered at Yorktown; the two light infantry battalions contributed 28 officers, two surgeons, 33 sergeants, 13 drummers, and 594 corporals and private soldiers to this total.[20] Three of the companies that surrendered at this last battle for British light infantry battalions had also been in the light infantry's first battle on 19 April 1775; in the 23rd's company, 11 men were in both engagements, in the 38th's company, 10; and in the 43rd's, 18. The 22nd Regiment's company, which arrived in Boston just after the Battle of Bunker Hill, brought 22 men to Yorktown who had been in the company in Boston, two of whom died during the siege; the 33rd's company had 14 men at Yorktown who had served in it the entire war. There were other men in the light infantry who had been in America for the entire war, but joined the light infantry more recently. These veterans of many American campaigns spent the next 18 months in captivity.[21]

* * *

In their final effort of the war, the grenadier battalions in New York boarded ships as part of a large relief force intended to rescue Cornwallis's trapped army at Yorktown. They boarded transports in early September and waited, disembarked two weeks later and waited, and embarked again on 12 October. A week later, still in New York harbour, the transports pulled alongside line-of-battle warships and the soldiers climbed from one ship to the other, where they 'were dispose'd of on the middle and lower decks, 6 to a mess between the guns,' wrote Captain Peebles. The fleet finally sailed after the army they sought to rescue had already capitulated, but were a week at sea before finally getting this news. The ships returned to New York, and off Sandy Hook the grenadiers and other troops clambered off the warships into small boats that took them once again to transports on 3 November, and finally onto land at Staten Island on the 10th.[22] There was nothing left to do but return to encampments, then huts, as winter approached.

After the capitulation at Yorktown the war carried on and the fighting continued, but not for the flank battalions. The grenadier battalions remained embodied and in garrison, spending most of their time on Long Island. Officers and soldiers transferred in and out, as did a few entire companies when their regiments arrived in or departed from the region. Training continued, as did all aspects of military routine, maintaining readiness for attack or defence should the need arise, but it never did.

The light infantry companies interned at Yorktown remained in captivity until a peace agreement in early 1783 allowed their release. Some of the prisoners escaped and made their way to British-held posts, some died in captivity, and some absconded to remain in America. Most returned to the New York garrison and rejoined their regiments; in the 17th Regiment's company, for example, about 40 men were taken prisoner, of whom four died in captivity and eight never returned after release; of about 40 prisoners in the 37th's company, three died and nine never returned.

Rather than disband with ceremony, the flank battalions faded away as individual companies rejoined regiments that left North America. The waning months of 1783 saw

20 *Pennsylvania Gazette*, 7 November 1781.
21 TNA: WO 12: muster rolls of the various regiments.
22 Gruber (ed.), *Diary*, pp.471, 476, 482–483, 491–492.

the final departure of British troops from the now-independent colonies. Some returned to Great Britain, some went to Canada, a few to the West Indies; many regiments raised during the war were disbanded. There were soldiers who had served in flank companies for the entire eight-year war – in the 23rd Regiment, 10 out of 38 grenadiers in the regiment on 19 April 1775 departed New York in November 1783, as did five out of 40 in the light infantry; another two of the latter accepted discharges and settled in Canada. The 38th Regiment had 45 grenadiers and 43 light infantry on the rolls in April 1775, of whom 11 and four, respectively, were still in the company in November 1783. Regiments that arrived in America later in 1775 or early in 1776 had a few more – in the 22nd, 16 out of 43 grenadiers remained, and 15 out of 38 light infantry; in the 33rd, there were 17 out of 49 grenadiers and 11 out of 49 light infantry. Some who left the flank companies during the war remained in the ranks of battalion companies in each of these regiments, and many served in the flank companies for only part of the war.[23]

In July 1778 Lieutenant William Hale of the 45th Regiment's grenadier company wrote, 'the Brigades have been looked upon as nurseries only for the flank Corps.'[24] This comment on the practice of sending select men from regiments to serve in the grenadiers and light infantry was both proud and cynical, albeit not entirely accurate; the battalion companies of most British regiments saw their share of active and heroic service during the war. It was the light infantry companies, newly-formed in 1771, that gained the most acclaim, so much so that for the rest of the 1780s soldiers going before the army's pension board often had annotations on their discharge forms pointing out light infantry service. The board saw that John Pitcher of the 17th Regiment, 47 years old when he went before the pension board in 1790 after 23 years in the army, was 'worn out thro' long & faithful service when in the light infantry during the greatest part of the late war'; 35-year-old John Gordon of the 55th Regiment, although having served only 15 years when he went before the board in 1787, was 'sickly and worn out in consequence of the very extraordinary fatigues he in the most soldier like manner went through in the light infantry during three years in North America & seven in the West Indies where he last had a severe fever which deprived him of his health'; John Hobson of the 22nd, 42 years old in 1788 with 20 years of service, was 'wounded in the left arm, worn out having served during the whole of the American War in the Light Infantry.'[25] In a few cases muster rolls reveal different service than claimed, such as John Vasey, a baker born in Oxford in 1748. After being drafted from the 3rd Regiment of Foot in May 1775, he served in a battalion company of the 22nd Regiment until joining the light infantry in October 1779; his 1788 discharge claimed that he 'served in the Light Infantry during the whole of the American War' and was 'worn out in the Service.'[26] Such was the prestige of the light infantry.

Like other British soldiers, men who served in the flank battalions often had lifelong careers in the army. James Rennison, wounded on 19 April 1775 (chapter 2), continued in the army until 1802 when, after service in several corps, he was discharged for the last

23 TNA: WO 12: muster rolls of the various regiments.
24 Wilkin, *Some British Soldiers*, p.245.
25 TNA: WO 121/9/323, WO 121/2/171, and WO 121/3/19: discharges of John Pitcher, John Gordon, and John Hobson, respectively.
26 TNA: WO 121/3/285: discharge of John Vasey.

time at the age of 58. Joseph Brooks, encouraged by another soldier to desert (chapter 5), remained in the army until 1793. Daniel Hollowell, tried by a court martial in 1777, served until 1798.[27] They and thousands of others had many adventures besides the campaigns in America, and yet barely anything is known of their careers beyond a few words on muster rolls, discharge forms, trial proceedings, and other military documents.

The tactical prowess attained by the flank battalions in the first years of the war, quickly emulated by other corps operating in America, was soon suppressed by conservative voices in the British army. As adjutant general in Ireland, David Dundas, an officer who had not served in America, advocated against the fast-moving formations that had seen such success on American battlefields, instead reverting to traditional close-packed, slow-moving formations. In his 1788 *Principles of Military Movements* he disparaged the 'loose and irregular system of our infantry,' attributing it to insufficient cavalry in America. He called the fast, open-order movements 'dancing about,' useful for show but impractical for large armies. He admitted that light infantry's 'service was conspicuous, and their gallantry and exertions have met with merited applause,' but in complaining that 'instead of being considered as an accessory to the battalion, they have become the principal feature of our army, and have almost put grenadiers out of fashion,' he failed to recognize that grenadiers had performed similar feats during the war. 'The showy exercise, the airy dress, the independent modes which they have adopted,' continued Dundas, 'have caught the minds of young officers, and made them imagine that these ought to be general and exclusive.' This assessment was accurate, as the light infantry themselves demonstrated several times in 1776 when they pursued with too much zeal and found themselves in danger. But Dundas's *Principles* overcorrected, advocating that flank companies 'when assembled in corps, they ought to act as other battalions do,' and should be held in reserve when attached to their regiments. 'There seems no reason why the light infantry should not conform to the same principles of order and movement as the battalion,' he wrote, 'The frequent dispersion and peculiarities they are taught, should be considered as occasional exceptions.' In asserting that 'their practice seems founded on a supposition of the spirit and exertion of each individual, more than on the real feelings by which the multitude are actuated,' he discounted the importance of the individual soldiers who had served so well in America.[28]

In Philadelphia in March 1778, Lieutenant William Hale of the 45th Regiment's grenadier company wrote 'Light Infantry accustomed to fight from tree to tree, or charge even in woods; and Grenadiers who after the first fire lose no time in loading again, but rush on, trusting entirely to that most decisive of weapons the bayonet; will ever be superior to any troops the Rebels can ever bring against them.'[29] They had the misfortune to prove this in a war that could not be won militarily, where battlefield victories did not compensate for an overall lack of strategy, foreign policy that could not adapt to the realities of managing powerful colonies, and the logistical demands of sustaining an overseas war in a vast terri-

27 TNA: WO 121/3/157, WO 121/17/127 and WO 121/147/89: discharges of James Rennison, Joseph Brooks, and Daniel Hollowell, respectively.

28 David Dundas, *Principles of Military Movements: Chiefly Applied to Infantry. Illustrated by Manoeuveres of the Prussian Troops, and by an Outline of the British Campaigns in Germany, During the War of 1757* (London: T. Cadell, 1788), pp.11–13.

29 Wilkin, *Some British Soldiers*, p.245.

tory. The exploits of the distinguished corps of grenadiers and light infantry were rendered moot by forces far beyond their influence. It is a sad testament that their 'gallantry and exertions' were eclipsed by the conflict's outcome.

Appendix I

Regimental and Non-Regimental Clothing for British Infantry

British uniform clothing can be divided into three general categories: regimentals, necessary items, and additional items procured for seasonal use. All were the property of the soldiers, paid for through withholdings from pay called stoppages.

Each soldier received new regimentals each year, consisting of a hat, coat, waistcoat (a snug-fitting sleeveless jacket worn under the coat), and knee-length breeches. A Royal Warrant enacted in December 1768 prescribed the general design and colours, and some distinguishing regimental variations; details varied in each regiment.[1] Most images of soldiers from this era depict this uniform. In practice, many factors led to deviation from the warranted uniform, so that each regiment had a specific look that changed with the time and place where it served.

Regimental clothing was manufactured by contractors in Great Britain to the general specifications of the clothing warrant. When received by regiments, it was tailored to fit each man and finished according to directions of local commanders. Regiments in Ireland and America typically received annual clothing late in the year, and fitted it during winter to be ready for the following year.

The coat was made of red wool and extended to just above the knees. A double-breasted design allowed it to be buttoned closed, with a collar that could turn up and cuffs that could unfold part way over the hands, forming a reasonably effective foul-weather garment.[2] The lapels, collar (also called the cape) and cuffs were lined with wool of a colour particular to the regiment; when folded back and buttoned for everyday use, they formed the distinctive 'facings' of the regimental coat. Lapels and cuffs were kept in place with cast white-metal buttons, roughly an inch in diameter and bearing the regiment's number, 10 on each lapel and four on each cuff. Buttonholes were bound with worsted woollen lace for strength. Each regiment had its own pattern of stripes or other designs woven into the white lace, and sometimes the lace arrangement and buttonhole spacing was also distinctive. Pocket flaps on the outside of the coat also carried lace and buttons, but did not open; instead, they provided strength and support for pockets cut into the lining. The coat was slit from the

1 TNA: WO 30/13B: 'His Majesty's Warrant for the regulation of the Colours, Clothing, &c. of the Marching Regiments of Foot,' 19 December 1768.

2 The clothing warrant directed that cuffs 'be made so that they may be unbuttoned and let down.'

waist down in the back and on each side, forming skirts that were usually 'turned back' and clipped together at the side; these turnbacks revealed the loosely-woven white or buff wool lining. Coats were tailored to fit each man snugly but comfortably.

Breeches and waistcoats were also of white or buff wool, depending on the regiment, calculated for the British climate. Breeches were tailored to fit snugly in the legs and waist, baggy in the hips and seat to allow for movement. A few buttons and a knee band, secured with a button or buckle, kept breeches closed on the leg just below the knee. The single-breasted waistcoat was tailored for a snug fit, secured with numbered metal buttons similar to coat buttons but smaller, spaced about an inch apart. The clothing warrant specified pockets without flaps or buttons, but period artwork often depicts pocket flaps.

The black felt hats, though much maligned, were consistent with period styles and had practical attributes. Made from a simple broad-brimmed, round hat blank, the brims were 'cocked,' folded up and tied to the crown. Cocking the back of the brim and tying it, then cocking the front and tying it in two places such that it formed a slight point in the middle, formed the typical military style. A strip of white binding around the edge protected the brim from fraying. A black fabric cockade on the left front was introduced during the reign of King George I and is sometimes associated with the house of Hanover. The resulting hat was fashionable and well-suited to modification -brims could be untied and let down for protection from sun and rain, or trimmed and reshaped to convert the hat into a cap.

Corporals wore the same regimentals as private men, with the addition of a white epaulet on the right shoulder. Sergeants' uniforms were of the same style but better materials. Higher-quality coating and dye resulted in a brighter red coat; buttons were sometimes silver plated and of a different pattern; white braid reinforced the buttonholes and silver lace bound the hat brim. A red sash with a stripe of the regimental facing colour was worn around the waist. Sergeants carried swords, and the clothing warrant prescribed a pole arm called a halberd.

Uniforms of drummers and fifers differed in that, for most regiments, the coat colours were reversed – lapels, cuffs and collars were red and the body of the coat was the colour of the lapels of the private soldiers. The lace used for the buttonholes also adorned other parts of the coat. In some regiments the breeches and waistcoats were red rather than white or buff. The clothing warrant prescribed fur caps for drummers, but drummers also received the same felt hats as private soldiers; use of fur caps and hats is discussed further in the section on grenadiers, below. The clothing warrant prescribed swords for drummers and fifers.

Necessary items were so called because each company commander provided them as often as needed. These included shirts, stockings and shoes, all of which required frequent replacement and could be procured from local sources. Large quantities were sent to America from Great Britain, and additional quantities were purchased from local merchants, so much so that some merchants advertised these items for soldiers.[3] Because they were procured as needed, styles varied. In general shirts were of white linen, fit very loosely like all shirts of the era, and might include a ruffle at the chest and cuffs. White woollen knit stockings were predominant, but other materials appeared occasionally. Low-topped buckle shoes had the rough side of the leather on the outside, waterproofed by polishing with blackened wax. Black canvas spatterdashes (gaiters) buttoned around the ankles to keep dirt and moisture out of shoes, a black neck stock kept the shirt collar stiff and neat, and black leather garters held stockings in place.

3 See, for example, *The Newport Gazette*, 21 May 1778.

Officers procured their own clothing at their own expense, including at least one suit conforming to the look of the regiment. Coats were similar in style to the soldiers, but of finer and brighter cloth, buttons plated with silver or gold depending on the regiment, and in many regiments buttonholes were trimmed with gold or silver lace. Most officers wore one epaulet on the right shoulder, again silver or gold, that secured a sword carriage. Hats were often trimmed with lace of the same metal as the buttons. Swords and pole arms called espontoons were prescribed for most officers.

That was the uniform described by the clothing warrant; there were many variations and adaptions, particularly in wartime.

Besides current regimentals and necessaries, a soldier might have several items of regimental clothing from previous years in various states of repair and alteration; some regiments followed strict regimens of 'wearing out' older clothing to preserve new clothing in the best possible condition.[4] Old clothing was altered: regimental coats were shortened or re-cut into single-breasted jackets; scraps were made into caps to wear off duty. Regiments procured additional clothing as local conditions dictated: heavy woollen overcoats and trousers, woollen leggings, fur caps and mittens for winter; hemp linen canvas trousers for summer campaigns, sometimes made from old tents; checked linen shirts and overshirts for work.[5] Regimental clothing was modified to suit local conditions, especially alterations to hats and coats to make them lighter and more convenient.

Besides clothing, each soldier received a 'stand of arms' and three items of 'camp equipage,' all property of the regiment. The stand of arms included a Land Pattern musket, a bayonet and scabbard, a waist belt with a frog to hold the bayonet, and a cartridge box that attached to the waist belt – a wooden block drilled to hold 18 cartridges in two rows, a leather flap to cover them, and leather belt loops nailed to the back. Regiments also procured cartridge pouches, leather boxes worn on a strap over the left shoulder with a wooden block inside, drilled to hold, typically, 26 to 32 cartridges in three rows; space underneath the block allowed carrying flints, tools, cleaning rags and other items.[6] The leather pouch flap was sometimes decorated by a brass plate bearing the regiment's number or the royal cipher.[7]

4 Some military textbooks contained extensive instructions for maintaining old clothing. See, for example, Cuthbertson, *System*,

5 'Caps, Capots, and Corduroy: European Troops Prepare for the Canadian Winter,' *The Brigade Dispatch* Vol. 30 No. 4 (Winter 2000), pp.13–15. For the 1778 campaign, the army in New York received a hemp canvas called Russia duck from which to make breeches. TNA: WO 4/274: p.9. For using old tents to make trousers, see: Lloyd W. Smith Collection, Morristown National Historical Park: orderly book of the Royal Regiment of Artillery, regimental orders, 7 March 1777; and LOC: George Washington Papers: examination of Joseph Driver, 33rd Regiment, 16 April 1777.

6 One design had a block with either 26 or 29 holes arranged in three rows, 9-8-9 or 10-9-10; an example from the 50th Regiment is in the National Army Museum, London. Another common design had a block with two rows of 8 holes on the top, and two additional rows of 8 holes on the bottom, for a total of 32; when the top 16 rounds were used, the block could be flipped over to access the remaining rounds. An example is described in 'A Revolutionary War British Cartridge Box,' William L. Brown III and Walter H. Bradford, *Military Collector & Historian* Vol. 38 (Spring 1986) pp.35–39. A variation of this type is called the Rawle Patent after London accouterment contractor William Rawle, but the style was in use before Rawle patented specific improvements to it.

7 For examples of pouch ornaments specific to grenadier and light infantry companies, see Don Troiani, et al., *Insignia of Independence: Military Buttons, Accoutrement Plates & Gorgets of the American Revolution* (Gettysburg, PA: Thomas Publications, 2012).

Each year the war office sent camp equipage to America for the campaign season consisting of a tent, kettle, and hatchet for every five men and a haversack and canteen for each man. These latter items transported food and drink on a march, but were not part of the uniform worn on duty. Knapsacks and blankets were included some years, such that each soldier, ideally, had one of each. [8] The knapsack held shirts, stockings and shoes, as well as pipe clay for cleaning white leather belts and white clothing, blackball for polishing shoes and pouches, brushes, combs, hair powder, spare soles and heels, and other items. Tin canteens were used almost exclusively throughout the war, until replaced by wooden ones in 1782.[9]

8 See, for example, TNA: WO 34/203: Return of camp necessaries shipped aboard the Juliana and Grand Duke transports, 1 March 1779.

9 Gilbert V. Riddle, 'From Tin to Wood: A Change in Canteens for the British Army,' *The Brigade Dispatch* Vol.26, No.3, p.16.

Appendix II

Distinctions of the Grenadiers

Grenadiers were armed in the same way as other infantrymen, but the grenadier's uniform prescribed by Royal Warrant in 1768 retained trappings of his original role: a 12-inch tall brimless cap that allowed a musket to be quickly slung so that grenades could be thrown, a tubular brass match case to hold a smouldering length of match cord to light grenade fuses (purely ornamental by the 1770s), and a lace-trimmed crescent of cloth on each shoulder called a wing, symbolic of grenadiers forming on the wing or flank of a regiment.[1] Caps were covered with black bearskin – a couple of regiments are believed to have used white instead – and featured a japanned tin front plate stamped with a royal crest and the motto *nec aspera terrant*, 'hardships do not deter us.'[2] Although not prescribed by the clothing warrant, each grenadier received the same cocked hat as other infantry soldiers, which appears to have been worn much of the time in favour of the expensive fur caps.[3] Grenadier officers and sergeants carried lightweight firelocks (muskets) – fusils for officers, specially-designed fusils for sergeants – instead of espontoons and halberds used by other company officers. Carrying firelocks meant slinging an ammunition pouch and bayonet scabbard, necessitating an epaulet on each shoulder to hold two shoulder belts instead of the single epaulet that held battalion officers' sword slings. As of the end of 1768, grenadiers were the only infantry private soldiers to carry swords.[4]

On service in America many of these things changed. Most notably, when men were transferred from the battalion to a grenadier company, clothing may not have been altered immediately to their new company's standard, if it was altered at all. Drafts from infantry and cavalry regiments may have continued to wear the clothing of their old regiment for up to a year after joining a new grenadier company.

1 TNA: WO 30/13B: 'His Majesty's Warrant,' 19 December 1768.

2 The 40th Regiment's grenadier caps were 'edged with white fur' in 1768. TNA: WO 27/15: inspection return, 40th Regiment, May 1768.

3 See, for example, TNA: T 14: 'Clothing for 17th Regt of Foot to be landed in Ireland duty free,' 22 July 1773, p.114, and 'Clothing for Sir Eyre Cootes Regt to be landed in Ireland duty free,' 15 August 1774, p.142.

4 TNA: WO 30/13B: 'His Majesty's Warrant,' 19 December 1768. Some authors call the sergeants' weapons carbines, but period sources use the term fusil. Hagist and Goldstein, 'Short Land Muskets for the British Light Infantry in America,' pp.18–25.

Grenadiers in Boston, 1775-1776

- Major John Pitcairn, commanding the battalion of Marines in Boston, wrote in December 1774, 'I have also beg'd [Lord Sandwich] to send us Caps for the Grenadiers, Light Infantry and Drummers. You can easily send us Grenadier Caps by the first ships. Light Infantry Caps must be bespoke as there are none at either of the Divisions; will you also mention swords for the Grenadiers and Drummers, the last have nothing to defend themselves but their Drumsticks.' An unidentified Marines grenadier wrote of the fighting on 19 April 1775, 'I had my hat shot off my head three times,' indicating that the Marines were not wearing grenadier caps if they had them at all.[5]
- The 10th and 38th Regiments' grenadier companies reported losing a few swords and sword scabbards on 19 April 1775, and the 38th lost three match cases; no other companies reported losses of these items.[6]
- Lieutenant Martin Hunter wrote that Captain Andrew Neilson of the 52nd's grenadier company at Bunker Hill, 'received a shot right through the head, and I was told that he had his hat off cheering his Grenadiers on into action when he received the shot.'[7]
- Lieutenant Francis, Lord Rawdon of the 5th's grenadiers wrote of the Battle of Bunker Hill, 'a ball passed through a close cap which I had made in imitation of the foreign travelling caps, and wore for convenience sake, for we no longer think of appearances at

A grenadier wearing a cocked hat, identifiable by the wings on the shoulders of his coat, sketched by Philip James de Loutherbourg in England, 1778. (Anne S.K. Brown Military Collection)

5 British Library (BL): add. Mss. 39190: John Pitcairn to Colonel Mackenzie in London, 28 December 1774; 'Extract from an Intercepted Letter of the Soldiery in Boston,' Peter Force (ed.), *American Archives* (Washington, DC: M. St. Clair Clarke and Peter Force, 1839), Series Four, Vol.2, p.440.

6 TNA: WO 36/3: 'return of the Arms & Accoutrements of the following Corps, Lost, and Broke, on the 19th April 1775'.

7 Hunter, *Journal*, p.11.

present.' Martin Hunter wrote, 'Lord Rawdon … received a shot through a cat-skin cap that he wore that day, and desired me to observe how narrowly he had escaped being shot through the head.'[8]

- The 5th Regiment's commanding officer prepared a list of deficiencies in the regiment's clothing that arrived in Boston in late 1775, including, 'The Light Infantry & Grenadier Wings too Short and Narrow'; missing from the clothing was 'Green Cloth to make Grenades for the Grendrs Coat Skirts,' the small decorations on the corners of the turnbacks.[9]
- In October 1775 Captain William Glanville Evelyn wrote from Bunker Hill that a cannon ball 'went through one of our tents, and fairly took the crown out of one of the King's Own Grenadier's hats. His head was not in it.'[10]
- On 28 February 1776 the commander of the grenadier battalion in Boston gave this order: 'Commanding Officers of companies are desired to compleat their men with slings for their greatcoats & according to the pattern of their own Corps.'[11]
- Two early 1776 returns of equipment belonging to the 55th Regiment, which arrived in Boston late in 1775, include 39 grenadier swords and 41 grenadier match cases.[12]

Grenadier battalions in General William Howe's army, May 1776–June 1777

- The 54th Regiment, which embarked for America in early 1776, did not take grenadier swords or match cases to America, according to their 1784 inspection report.[13]
- At a trial on Staten Island in July 1776, a witness testified to recognizing that soldiers of the 46th Regiment were grenadiers 'from the wings on their coats, and their size.'[14]
- At a trial on Long Island in late August 1776, a witness described a grenadier of the 57th Regiment as wearing a white waistcoat and breeches.[15]
- In November 1782 an officer of the 71st Regiment wrote that 'Our Grenadier and Light Infantry Caps are all lost.' He did not say when they were lost; they may have been captured at sea with other equipment in 1776, or later in the war.[16]
- Captain William Harris of the 5th's grenadiers wrote of the Battle of Harlem Heights on 16 September 1776, 'a man of my company had his hat shot through nearly in the direction of my wound; but the ball merely raised the skin.'[17]

---

8 Francis Bickley (ed.), *Report on the Manuscripts of the late Reginald Rawdon Hastings, Esq.* (London: Historical Manuscripts Commission, 1934), p.155; Hunter, *Journal*, p.11.

9 Alnwick Castle, Northumberland , Mss. of the Duke of Northumberland, Volume 150: Letters & Papers of the Percy Family, July 1774 – December 1776, American War, No. 50, 23/3: 'Return of the Deficiencies in the Cloathing of the 5th Regimt of Foot for 1775.'

10 Evelyn, *Letters*, p.70.

11 LOC: Orderly book of Captain John Hatfield: battalion orders, 23 February 1776.

12 BC: James Grant Papers: 'Return of the State & Condition of the Accoutrements of His Majesty's 55th Regiment of Foot,' 10 January and 15 May 1776.

13 TNA: WO 27/52: inspection return, 54th Regiment, 7 July 1784.

14 TNA: WO 71/82: trial of John Riely, pp.388–402.

15 TNA: WO 71/82: trial of John Dunn and John Lusty, pp.405–425.

16 TNA: WO 72/10: Simon Fraser to Thomas Stirling, November 1782.

17 Wilkin, *Some British Soldiers*, p.186.

- Captain John Peebles of the 42nd, in the 3rd Battalion of Grenadiers, wrote upon arrival off Rhode Island on 7 December 1776, 'received orders to be ready to land at day break caps on.'[18]
- In December 1776 General Howe wrote to General James Grant, 'Pray make my Compliments to Lieut. Bunbury of ye 49th Grendrs. I have got a Fusee here made after ye pattern of those in ye Company, which I beg to present to him to replace that he lost at Boston.'[19]
- Lieutenant David Howell said that, at the Battle of Princeton on 3 January 1777, Captain John Hatfield of the 43rd's grenadiers 'waved his hat' to get the attention of a detachment of dismounted dragoons. Cornet Henry Evatt referred to Hatfield as 'an officer with white facings,' indicating that Hatfield wore a regimental coat that day.[20]
- The 3rd Battalion of Grenadiers put their heavy baggage ashore in New York on 10 February 1777 after returning from Rhode Island; they then went to New Jersey, and on 22 February Lieutenant Peebles of the 42nd's grenadiers 'sent to New York for our Grenadier Caps & some other articles.'[21]

Grenadier battalion in Canada, May 1776 – October 1777

- In July 1776, Lieutenant William Digby of the 53rd's grenadiers wrote, 'we all went as thinly clothed as possible, wearing large loose trousers to prevent the bite of the moscheto, a small fly which was then very troublesome.'

Grenadier battalions in General William Howe's army, August – December 1777

- Lieutenant William Hale of the 45th Regiment's grenadiers wrote that during the Battle of Brandywine, 'the grenadiers put on their Caps and struck up their march.'[22]
- A sketch by Lieutenant Richard St George Mansergh St George of the 52nd Regiment depicts Captain John West of the 4th Regiment in the same style of jacket that he rendered in several sketches of light infantry during the 1777 Philadelphia campaign – snug-fitting red single-breasted jackets extending only to the waist, cuffs and collars in the colors of each regiments' lapels, shoulder wings, and no lapels. He wears brown linen trousers with the legs tucked into spatterdashes; the billowy fit is typical of linen that has been worn for a long time without washing.[23]
- Lieutenant William Hale of the 45th's grenadiers wrote from Philadelphia in January 1778, after over four months on campaign, 'My jacket (an old coat turned) cannot now be resembled to any earthly clothing; transparent as that of the inhabitants of light.' On 5 June, preparing for the next campaign, he wrote what appears to refer to his garb from the time he joined the grenadier battalion at the beginning of 1777: 'two coats have

18 Gruber (ed.), *Diary*, p.70.
19 BC: James Grant Papers: William Howe to James Grant, 23 December 1776.
20 TNA: WO 71/87: trial of Henry Evatt, pp.343–361.
21 Gruber (ed.), *Diary*, pp.88, 95.
22 Wilkin, *Some British Soldiers*, p.231.
23 'My triumphal entry into Philadelphia,' colored drawing by Richard St George Mansergh St George, Harlan Crow Library.

constituted the whole of my wardrobe'; one of these presumably became the jacket he wore in the autumn 1777 campaign.

Grenadier battalions in General Sir Henry Clinton's army, June – October 1778

- To replace equipment captured in 1775, in summer 1777 the colonel of the 7th Regiment purchased, among other things, 3 each of 'grenadier serjeants pouches & boxes with tutenage ornaments,' 'buff should belts,' 'cross belts & tutenage plates engraved,' 'fuzee slings,' 'tutenage match cases,' 'matches & tutenage rings,'; and 56 each of 'grenadier pouches & boxes with ornaments,' 'buff shoulder belts,' 'waistbelts & plates engraved in a cypher,' 'match cases,' 'matches & rings.'[24]
- Lieutenant William Hale of the 45th's grenadiers wrote from Philadelphia in early June 1778: 'I purchased a coat which is now turned and made into a jacket for the campaign at present on my back,' and suggested that he had a new regimental coat made in Philadelphia: 'the cloth you sent me, arrived time enough to be worn about a dozen times, with the addition of another epaulet (2–15–0) and is now deposited in my chest.' After returning to England that year, he wrote on 2 December, 'To say the truth I have but one coat and an old campaign jacket.'[25]
- In July 1778 in New York, Lieutenant Hale purchased fabric for 'two pairs of waistcoats and trowsers of brown linen.'[26]
- At a trial of Lieutenant Robert Jackson of the 57th's grenadiers, several witnesses mentioned Jackson wearing a hat in camp on 6 October 1778.[27]

Grenadier battalion in New York, November 1778 – December 1779

- An artillery officer attached to the grenadiers wrote on 12 December 1778, 'The Light Infantry wear a green feather in their Caps & we the Grenadiers a White one in our Hatts.'[28]
- Captain Peebles of the 42nd's grenadiers 'went to New York to look at the Companys Caps' on 24 March 1779, but discovered them 'almost all spoil'd by putting salt on them last year at Philadelphia,' indicating that they had been in storage since early 1778 at least. He also described purchasing 'stuff' to make 'summer trousers' for his company in March 1779, which were ready to wear in May and 'beginning to go already' in August. That November he wrote, 'the taylors at work on brown cloth trousers.'[29]
- On 14 December 1779 the 1st Battalion of Grenadiers received '6 Serviceable Light Infantry Carbines,' presumably for sergeants.[30]

24 Berkshire Record Office (BRO): D-ED O37 part 1: Trotter & Macintosh, Lord Robert Bertie's Vouchers, 'Messrs Ross and Gray for the 7th Regiment Foot. Tutenage is a copper-brass alloy.
25 Wilkin, *Some British Soldiers*, pp.234, 253–254, 257, 270.
26 Wilkin, *Some British Soldiers*, p.264.
27 TNA: WO 71/87: trial of Robert Jackson, pp.362–384.
28 NAM: 6807-154: Francis Laye letters.
29 Gruber (ed.), *Diary*, pp.252, 258, 289.
30 WLC: Henry Clinton Papers: Vol. 155:7.

Grenadier battalions in New York, June 1780 – November 1783

- A German general wrote in November 1780 that the General Clinton 'expressed the wish some time ago that the Hessian grenadier brigade might have white plumes like the English, as the same is necessary as a distinguishing token in a battle or in the army on the whole.'[31]
- In March 1781 Lieutenant Colonel Henry Hope directed the 2nd Battalion of Grenadiers to wear 'linen breeches and black cloth gaiters' during summer. In November Captain Peebles purchased 'grey cloth for trousers' for the 42nd's grenadiers.[32]
- In June 1783 an officer of the 71st's grenadiers purchased 103 ½ yards of 'sheeting' for 60 pair of trousers, and '39 white feathers' for his company. The same receipt includes '185 ostrich feathers,' ornaments typical of highland regiments.[33]

31 Lidgerwood Collection of Hessian Transcripts, Morristown National Historical Park, NJ: Wilhelm von Knyphausen wrote Landgraf Friedrich II, 10 November 1780, Letter GG, pp.304–305.

32 Gruber (ed.), *Diary*, pp.431, 494.

33 NRS: GD153/1/5/5: necessaries for the Grenadier Company.

Appendix III

Distinctions of the Light Infantry

Light infantry companies became part of the regimental establishment in 1771; as such, their clothing was not prescribed by the 1768 clothing warrant. A board of general officers convened in 1771 'to consider the Cloathing & Accoutrements best adapted for the use of the Light Company belonging to each of the Marching Regiments of Foot on the British Establishment.'[1] They prescribed attributes that most regiments appear to have followed for most of the American Revolution years, but there were many exceptions as these new companies evolved.

The typical uniform differed from other companies in several ways: the coat was about three inches shorter with pocket flaps, horizontal for grenadiers and battalion soldiers, affixed vertically (these flaps on the outside of the coat were ornamental, but reinforced the body of the coat at the pocket opening inside the coat). Like grenadier coats, light infantry coats had wings on the shoulders denoting flank companies. The 1771 board of general officers prescribed red waistcoats with laced instead of plain buttonholes; they did not state the reason, but it may have been so sleeves could be affixed for use as jackets. The board prescribed spatterdashes – which they described as a gaiter 'up to the calf of the leg & no higher'; by 1774 all companies were wearing 'black spatterdashes according to order.'[2] The board recommended that 'accouterments be conformable to Col Howe's pattern, with a small cartridge box to contain 9 rounds in one row, to be worn before with a belt of tanned leather round the waist,' and 'the Belt to be furnished with 2 frogs, one for the bayonet, the other for the hatchet occasionally, which at other times will be tyed upon the knapsack.'[3]

In 1771, armouries sent 'two Sergeants' Fuzils' and 39 'New Short Arms for Light Infantry' to regiments in England and Scotland; regiments in Ireland received the same in 1772. Artifact examples prove that the fusils were of the same pattern authorized for grenadier sergeants in 1770, while the 'new short arms' were the 1769 land pattern firelocks issued universally in the 1770s and 1780s.[4]

The most distinctive and most varied feature of the light infantry uniform was the cap. Military author Thomas Simes in 1772 described 'black leather caps, with 3 chains round

1 TNA: WO 71/10: Report of a Committee of the Board of General Officers, ff.295–301.
2 See, for example, inspection returns of the 22nd and 24th Regiments, TNA: WO 27/32.
3 TNA: WO 71/10: Report of a Committee of the Board of General Officers, folio 297–279.
4 Hagist and Goldstein, 'Short Land Muskets for the British Light Infantry in America.'

Light infantryman sketched by Philip James de Loutherbourg in England, 1778, wearing the uniform recommended in the early 1770s. His coat has wings on the shoulders, and he carries a powder horn, a shot bag, and a tomahawk with a case is visible under his right forearm. Note the cap-hat made by altering a broad-brimmed felt hat. (Anne S.K. Brown Military Collection)

them, and a piece of plate upon the centre of the crown; in the front, G. R. a crown, and the number of the Regiment.'[5]

Some variations to these recommendations can be readily documented, others implied or inferred, and often it is not clear exactly how light infantry companies were clothed or whether different companies in a light infantry battalion were clothed uniformly. Only months after the board of general officers made recommendations, the Lord Lieutenant of Ireland advised making gaiters of 'course cloth, such as were worn in America,' apparently

5 Thomas Simes, *The Military Guide for Young Officers* (London: Millan, 1772), p.258.

referring to the French and Indian War.[6] Portraits of light infantry officers sometimes feature white waistcoats instead of red, and accoutrements with white or buff belts instead of the black usually used on 'tanned leather.'

Pre-war light infantry caps

- A newspaper account of the 23rd Regiment reviewed at Hyde Park mentioned the light infantry wearing 'leather caps.'[7]
- Two deserters from the 38th's light infantry wore 'caps fronted with bears-skin, a black band round the cap with white and red tossels.'[8]
- In summer 1771 the colonel of the 7th Regiment of Foot purchased 'accoutrements &c. for the Light Company' including 39 each of 'setts of waist belts, cartouch boxes, hatchet cases, frogs, powder horns & belts, ball bags & slings,' 'hatchets,' 'private caps & feathers,' three each of 'serjeants waist belts with running carriages & buckles,' 'cartouch boxes with brass ornaments,' serjeants caps with silver lace & tassels &c,' and one 'drummers cap with a white bear skin front, a drum embroider'd & a variegated feather.'[9]
- In February 1773 the colonel of the 7th Regiment purchased '40 Light Infantry Cap Hats Laced with Tape & Tape Bands,' '2 Light Infantry Serjts Cap Hats Laced with Silver & Silver Bands,' and 42 'Black Ostrich Plumes'; the terms 'cap hats' and the pricing of 2s 9d each indicates that these were felt caps.[10]
- In July 1773 the 17th Regiment, in transit from Great Britain to Ireland, shipped '40 plain hats for the light company.'[11]
- In August 1774 the 37th Regiment, in transit from Great Britain to Ireland, shipped '40 private centinel Hatts for the light infantry, 2 serjeants Hatts for ditto.'[12]

Light Infantry in Boston, 1775–1776

- A powder horn taken from a dead British soldier on 19 April 1775 was described as 'quite a nice piece of work, and held just one pound of powder. It had a peculiar stopper; and at the large end, on the under side, was engraved the English coat-of-arms, and on the upper side what they called the British ensign. The bottom of the horn was made of brass, saucer-shaped, with a hole half an inch in diameter in the centre serving as a tunnel to pour in the powder, with a wooden stopper.'[13]

---

6 TNA: SP 63/434: George Townsend to Lord Rochford.
7 *Kentish Gazette*, 18 June 1771.
8 *Newcastle Courant*, 4 April 1772.
9 BRO: D-ED O38 Vol. 1: Lord Robert Bertie to John Hume, 7 February 1772.
10 BRO: D-ED O38 Vol. 2: 'Hats deliver'd for the 7th Regt of Foot,' 26 February 1773.
11 TNA: T 14: 'Clothing for 17th Regt of Foot to be landed in Ireland duty free,' 22 July 1773, p.114.
12 TNA: T 14: 'Clothing for Sir Eyre Cootes Regt to be landed in Ireland duty free,'15 August 1774, p.142.
13 Abram English Brown, *Beneath Old Roof Trees* (Boston: Lee and Shepard, 1896), p.297. The description was given to the author by a descendant of the man who took the horn. The author added a parenthetical phrase that the stopper was 'probably a spring snapper like some now known.'

- The 22nd Regiment purchased '42 small Hats and Looping for the Light Infantry Company' before embarking for Boston[14]
- New clothing received by the 55th Regiment included '2 sergeants laced caps' and '40 private laced cap hats,' as well as similar quantities of 'waist coat fronts red cloth' and 'jackets' for sergeants, privates and drummers. For one drummer, there was a 'drummer's jacket' and 'drummers waist coat green cloth', in keeping with the typical practice of reversing colours for drummers. The date of shipment and receipt is not specified, but quantities reflect the 1775 company strength.[15]

Light Infantry battalions in General William Howe's army, May 1776–June 1777

- In Halifax in May 1776, the 55th's light infantry had 41 each of caps, powder horns, horn slings, shot bags, and 39 tomahawks; they were 'wanting' three 'light infantry swords' for sergeants.[16]
- A return of accoutrements lost between 1 January 1776 and 24 May 1778 includes shot bags, cartouch boxes and powder horns (15 each for the 10th Regiment; 38 each for the 15th; 27 each for the 28th; 41 each for the 37th; 39 shot bags, 22 cartouch boxes and 37 powder horns for the 46th; 29 each for the 55th); the cartouch boxes are presumed to be for light infantry because numbers are the same as shot bags and powder horns.[17]
- On Staten Island in June 1776, light infantry battalions were directed to send for loose powder to fill horns.[18]
- In August, general orders read: 'Forty Cartridge Boxes, containing 18 Rounds of Ball Cartridge each, to be delivered from the Artillery to Major Johnson, for the use of the Light Company of 28th Regiment.'[19]
- Captain James Murray of the 57th Regiment, preparing to sail for America, wrote, 'being appointed to the Light Infantry I have got a double barrel fusee.'[20]
- The day before the Battle of Long Island on 27 August 1776, an American observer wrote, 'many of the regulars are in rifle dress'; in the days after the battle one American officers wrote, 'Several Companies of their Light Infantry are cloathed exactly as we are, in hunting shirts and trowers,' presumably meaning 'trousers'; another wrote, 'I discovered as I thought, our battalion on a hill coming in, dressed in hunting shirts, and was going to join them, but was stopped by a number of our soldiers, who told me they were the enemy in our dress.' It is not clear that they referred to British light infantry (one

14 LBA: Cox & Company Accounts: Agent's Ledgers, 22nd Regiment of Foot. The payment for these hats was in 1776; payments recorded in the ledgers are typically a year or two after equipment was obtained.

15 BC: James Grant Papers: 'For Cloathing Supplied to the 55th Regiment'. This receipt is dated 1777 but is clearly for clothing delivered before that year.

16 BC: James Grant Papers: 'Return of the State & Condition of the Accoutrements of His Majesty's 55th Regiment of Foot'.

17 WLC: Frederick Mackenzie papers: vol. 1 folio 1, 'Return of Accoutrements lost in Action by Desertion & by Accidents by the following Corps fm 1st Jany 76 to 24th May 1778'.

18 TNA: WO 36/5: general orders, 30 June 1776.

19 TNA: WO 36/5: general orders, 11 August 1776.

20 Robson (ed.), *Letters*, p.29.

passage follows a sentence about German riflemen), and no British source corroborates British light infantry companies wearing this type of clothing.[21]

Light Infantry battalion in Canada, May 1776 – October 1777

- A 1781 inventory of clothing left in Canada by regiments captured at Saratoga includes 'hat caps' for the 9th and 24th Regiments and 'light infantry wire bound caps' for the 21st Regiment.[22] These were left in Canada, indicating that light infantry companies wore similar caps to those of battalion companies on this campaign.

Light Infantry battalions in General William Howe's army, August – December 1777

- Sketch by Lieutenant Richard St George Mansergh St George of the 52nd Regiment depict himself and soldiers in the 2nd Battalion of Light Infantry in snug-fitting red single-breasted jackets extending only to the waist, cuffs and collars in the colours of each regiments' lapels, shoulder wings, and no lapels. They wear brown linen trousers with the legs tucked into spatterdashes; the billowy fit is typical of linen that has been worn for a long time without washing.[23]
- On 16 September 1777, a British officer wrote, 'the Violence of the Rain was so lasting that it was afterwards known the Rebels had not a single Cartridge in their Pouches but was Wet, the Light Infantry Accoutrements being mostly Rebel were in the same Situation.' No other British source corroborates British light infantry using captured accoutrements.[24]
- A newspaper advertisement offered a reward for 'A handsome silver-mounted Fusee marked on the thumb-piece 15th light infantry and the stock was broke a little about the muzzle.'[25]

Light Infantry battalions in General Sir Henry Clinton's army, June – October 1778

- New York hatter Peter Lynch advertised 'Light-Infantry caps of all sorts.'[26]
- To replace equipment captured in 1775, in summer 1777 the colonel of the 7th Regiment purchased, among other things, three each of 'light infantry serjeants pouches with tutenage ornaments,' 'buff should belts,' 'cross belts & tutenage plates engraved,' 'fuzee slings,' 'horns mounted with brass,'; and 56 each of 'light infantry pouches & boxes with

21 'New York, August 26, 1776,' *Freeman's Journal* (Portsmouth, NH), 7 September 1776; Henry P. Johnston, *The Campaign of 1776 Around New York and Brooklyn* (Brooklyn: Long Island Historical Society, 1878), p.50; 'Extract of a letter from Long Island, 28 August 1776,' in Peter Force (ed.), *American Archives* (Washington, DC: M. St. Clair and Peter Force, 1848), Series Five, Vol.1, p.1195.

22 TNA: WO 1/11: pp.478, 480.

23 Coloured drawings by Richard St George Mansergh St George, Harlan Crow Library; paintings of the battles of Paoli and Germantown by Xavier della Gatta, Museum of the American Revolution, Philadelphia.

24 APSL: Sol Feinstone Collection No. 409: Anonymous British Journal, 1776–78.

25 *Pennsylvania Ledger*, 3 December 1777.

26 *Royal Gazette* (New York), 9 May 1778.

ornaments on the flaps,' 'buff shoulder belts,' 'cross belts & plates engraved with hatchett cases bullet bags & bayonet carriages,' 'neat polished hatchetts,' 'horns mounted with brass & box spring chargers.'; also '3 serjeants light infantry caps, silver orris bands bound with silk' and 32 'private light infantry caps, bound black & tape.'[27]

- The 22nd Regiment purchased three 'Light Infantry Scymeters,' presumably for the company's officers, from London swordsmith James Cullum; the purchase was ordered by Lieutenant Colonel John Campbell, who resigned in October 1778, but payment was made in March 1779, so it is not clear when these 'scymeters' were used in America.[28]

Light Infantry battalion in the West Indies, December 1778

- An unidentified officer wrote a memorandum titled 'Light infantry soldiers necessaries – West Indies.' It read: 'Sleeves of the jacket sewed to the waistcoat; shell laid aside. One or two pockets in the waistcoat below the breast. Linen trowser and socks. One pair trowsers died uniform; two, or three pair socks; 2 flannel shirts; 1 pair drawers ditto. 1 pair shoes off 1 on in a bag rolled in blanket, carried up and down: if across men cannot get through thickets. Haversack for provisions; tomahawk; camp kettle for each mess.'[29]
- Captain Colin Lindsay of the 55th Regiment wrote of a fellow officer, 'The coat he happened to have on was not exactly new, nor was the appearance of it probably the better for the soaking it had had for many days and nights. He wore no shoulder-knot, it being often the custom of our light-infantry officers to wear, instead of them, a sort of fringe called wings.'[30]
- Lieutenant William Robertson of the 55th Regiment wrote that he landed on St Lucia 'without proper Clothing having on only a Waist Coat with sleeves (such as the LI wear) with a pair of Trousers.'[31]

Light Infantry battalion in New York, November 1778 – December 1779

- An artillery officer attached to the grenadiers wrote on 12 December 1778, 'The Light Infantry wear a green feather in their Caps & we the Grenadiers a White one in our Hatts.'[32]
- The captain of the 37th's light infantry kept a ledger of purchases including 'moulds for the caps,' 'hair for the caps,' '4 pieces yellow binding,' '50 green feathers,' 'to Watson for working the hair for the caps,' 'to the hatter for dying the hair,' 'to making the companys caps,' 'paint and oyl for the haversacks,' 'painting 54 haversacks,' 'making 50 haversacks,' and 'making 40 pair trowsers.' Also mentioned are leggings and breeches.[33]

27 BRO: D-ED O37 part 1: 'Messrs Ross and Gray for the 7th Regiment Foot' from Trotter & Macintosh,' and 'Bought of J. Burgess Hatter, Hosier & Glover,' 20 March 1777.
28 LBA: Cox & Company Accounts: Agent's Ledgers, 22nd Regiment of Foot.
29 APSL: Sol Feinstone Collection No. 111: this is written on the reverse of 'Memo battle of Brandiwine. 11t Sepr 1777.'
30 Lindsay, 'Narrative,' p.348.
31 NRS: GD 132/774/3: William Robertson to James Robertson, 29 February 1780.
32 NAM: 6807-154: Francis Laye letters.
33 WLC: 6912/14-40: Eyre Coote Orderly Book.

- The light infantry battalion paraded for inspection on 19 November 1779 'with tin boxes to be left behind'[34]
- An officer sent a wooden canteen to the War Office in England, 'which sort are universally esteem'd by the Army here as far superior to the tin ones send from England,' noting, 'The Flank Companies of the 70th Regt are already furnished with a similar sort to the model, (at the General's expense) ... a narrow black leather strap, nearly an inch broad with a small buckle, will be necessary for each canteen.'[35]
- Light infantry battalions received '47 serviceable shortland musquets' on 8 December 1779, apparently as replacements.[36]

Light Infantry battalions in New York, June 1780 - March 1781

- The commander of the 1st Battalion of Light Infantry ordered inspection of 'the tin boxes of the light infantry' on 30 September 1780.[37]
- For an inspection on 22 November 1780 the light infantry were to appear in breeches and gaiters.[38]

Light Infantry battalions in Virginia, April - October 1781

- On 8 March the two light infantry battalions received orders for 'the taylors to be kept constantly at work in order that the soldiers may be completed with trowsers.'[39]
- On 13 April the light infantry officers were directed to 'only carry their canteens, bear skins and what they usually carry on campaign' when embarking for an expedition.[40]
- On 19 April the light infantry marched 'in their trowsers, carrying their breeches and leggings with them.'[41]

34 WLC: 6912/14-41, Eyre Coote Orderly Book.
35 TNA: WO 34/119: B. J. Johnson to 'Mr. Elwin,' 10 October 1779, p.85.
36 WLC: Henry Clinton Papers: Vol. 155:7.
37 WLC: 6912/14-42: Eyre Coote Orderly Book.
38 WLC: 6912/14-43: Eyre Coote Orderly Book.
39 WLC: 6912/14-43: Eyre Coote Orderly Book.
40 WLC: 6912/14-43: Eyre Coote Orderly Book.
41 WLC: 6912/14-43: Eyre Coote Orderly Book.

Appendix IV

Rules and Orders for the Discipline of the Light Infantry Companies in His Majesty's Army in Ireland, 1772

Soon after light infantry companies were added to the strength of British infantry regiments, the Lord Lieutenant of Ireland distributed 'rules and orders' for them. This version was published in 1894; no manuscript copy is known to exist.[1]

The Light Infantry Companies are always to be drawn up two Deep with a space of Two Feet between the Files. Marching in a Wood upon any Service of a Secret Nature, they are to be taught to lower their arms in two motions and carry them in a diagonal Position, with the hands on the swell of the firelock; and they are to shoulder in three Motions. They are to perform all Evolutions by Files and never to wheel any part of the Circle by Platoons or subdivisions much less by a larger Body. When marching through a Wood or any Strong Country by Files and ordered to form a Front to the Left, the Right Hand File is to face to the Left and the others to run up briskly and dress by it, If to form a Front to the Right the Right Hand File is to face to the Right, and the other Files are to form briskly to the Right of it; and then the Rear Rank of the Detachment becomes the Front, when a few files are formed the Commanding Officer is to order an Irregular Fire to begin, and to Continue untill the signal shall be given for Ceasing. It is to be particularly observed that each file has an entire dependence upon itself and that the Firelocks of the front and rear Men, are never to be unloaded at the same time, When the front Rank Man Fires, the Rear Rank Man is to make Ready and step up briskly before his Comrade, but is by no means to discharge his Firelock untill the other has loaded, and then he is to step briskly before the Rear Rank Man, and this method to be followed untill a signal shall be given for ceasing to Fire. This Mutual Defence and Confidence is one of the most Essential Principles of Light Infantry. The Men when in a Wood are to be taught to Cover themselves with Trees by placing the Right Foot about six inches behind the left, and presenting to the Right of the Tree, and after Firing to step back two paces, and give Room to the Rear Rank man to come up to the same Tree and to fire alternately, according to the directions before mentioned. All Officers Commanding

1 R.H.R. Smythies, *Historical Records of the 40th (2nd Somersetshire) Regiment*, pp.549–552.

Companies, or any body of Light Infantry, are to fix upon signals for extending their Front to the Right or to the Left, or to both Flanks, or to Close to the Centre, to retire, or to advance, and these signals must be made by a loud whistle, a posting horn, or some other instrument capable of conveying a sufficient sound to be heard at a considerable Distance, and the stoutest of the Drummers is to be taught to sound these instruments by directions from the Commanding Officer, who is to give the strictest Orders to the Men to be silent and attentive without which it is scarce possible that any action in a wood can be successful.

Tho' the posting of guards depends upon the ground yet in general, Officers who command Light Infantry, must never place their outposts at too great a distance from the Main Body. If it should be necessary to occupy an height, which Commands the Country, Care must be taken to post other guards near to the most advanced, which may Aid its retreat.

When a Corps of Light Infantry is composed of Companies from different Regiments they must do Duty by Companies with their own officers, and as double Centries are always to be posted, the file must mount together; to be relieved every hour Messes are to consist of a Non-Commissioned officer and three File and where it is necessary to detach a Corporal's Command the Men are to go together.

The Light Infantry must also be taught to take Advantage of large stones, broken Inclosures, old Houses, or any strong feature which presents itself upon the face of a Country. But they must take particular Care not to run in Crowds to these objects.

When a Corps of Light Infantry shall be employed in this Kingdom a small Waggon loaded with Intrenching Tools will be Ordered to attend it, and the officers are therefore to make themselves acquainted with the usual Method of Constructing Redans, Square Redoubts, and other parts of Field Fortification, likewise the Manner of felling and Freizing Trees for making abattis D'Arbres and to turn their Thoughts upon fortifying Church Yards and making Creneaus in Houses.

When there is appearance of service the Men must be instructed in the Use of the Intrenching Tools and to make Fascines and Gabeons of different sizes.

The Light Infantry must be Carefull not to fall into Ambuscades when they are marching through a Wood or any inclosed Country and Care must be taken to Advance a Guard, and to detach flanking parties The flanking parties to March in front and the Files to move at the distance of ten yards from each other, when either of these parties shall discover an Enemy, They are not to run into the Main Body, but to take posts immediately and begin an attack according to the directions before mentioned, and the Commanding Officer is to form his Detachment to the flank that is Attacked and to support his party by sending a few Men under the command of a Subaltern Officer, and to repeat this reinforcement as frequently as the Exigency of the Case may require. He is also to be very Carefull that the Men do not Crowd, and that the Enemy do not turn his flank, when there is any likelihood of that being the Case he must order a Signal to be Sounded for extending the Front. If he should Command a Considerable Corps he should keep a small Reserve disengaged as long as possible.

The success of any Engagement in a Wood or Strong Country depends upon the Coolness and presence of Mind of the Commanding Officer, and the Silence and Obedience of the Men fully as much as upon their Bravery.

The Light Infantry are to be taught to fire at Marks, and each Soldier is to find out the proper Measure of Powder for his own Firelock and to make up his Cartridges accordingly.

The Arms of every Soldier should be always be kept in good Order, But the Light Infantry Man, in particular, must not neglect his Arms, his Ammunition or throw away his Fire, as his Existence may depend upon a Single Shot's taking place. The Light Infantry must consider that the Service upon which they are likely to be Employed, is very different from that of heavy Troops. The former being always to Engage in open Order and the Attack may frequently become personal between Man and Man, It is therefore necessary to be particular in selecting Men for this Service not only of Activity and Bodyly Strength but also of some Experience and approved Spirit.

Each man must have a sufficient Number of Cartridges made up, But as it may be necessary to have recourse to the Horn, The Men are to be taught to load from it. Every part of the Accoutrements must be kept in Constant repair, the Tomahawks Sharp, and fit for Use. The Hatchet Men of the Light Infantry Companies must be able Active Men and they should know how to Make Use of their Axes. When a considerable Corps of Light Infantry is to march through a Wood or inclosed Country that can admit of it, The Commanding Officer may Order it to move from the Right or Left of Companies by Files the Companies are then to March in parallel Lines, but the flanking Companies must march in Front and form flanking Parties.

An Officer Commanding a Corps of Light Infantry and marching thro' an open Country may shorten his line of March, or move them in whatever manner he may think best.

Should any of the Enemy's Cavalry appear near a Corps of Light Infantry they must endeavour to retire to a Wood or some Strong Ground, in good Order and with a firm Countenance. But if that cannot be effected they must disperse by Files, at Considerable distances from one another, fix their bayonets, take great Care not to throw away their Fire untill they are shure that a shot shall take place, still endeavouring to gain a Hedge, Broken House, Ravin, Wood or large Stone, Cavalry seldom attacks Infantry in this dispersed situation if Men are resolute and determined not to throw away their Fire, and the files are attentive to the directions before given. The Light Infantry Companies are to practice Marching very frequently in quarters.

Besides what is before directed the Light Infantry Companies are to be instructed in the manual and every other Evolution which the Battalion may be ordered to perform.

And Officers Commanding Regiments may employ the Light Infantry Companies in the manner which shall appear to them most proper, for the safety and protection of the Battalion whether upon a March or in the Field. And We do hereby direct and require the Commander in Chief of His Majesty's Forces in this Kingdom to cause these Rules and Orders to be duly observed and executed and he is to direct the Adjutant General to send Copies thereof to the General Officers upon the Staff and to the commanding Officer of every Regiment of Foot upon this establishment.

Given &c. the 15th Day of May 1772

George Macartney

Appendix V

Discipline established by Major General Howe for Light Infantry in Battalion, Sarum September 1774

Major General William Howe trained light infantry companies from seven regiments to operate as a battalion in England in August and September 1774. These are the manoeuvres he taught, the first known set of manoeuvres for a composite battalion of light infantry companies.[1]

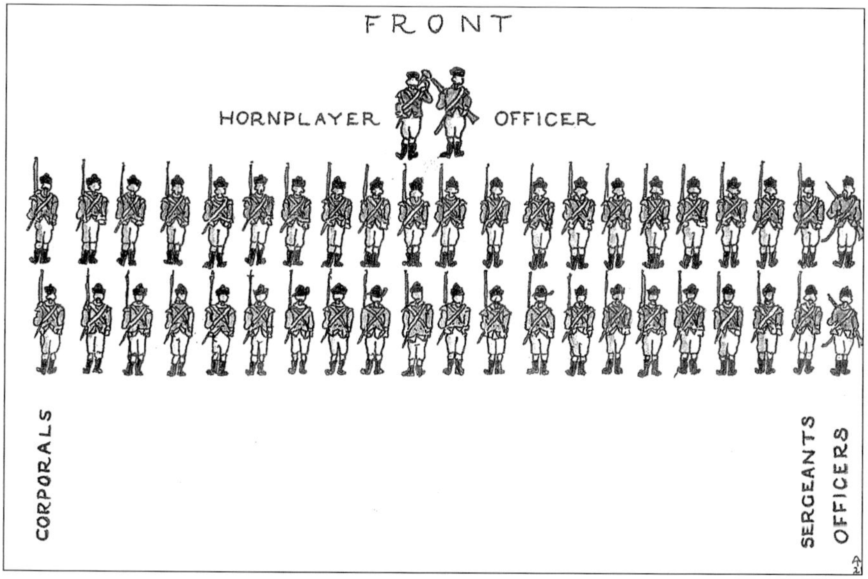

A light infantry company in General William Howe's army formed for battle, August 1776. At this time the established size of a company included three officers, three sergeants, three corporals, two drummers and 54 private soldiers, but most companies had only about 40 private men and one drummer. Often one or two of the officers, and sometimes one of the sergeants, had other duties or were otherwise indisposed. In light infantry companies, the drummer played a horn or bugle instead of the drum. There were no prescribed positions in the formation for the officers or horn man. In August 1776, most flank companies had recently received a few new men from their own regiment, and a few transfers from other regiments, meaning there was probably some variation in the uniforms – as we see here, with a few men in round hats while the majority wear caps. (Artwork by Alan Turton, © Helion and Company 2021)

1 NAM: 6807-157-6: Discipline established by Major General Howe for Light Infantry in Battalion, Sarum September 1774.

Words of Command	Explanation
Battalion form at order at open order at extended order	The files to be at two feet Interval at four feet Interval at ten feet Interval
To the Right or to the Left form the line of 'March,' 'March, March,' or 'Advance'	The whole faces as directed and the Men of the Rear ranks step to the Rear of their File leaders upon the word 'March & c.' and then the Column follows their leading officer as directed. NB: the Command 'March' signifies slow time, 'March, March' quick time, and 'Advance' run.
To the Front To the Right Form To the Left	If to the front when marching to the Right, the leading Company forms to the left of the leading file; the other Companys when the ground will admit (Advance) in File obliquely to the Left and form in their proper order as soon as the leading files halt in their places in Battalion. If to the Right when marching to the Right the Files run up and face to the Right, the order of Files and Company will then be reversed, what was before the left Company will become the Right. If to the left when marching by the Right the Files run up and Face to the Left.
Or Forward to the Right Form.	When marching by the Right; the leading File turns to the Right; the other Files form upon the Left of the first file, and so in successive order, until the whole is formed.
Or Forward to the Left Form.	When marching by the Right, the leading file turns to the Left, the other files form upon the Right, in this order the Front and Companys will be reversed as before.
Or (when marching by the Right) oblique to the Right, and to the Front form.	The first or leading file halts, the other files move in the shortest line and forms upon its Right, the other Companys march in file obliquely to the Right and form in the same order, which reverses the order of files and Companys. The same directions Vice Versa, marching from the Left.
From the Right or Left of Companys, Division, or Platoons, March &c.	The Companys face and lead to the front in file, as directed, in parallel directions the leading file does not face.
To the Front, Right, or Left Form	If to the Right when marching by the Right, the Captain of the Right Company orders his Company to form to the Right, the other Companys take the shortest line, and form on the Right of the Company as before mentioned. The same directions Vice Versa, if ordered to form to the Left, when marching by the Left, and the order of Files and Companys will be reversed.
Or Forward to the Right, or to the Left Form.	When marching by the Right, if ordered forward to the Right form, the Companys then form in their proper order, and so Vice Versa if marching by the Left.
From the Right or Left of Companys to the Center form the line of March.	The Center Company leads, followed by the other Companys alternately, the Left Company closing the Line.
Of Battalion to the Center form the line of March.	The Center files of the Battalion stands fast, the Companys upon the Right face to the Left, and those upon the Left to the Right, the rear rank men stepping into their places.
March, &c.	The Column proceeds.
To the Right & Left form	The files move briskly up and face outwards.

Words of Command	Explanation
Resume the Line of March.	The Wings Face and move as before.
To the Rear Form.	The two rear Companys wheel to the Right and Left and form to the Rear, the Companys of the Right Wing march in file from their Right flanks, taking the nearest line to form to the Left of the Rear Companys of that Wing, the Companys of the Left Wing march from their Left Flanks and form to the Right of the Rear Companys of that Wing; the Front Rank men in the Front.
Resume of the Line of March.	The Companys of the Right Wing (when faced to the rear) turn to their Right from their Right Flanks, and those of the Left Wing turn to the Left, from their Left Flanks, the two Flank Companys meeting in the Rear of the Center, the other Companys taking the nearest line to form the order of march as directed the Front Rank men lead.
Or to the Rear form the Line of March.	The Wings face and the Front Rank men lead at the word 'March &c.'
To the Front, Right or Left Form.	If to the Right, the Right Wing forms as before, the Companys of the left taking the shortest line in File to form in their proper order. The Right Wing doing the same if ordered to form to the Left, and the whole follows the same direction, when ordered to form to the Front.
From the Center of Companies to the Center form the line of March, March, March	At the word 'March, March' the Companies face to their own Centers, the two Center files of each Company excepted, the Rear Rank men stepping to the Rear of their File leaders, the Center Company leads the line followed by the other Companys alternately from the Right to Left, the Left Company of the Battalion closing the line of March.
To the Rear form.	The Rear Company wheels by Files to the left about and forms to the Rear, the Companys of the Left Wing wheel by files to the Left about, and form to the Right of the first formed Company. The Companys of the Right Wing wheel by files to the Right about, and form to the Left of the first formed Company.
Resume the Line of March.	The Companies form into Columns, from their Centers, the Left Company which is the leading Company, wheels to the Right about, the other Companys of the Left Wing doing the same, and those of the Right Wing wheel to the Left about and take up the order of March.
To the front or to the Front Company; and to the Right or to the Left form.	If to the Front, the leading Company forms; the next obliquing and dressing to it in Battalion; if to the Right the front Company forms as ordered, the Right Wing then forms to it, on its Right, the Left Wing forms on its Left. If to the Left, the Wings form on its Right and Left as before.
Or Form two Fronts.	The Companies of the Right Wing form to the Right, dressing to the Right of the Front or leading Company. The Companies of the Left Wing form to the Left, the most advanced Company covering the Rear of that which was the leading Company in Line of March, the other Companys of the Left Wing, dress to the Left of the first formed Company of that Wing.
Resume the line of March.	As before explained.

Words of Command	Explanation
To the Right or to the Left and to the Front form.	If to the Right and to the Front, the Right Wing form to the Right, and the Left to the Front. Vice Versa if to the Left and to the Front form.
Resume the Line of March.	As before explained.
Or Form Battalion.	The Flank Wing dresses by the Front Wing, already formed.
From the Center of Companys to the Right of to the Left form the Line of March.	The Companies (the two Center Files excepted) face to their own Centers, the Right of Left Company leads as directed followed in line by the other Companies.
To the Front, Right or Left Form.	As before explained.
Or Forward to the Right or to the Left form.	As before explained.
Or Oblique to the Right and to the Front Form.	As before explained if marching to the Right.
Or Oblique to the Left and to the Front form.	If Marching by the Left
From the Center of Companies March &c.	The Companies leads out from their Centers to the Front, and March in parallel directions.
To the Front, Right or Left Form.	As before explained.
Or Forward to the Right or to the Left Form.	Ditto.
Battalion upon the Center to the Right or to the Left change the Front.	The Wings as directed goes to the Right about at the word 'March,' and the other Wing wheels by Files, and the Wing that faced about does the same to the Rear, these Files turning to their proper Front, as soon as they get to their ground.
Battalion to the advanced Company or Companies Form, or to the advanced File Form.	The Companies that are to fall back go to the Right about, and the Files front as soon as they are in their places, the Companies receive the necessary words of Command from their respective Commanding Officers.
Battalion to the Right about Change the Front	The front Rank men goes to the Right about, the Rear Rank men moving round to cover their File Leaders. The Companies are then reversed. Repeated brings the Battalion to the former Front.
From the Center of Companys to the Right or to the Left oblique.	Each Company marches from its Center, in an oblique direction as ordered.
Forward to the Front Form.	They march straight to the Front as before explained.
By Companies to the Center, form a Column, or by Division, or by Platoons to the Center, form a Column.	The two Center Companies, Divisions or Platoons march forward, those of the Right Wing wheels half to the Left, and those of the Left Wing, a half wheel to the Right, and Cover to the Rear of the two in Front. To form Battalion the Divisions March obliquely to the Right and Left. NB: the leading Company, File or Files of a Column of March is the Front; and when the Column is ordered to form to the Front, the whole dresses to the leading point in whatever direction it may be, at the time it halts.
To the Center of Companys form Column.	The Companies form into Columns to the Rear of their two Center files.

Words of Command	Explanation
To the Right or to the Left 'March, March'	The Companies move as hereafter directed.
Advance	To turn the Enemys Flank.
Or from the Center of Companys to the Right and Left form Columns, Advance.	To turn both Flanks, the Companys advance from their Center. If to the Right, the Right Company marches obliquely to the right, the next Company marching with its front in a parallel Line, about four paces to the Right of the Rear of the leading Company; the other Companys following in a similar and parallel direction.
To the Left Form.	The leading Company turns its Front to the Left and forms, the other Companys do the same, and form on the Left of the leading Company. Similar directions Vice Versa in advancing by the Left.
Advancing to the Right and Left.	The Companies upon the Right of the Center, move to the Right as abovementioned and those of the Left, march to the Left. When marching from the Center of Battalion, to form two fronts at Right Angles.
To the Right and to the front Form, to the Left and to the Front Form.	If to the Right and to the Front form, the Right Wing forms to the Right and the Left to the Front. If to the Left and to the Front, the Left Wing forms to the Left, and the Right to the Front.
Battalion Resume the Line of March	The Wings face and the Battalion proceed from the Center by Files.

Retreating Movements

From the Right or from the Left of Companys Retreat, March &c.	At the word 'March &c.' the Companies face as directed, the Front Rank men stepping immediately behind their respective Rear Rank Men and March to the Rear.
Front Form.	The whole comes to the Right about. As before explained.
To the Center of Companies form Columns.	The Companies form into Columns, to the Rear of the two Center Files.
To the Right about Face, March, March	The whole faces to the Rear.
Front Form.	As before explained.

Appendix VI

General Howe's Manoeuvres for the Light Infantry

Published by popular military author John Williamson in London in 1778, these manoeuvres are similar but somewhat simpler than those described by General Howe at Sarum in 1774 (Appendix V); as such, they may represent the movements taught in Halifax in 1776 and used in American campaigns thereafter.[1]

From the center of	Battalion Grand divifions Sub divifions	To the front. To the rear. To the right. To the left.

The different formings are	To the front. To the front and right. To the front and left.

Wings and platoons might be added in the table, and the fame movements might take place from them; but as the above will anfwer all the purpofes that can be intended, to add any more would only ferve to increafe the trouble and confufion in the telling off.

Text from the description of 'General Howe's Manoeuvres for the Light Infantry.' (John Williamson, *The Elements of Military Arrangement, comprehending the Tactick, Exercise, Manoeuvres, and Discipline of the British Infantry*)

These manoeuvres are principally calculated for a close or woody country. They are all done from the center [sic], and the two center files of battalion, grand, and sub-divisions must be told off for the purpose. They are comprehended in the following table.

1 John Williamson, *The Elements of Military Arrangement, comprehending the Tactick, Exercise, Manoevres, and Discipline of the British Infantry* (London: printed for the author, 1781), pp.111–119.

From the center of	Battalion Grand divisions Sub-divisions	To the front To the rear To the right To the left

The different formings are	To the front To the front and right To the front and left

Wings and platoons might be added in the table, and the same movements might take place from them; but as the above will answer all the purposes that can be intended, to add any more will only serve to increase the trouble and confusion in the telling off.

These movements are nothing more than double Indian files from the center of the battalion, or one file from the left of the right wing, and another from the right of the left wing. When the whole battalion has filed off, the right wing is in one file, and the left wing in the other.

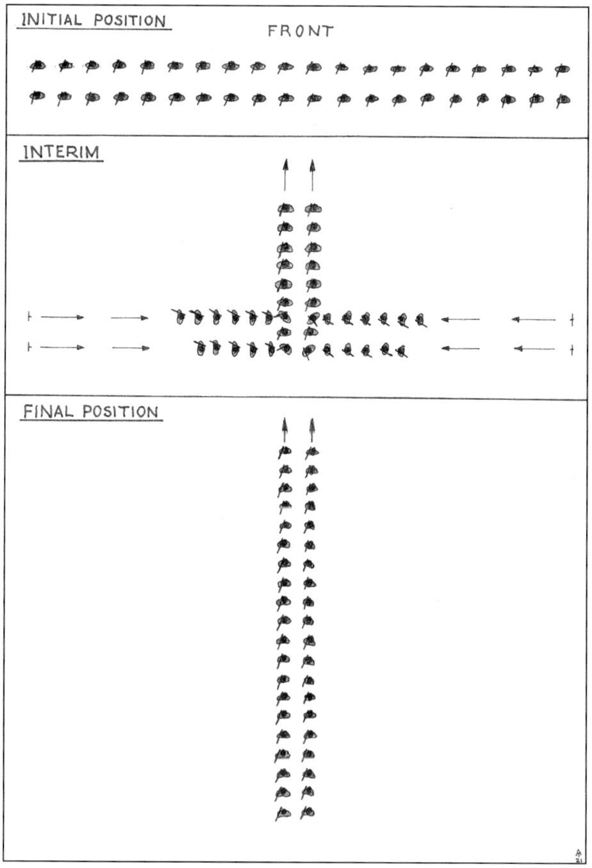

A company moving from line into column, as described in General Howe's maneuvers for light infantry. The men in the centre marched forward, the remainder faced inward, marched to the center, then turned and continued forward. Forming the line again was accomplished by the front of the column halting and the remainder forming on either side. Similar movements allowed changing fronts and retreating; all were done at a trot or run when required. (Artwork by Alan Turton, © Helion and Company 2021)

No. 1. *Battalion! from the center to the front— March.*

The two center files march out, and all the others face inward and march to the center: as soon as they come on the ground on which the center files stood, each file on the right of the center turns to the right, and each file on the left of the center to the left, and march out to the front abreast, covering the two center files of battalion.

To the front, form battalion.

The two center files stand fast; all the others ran up in charging time, and form on the right and left of them, dressing by the center.

No. 2. *Battalion! from the center to the right, march.*

The two center files lead out, and wheel to the right; the other files follow the center files as before, and wheel where they did.

To the front, and to the right, form battalion.

The left center file stands fast, and the whole left wing runs up by files, and forms on the left of it. The right center file faces to the right, and the whole right wing runs up by files, and forms on the right of it.

No. 3. *Battalion! from the center to the left, march.*

The two center files lead out as before, and, when clear of the front rank of the battalion, wheel to the left. The wings file off, as above directed.

To the front, and to the left, form battalion.

The right center file stands fast, and the right wing forms on the right of it, running up by files. The left center file faces to the left, and the remaining files of the left wing run up, and form on the left of it.

No. 4. *Battalion! from the center to the rear, march.*

The two center files go to the right about, and march out to the rear. The wings file off as before and follow them.

To the rear, form battalion.

The battalion is formed as in No. 1.

This manoeuvre should seldom or never be practised; not only on account of the danger in forming the battalion with its rear to the enemy, in which situation it is well known by experience that a few shot will discourage men more than a much heavier fire in front – but likewise on account of the length of time required for the whole battalion to file off. As was before observed of columns in retreating, a battalion should file off from the flanks, and the less the columns are, the sooner will the manoeuvre be completed: therefore in retiring before the enemy, it should be from right or left of sub-divisions.

When the battalion is to change its front to the right or left, it is likewise best done by sub-divisions.

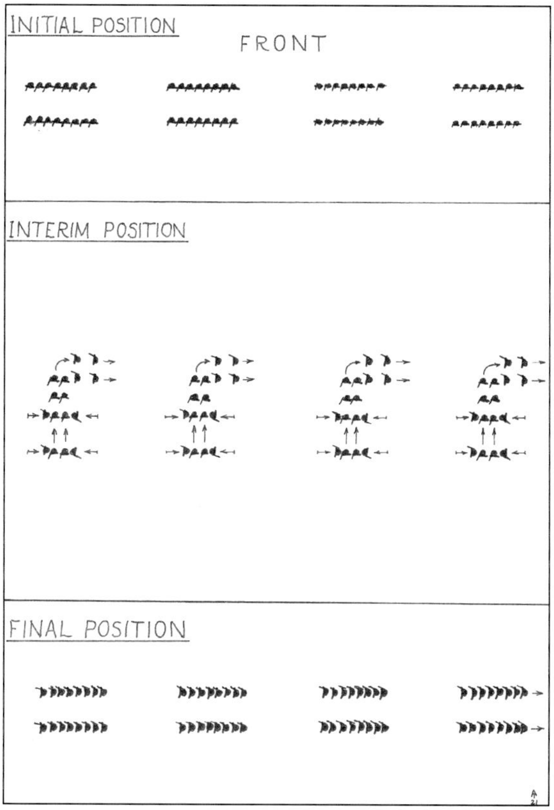

A formation marching to the right by subdivisions, as described in General Howe's maneuvers for light infantry. 'Subdivision' could refer to a pair of companies, a single company, or a half-company depending on the context. Here, four subdivisions are shown, while a battalion typically contained many more subdivisions. The centre men of each subdivision march forward then wheel to the right, and the remainder close to the centre then follow to the front and then wheel right, so that the entire battalion has quickly formed into a column. (Artwork by Alan Turton, © Helion and Company 2021)

No. 5. *Sub-divisions! from the center to the right, march.*

The two center files of each sub-division lead out, and wheel to the right, and each sub-division acts in the same manner as was described in No. 2 for the whole battalion.

Form battalion.

The two center files of the right sub-division halt, and the other files run up and form to the right and left of them. All the other sub-divisions march obliquely to the left, and when the leading files are arrived upon their ground, the officers commanding sub-divisions order their respective divisions to form, and dress by the right,

No. 6. *Sub-divisions! from the center to the left, march.*

This is done in like manner with the above, when the battalion is to change its front to the left.

When a double front is to be formed, it is indifferent whether the movement be made from the center of grand or sub-divisions, or from the center of battalion. It should be remembered, that when the battalion forms to the front and right, the left wing forms to the front, and the right wing to the right; if to the front and left, the right wing forms to the front, and the left wing to the left. That wing which is to form to the flank will be always the first formed, as the rear files of it will have the least ground to go over.

Thus we have taken a view of nearly all the manoeuvres now practiced by the regiments of infantry; the greater part of which, it must be confessed, are more curious than useful, more calculated to please the eye on a parade, than to answer any good purpose in action. Very few manoeuvres will suffice for a battalion, if their utility upon service be the only object considered, and those few judiciously chosen and well performed will do a regiment more credit, even on the parade, than twice the number here collected slatterned over in an imperfect manner. Yet numerous as the particular movements are, if we consider them attentively, we shall find that the general intentions are but few, and that practicing a variety of manoeuvres is nothing more than employing a number of different means in order to attain the same end. For the different kinds or species of manoeuvres may be reduced to the following heads:

1. Moving in file.
2. Moving in column.
3. Changing front.
4. Changing order or disposition.
5. Forming square and oblong.

In treating of the manoeuvres we have insisted the more, as they depend more on principle than any other part of the exercise: and further, as it is incumbent on every officer to study the theory before he attempts to enter upon the practice of them. The former may be acquired to a tolerable degree in the closet: the latter is to be acquired only in the field.

No rules have been laid down for the time or step with which the different movements are to be made; but none certainly should be done slower than with the common quick step; some, and particularly in forming, should be conducted in charging time. When a battalion, being already in motion, is to perform any manoeuvre, the word march, should not be given, unless when meant as an order to take up a quicker step. Thus, if a battalion marching forward in slow time is to retire in quick time from the right of sub-divisions, the word of command may be given.

> Sub-divisions! from right retreat by files, march.
> On which they march out to the rear with the quick step.

Many of the manoeuvres are useful only in particular circumstances of ground and position. Therefore when regiments are taken out to exercise, it should not be confined, as is but too frequently the case, to plains and level country; but the scene should be varied to every situation in which they may find themselves on real service. By this means they will learn the application as well as the practice of the manoeuvres, and will discern the occasions on which they may be found useful.

Appendix VII

Notes on the Practice of the 1st Battalion of Light Infantry

In 1788, David Dundas, an officer who had not served in the American War, published *Principles of Military Movements*, presenting 18 manoeuvres that contemporaries called the Dundas System. An unidentified officer who had served with General Howe's army in America wrote some notes entitled 'Examination of the Dundass System' on the back of his own account of the Battle of Brandywine, comparing aspects of Dundas's manoeuvres with 'the practice of the 1st Battalion of Light Infantry.'[1] These notes do not fully describe the 1st Battalion's practices but provide useful details for understanding how General Howe's manoeuvres were put into practice, and make it clear that expedience and practicality took precedence over formalities.

In response to Dundas's terminology of referring to company sometimes as one platoon and sometimes as two, the officer wrote, 'A company is a company, weak or strong a company.'

Where Dundas advocated a traditional method of 'sizing,' arranging ranks of soldiers with the shortest men on the flanks and the tallest in the centre, the officer wrote, 'Upon service the front rank man to be permitted to chuse his comrade and always to cover him; this will prevent the exact sizing of the men, which certainly adds to the appearance of the company. The front rank may be sized.'

Dundas based his manoeuvres on the old formation of three ranks, with soldiers close together, 'lightly to touch'; the officer wrote, 'Usual order two men. Men instructed to form single rank or four deep. Files by day always loose; usual order 11 inches; open order arms length, extended order from five yards to fifty. In danger men like all animals crowd together.'

Dundas described dividing companies into 'subdivisions,' and those into 'sections.' The officer shunned these terms, writing, 'The company to be divided in plain familiar language – in half, quarters and if this is not sufficient, into eights.'

1 APSL: Sol Feinstone Collection No. 111: 'Examination of the Dundass System.' This is written on the reverse of 'Memo battle of Brandiwine. 11t Sepr 1777.'

Dundas advocated arranging companies in order of seniority, from the flanks to the centre, which had been the common practice in America. The officer agreed, but with a caveat: 'The precedency of companies being well understood to be established as the parade order – but in formation of line from column conveniency, or rapidity of movement, to supersede seniority.'

Appendix VIII

General Rules for Manoeuvring the 1st Battalion of Grenadiers, 1780

On 22 August 1780 Lieutenant Colonel Henry Hope distributed 'general rules' for the 1st Battalion of Grenadiers to practice while encamped on Long Island. It is not known whether they were entirely new or reflected common practice from previous years.[1]

General Rules for Manouvring the Battalion by the Commanding Officer

Whatever Company or Division in the Battalion may be first order'd by the Commanding Officer to perform any Movement, the same is always to be immediately followed by the two next on their right & left, & so on through the whole Battalion without waiting for further directions, the Men receiving the word of Command from their own Officers which should be given in that tone of Voice & to be distinctly heard by whatever member their respective divisions consists of.

In Marching by Companies or division the Officers Commanding each should at all times caution his division to which flank he would have his men dress. Which is to be regulated by different circumstances, remembering always that they should never be required to look in a different direction from that which is intended they should incline to and to facilitate this still more, there should be always either an Officer or Serjeant on each flank when the Battalion breaks off into Companys or divisions as far at least as the Numbers will admit of their being so distributed, that the men may have some superiour to look to for regulating their movement & Dress by; and When there is only one with each division he should run to the Opposite flank when it is necessary to make his division dress that way: or Otherways it can never be done with precision.

1 NRS: GD 21/492: Cunninghame of Thorntoun Papers, book #11, Papers of John Peebles of the 42nd Foot, pp.16–21.

Marching in Line

When the Battalion is order'd to march in Line, the whole is order'd to march by that particular division in front of which the Commanding Officer Marches; the Officer of which will give the greatest Attention to keep the direction in which he moves, that the same file continue to cover him as when first put in motion.

The Charge

When the Line is order'd to Charge, either by word of Command from the Commanding Officer or by signal of Drum, each Officer will repeat the word to his own Company & will endeavour as much as possible in rushing forward to prevent his men from breaking their Order; that either upon being order'd to halt, or after coming up with & forcing the first Body of the Enemy, the Line may be reform'd again with as little confusion & loss of time as possible; so as to throw in a fire upon such of the broken flying Enemy as they can't come up with, or to be in order to charge any second Body that may present itself.

Advancing in Column by Companys or Divisions

When the Battalion is order'd to advance in Column from any particular Company or division, the Officer Commanding it will give the word to March: every other Alternately doing the same when the preceeding one has got to a proper distance and carrying his Division into the line of March; remembering always to caution his Men to which flank they are to oblique and dress: if the Company first put in Motion is of the Right Wing it is to be followed by the next upon its left; if it belong to the Left Wing of the Battalion by the next upon the right and so on Alternately, but if the Column moves in a smaller front than of a Company, the divisions of one Company are never to intervene between those of another. N.B. the Center of the Battalion (as it now consists) is consider'd to be at the left of the 42d & right of the 76th Companies.

To form the Line from the Column

When order'd to form the Battalion upon any given Company or Division, the Officer of that Company or division Orders it to halt and immediately see that his line is dress'd in such direction as may be pointed out by the Commanding Officer; the Other divisions either advance obliquely or go about & retire obliquely in the nearest line to their proper front in Battalion. N.B. this is never to be done by files except when the Column is quite in close order, at all other open distance the divisions are to keep a front & move to their ground obliquely.

Retreating in Column by Companies or Divisions

When the Battalion is order'd to retire in one or more Columns from any particular Company; the Officer Commanding that, orders it to the Right about, & march & moves straight to the Rear, or in such other particular direction as he may have been commanded, the other Divisions doing the same alternately; Marching obliquely to the Rear by the nearest Route in the Line of March; remembering not to make his Division go About till the one preceding him is got to a proper distance, & then not to hurry; if they are order'd to fire before they Retreat they shoulder without loading & no Company is to give their fire till their preceding one has shoulder'd. When the Column is retreating the greatest Attention must be given by the Officer Commanding each Division to what the one in his rear may be order'd to do, that if the Rear is directed to halt & come about to the front, the word of Command may pass from one to the Other & the movement be perform'd without noise hurry or confusion.

Columns by files

In Advancing or Retreating by files from the flanks or Center of Companies, the several Columns are to be directed in their March by dressing on that led by the Commanding Officer, & they are to endeavour always to preserve the distance for forming; of obliged to close or open at any time by the nature of the Country, the proper distance to be regain'd as soon as possible without hurrying the men too much. N.B. The same rule is to be observed at all times when any part of a line may have been obliged from particular impediments in the way to double to its Right, or Left, the manner of doing which will always shew the Attention & judgement of the Officer Commanding that Division obliged to break off; in forming again from files that have either advanced or retired, it is always to be done upon the leading file which halts or fronts to any direction the Commanding Officer chooses, and form upon it.

Signals by Drum

Preparative: to begin firing by Companies, which is to go on as fast as each is loaded till the first part of the General when not a shot more is ever to be fired.

Grenadiers March: to advance in Line.

Point of War: to Charge.

To Arms: to form the Battalion (whether advancing or Retreating in Column) upon the leading division.

Double flam: to halt. Upon the word forward, in forming, the Divisions to run up in Order.

Appendix IX

Signals for the Drum Bugle or Whistle

Major Patrick Ferguson developed these signals for his corps of rangers created for the expedition to Charleston, South Carolina in 1780. Ferguson had been on campaign with General Howe's army in 1777, but it is not known whether these signals are representative of those used by British flank battalions.[1]

Signals for the Drum Bugle or Whistle

1st. 1 Short sound – Flankers to go out
2nd. 1 long sound – Flankers & all other partys to come in
3rd. 2 short sounds – to march
4th. 2 (very) long sounds – to form the Battalion & to prepare for action.
N. B. whenever this signal is used the utmost silence, steadiness and attention to be observed
5th. Three short sounds – to run or advance without dispersing in rough fighting order
6th. The same frequently repeated – Rangers to pursue at full speed
7th. A short sound followed by a long – if marching to halt; if firing to cease
8th. The same three repeated – to retreat
N. B. when a signal is not generally heard it will be repeated one time after

When the above signals are not used or cannot be heard the men will cast their eye on the officer commanding the division. When he waves his hat with an extended arm above his head they will form upon him in the direction in which he faces. If he holds his hat towards the ground they will lay down in the utmost silence – if he points to the front, rear, right or left they will immediately face & march in the same directions.

1 NYHS: Orderly book of Captain Frederick DePeyster.

Bibliography

Primary Sources

Manuscripts

American Philosophical Society Library, Philadelphia (APSL)
  Memo Battle of Brandywine, Sol Feinstone Collection no. 111
  Anonymous British Journal, 1776–78, Sol Feinstone Collection no. 409
Archives of Ontario (AO)
  Peter Russell Fonds
Ballindalloch Castle (BC)
  James Grant Papers
Centre for Kentish Studies, Maidstone, Kent (CKS)
  U1350: Amherst Manuscripts
Firestone Library, Princeton University, Princeton, New Jersey (FL)
  Thomas Glyn Journal
Historical Society of Delaware, Wilmington (HSD)
  William Dansey Letters
Huntington Library, San Marino, CA (HL)
  Journal of an officer of the 47th Regiment of Foot
Library of Congress, Washington, DC (LOC)
  George Washington Papers, British Account Ledger
  George Washington Papers, Orderly book, 40th Regiment of Foot
  George Washington Papers, Orderly book, 2nd Battalion of Light Infantry (64th Regiment's company)
  Journal of Christopher French
  Map, 'A map of the country in which the army under Lt. General Burgoyne acted in the campaign of 1777, shewing the marches of the army & the places of the principal actions'
  Map, 'Battle of Bunker Hill'
  Map, 'British Camp at Trudruffrin with The Attack made by Major General Grey against the Rebels near White Horse Tavern'
  Map, 'Plan of New York and Staten Islands with part of Long Island, survey'd in the years 1781, & 82'
  Map, 'Plan of St. Lucia, in the West Indies: Shewing the positions of the English and French forces with the attacks made at its reduction in Decr. 1778'
  Map, 'Plan of the Isle aux Noix, in the River Richelieu, and Province of Canada'
  Map, 'The encampment & position of the army under His Excy. Lt. Gl: Burgoyne at Swords's and Freeman's Farms on Hudsons River near Stillwater, 1777'
Lloyds Bank Archives, London (LBA)
  Agent's Ledgers, Cox & Company Accounts
The National Archives, Kew, UK (TNA)
  ADM 36: Ship muster books
  CO 5: Board of Trade and Secretaries of State: America and West Indies, Original Correspondence

SP 63: State Papers Office: State Papers of Ireland
T 14/15: Out Letters concerning Ireland
WO 12: General muster books and pay lists
WO 27: Inspection Returns
WO 30/13B: Register of Warrants
WO 34: Jeffrey Amherst Papers
WO 36: Entry Books, American Revolution
WO 43: Secretary-at-War Correspondence, Very Old Series
WO 71: Judge Advocate General's Office: Courts Martial Proceedings and Board of General Officers' Minutes
WO 121: Royal Hospital, Chelsea: Discharge Documents of Pensioners
WO 379/1: Army establishments, 1737–1788

National Army Museum, London, UK (NAM)
Discipline established by Major General Howe for Light Infantry in Battalion, Sarum September 1774
Francis Laye Letters

National Library of Scotland (NLS)
Correspondence of Andrew Stuart

National Records of Scotland, Edinburgh (NRS)
GD 3: Papers of the Montgomerie Family, Earls of Eglinton
GD113: John Row letters
Orderly book, 4th Battalion of Grenadiers, in Papers of John Peebles, 42nd Regiment.
Papers of John Peebles of the 42nd Foot, Cunninghame of Thorntoun Papers

New York Historical Society, New York (NYHS)
Orderly book, Major Acland's Grenadier Battalion
Orderly book of Captain Frederick DePeyster

Parliamentary Archives, Houses of Parliament, London (PA)
HL/PO/JO/10/7/544: Return of Courts Martial held in Ireland

Public Archives of Canada, Ottawa (PAC)
MG23, K6(2): Punishment Book of the 44th Regiment of Foot

Society of the Cincinnati, Washington, DC (SC)
Orderly book, Major Acland's Grenadier Battalion

William L. Clements Library, University of Michigan, Ann Arbor (WLC)
Loftus Cliffe Papers
Sir Henry Clinton Papers
Eyre Coote Papers
Thomas Gage Papers, American Series
William Howe orderly book, 1776–1778
Frederick Mackenzie Papers
George Wray Papers

Newspapers

British
Caledonian Mercury (Edinburgh), 1772
Edinburgh Advertiser, 1775–1776, 1779
General Evening Post (London), 1771
Kentish Gazette, 1771
Newcastle Courant, 1772
North British Intelligencer (Edinburgh), 1776

American
Connecticut Courant, 1771
Freeman's Journal (Portsmouth, NH), 1776
New York Gazette and Weekly Mercury, 1778

Newport Gazette, 1778
Pennsylvania Gazette, 1781
Pennsylvania Ledger, 1777
Royal Gazette (New York), 1778–1779

Published Primary Sources

Almon, J. (ed.), *The Remembrancer, or impartial repository of public events* (London: J. Almon. 1775–1780)
Anbury, Thomas, *Travels through the Interior Parts of North America* (Boston: Houghton Mifflin, 1923)
Anon. (ed.), 'British Army Orders.' *Collections of the New York Historical Society for the year 1883* (New York: New York Historical Society, 1884)
Anon. (ed.), 'Journal of Rev. Joshua Wingate Weeks', *Historical Collections of the Essex Institute*, Vol.LII, No. 1 (1916), pp.1–16
Anon. (ed.), 'Journals of Lieut.-Col. Stephen Kemble.' *Collections of the New York Historical Society for the year 1883.* New York: New York Historical Society, 1884
Anon. (ed.), *Military Journal of Major Ebenezer Denny* (Philadelphia: J. B. Lippincott, 1859)
Anon., *The Manual Exercise, As ordered by his Majesty, In 1764. Together with Plans and Explanations Of the Method generally Practis'd At Review and Field-Days, &c.* (London: Adjutant-General's Office, 1764)
Anon., *The Volunteers Companion* (Dublin: W. Coles, 1784)
Bain, James (ed.), 'The Siege of Charleston: Journal of Captain Peter Russell,' *American Historical Review*, Vol. IV, No. 3 (April 1899), pp.478–501
Barker, John, *The British in Boston, being the Diary of Lieutenant John Barker of the King's Own Regiment* (Cambridge, MA: Harvard University Press, 1924)
Bickley, Francis, *Report on the Manuscripts of the late Reginald Rawdon Hastings, Esq.* (London: Historical Manuscripts Commission, 1934)
Bolton, Charles Knowles (ed.), *Letters of Hugh Earl Percy from Boston and New York 1774–1776* (Boston: Charles E. Goodspeed, 1902)
Boyle, Joseph Lee (ed.), *From Redcoat to Rebel: The Thomas Sullivan Journal* (Bowie, MD: Heritage Books, 1997)
Bradford, Sydney S., 'Lord Francis Napier's Journal of the Burgoyne Campaign,' *Maryland Historical Magazine*, Vol.57, no. 4 (December 1962): pp.285–333
Burgoyne, John, *A State of The Expedition From Canada, as Laid Before The House of Commons, by Lieutenant-general Burgoyne, and Verified by Evidence; with a Collection of Authentic Documents ...* (London: J. Almon, 1780)
Cometti, Elizabeth (ed.), *The American Journals of Lt. John Enys* (Blue Mountain Lake, NY: Adirondack Museum, 1976)
Cubbison, Douglas, *Burgoyne and the Saratoga Campaign: His Papers* (Norman, OK: University of Oklahoma Press, 2012)
Cuthbertson, Bennett, *A System for the Compleat Interior Management and Œconomy of a Battalion of Infantry* (Dublin: Boulter Grierson, 1768)
Dansey, Paul (ed.), *Captured Rebel Flag: The Letters of Captain William Dansey, 33rd Regiment of Foot, 1776–1777* (Godmanchester: Ken Trotman Press, 2010)
De Berniere, Henry, 'Transactions of the British troops previous to, and at the Battle of Lexington,' in Anon. (ed.), *General Gage's Instructions of 22d February 1775, to Captain Brown and Ensign D'Berniere, (of the army under his command) whom he ordered to take a sketch of the roads, passes, heights, &c. from Boston to Worcester, and to make other observations, with a curious Narrative of Occurrences during their mission, wrote by the Ensign* (Boston: J. Gill, 1779) pp.17–20
Digby, William, 'Lieut. Digby's Journal.' in James Phinney Baxter, *The British Invasion From the North: The Campaigns of Generals Carleton and Burgoyne from Canada, 1776–1777, with the Journal of Lieut. William Digby* (Albany, NY: Joel Munsell's Sons, 1887)
Dundas, Thomas, *Principles of Military Movements: Chiefly Applied to Infantry. Illustrated by Manoeuveres of the Prussian Troops, and by an Outline of the British Campaigns in Germany, During the War of 1757* (London: T. Cadell, 1788)
Force, Peter (ed.), *American Archives* (Washington, DC: M. St. Clair and Peter Force, 1839) Series Four, Vol.2
Force, Peter (ed.), *American Archives* (Washington, DC: M. St. Clair and Peter Force, 1848) Series Five, Vol.1
Fortescue, John (ed.), *Correspondence of King George III* (New York: McMillan & Co., 1927) Vol. 3

Graydon, Alexander, *Memoirs of a Life, Chiefly Passed in Pennsylvania* (Harrisburg: John Wyeth, 1811)

Gruber, Ira D. (ed.), *John Peebles' American War: The Diary of a Scottish Grenadier, 1776–1782* (Mechanicsburg, PA: Stackpole Books, for the Army Records Society, 1998)

Hagist, Don. N. (ed.), *A British Soldier's Story: Roger Lamb's Narrative of the American Revolution* (Baraboo, WI: Ballindalloch Press, 2004)

Hattendorff, John B. (ed.), *A Redcoat in America: The Diaries of Lieutenant William Bamford, 1757–1765 and 1776* (Warwick: Helion, 2019)

Hunt, Gaillard, *Fragments of Revolutionary History. Being hitherto unpublished writings of the men of the American Revolution* (Brooklyn: Historical Printing Club, 1892)

Hunter, Martin, *The Journal of Gen. Sir Martin Hunter* (Edinburgh: Edinburgh Press, 1894)

Inman, George, 'George Inman's Narrative of the American Revolution.' *Pennsylvania Magazine of History and Biography* 7, no. 3 (1883), pp.237–248

Kingsley, Ronald F., 'Letters to Lord Polwarth from Sir Francis-Carr Clerke, Aide-de-Camp to General John Burgoyne,' *New York History* Vol.79, no. 4 (October 1998), pp.393–424

Lister, Jeremy, *Concord Fight* (Cambridge, MA: Harvard University Press, 1931)

Mackenzie, Frederick, *The Diary of Frederick Mackenzie* (Cambridge, MA: Harvard University Press, 1930)

Morgan, William James et. al. (ed.), *Naval Documents of the American Revolution* (Washington, DC: Government Printing Office, 1964–2019) 13 Vols.

O'Callaghan, E.B. (ed.), *Orderly Book of Lieut. Gen. John Burgoyne.* (Albany, NY: J. Munsell, 1860)

Partridge, Eric (ed.), *A Classical Dictionary of the Vulgar Tongue* (New York: Dorset Press, 1992)

Pell, Joshua, 'Diary of Joshua Pell Junior an Officer of the British Army in America.' *The Magazine of American History with Notes and Queries* Vol. 2 (February 1878), pp.107–112

Robson, Eric (ed.), *Letters from America, 1773 to 1780* (New York: Barnes & Noble, 1950)

Rogers, Horatio (ed.), *Hadden's Journal and Orderly Books* (Albany, NY: J. Munsell's sons, 1884)

Scull, G.D. (ed.), *Memoir and Letters of Captain W. Glanville Evelyn, of the 4th Regiment, ('King's Own,') from North America, 1774-1776* (Oxford, UK: Parker & Co., 1879)

Seybolt, Robert Francis, 'A Contemporary British Account of General Sir William Howe's Military Operations in 1777', *Proceedings of the American Antiquarian Society* 40 (April 1930), pp.69–92

Simes, Thomas, *The Military Guide for Young Officers* (London: Millan, 1772)

Smith, George, *An Universal Military Dictionary* (London: Millan, 1779)

Smith, S. (ed.), *At General Howe's Side, 1776–1778: The Diary of General William Howe's Aide de Camp, Captain Friedrich von Muenchhausen.* (Monmouth Beach, NJ: Philip Freneau, 1974)

St George, Richard St George Mansergh, 'The Actions at Brandywine and Paoli, described by a British Officer', *Pennsylvania Magazine of History and Biography*, Vol. 29 No. 3 (1905), pp.368–369

Stedman, Charles, *The History of the Origin, Progress and Termination of the American War* (London: by the author, 1794)

Stevens, B.F. (ed.), *General Sir William Howe's Orderly Book* (Port Washington, NY: Kennikat Press, 1980)

Stirke, Henry, 'A British Officer's Revolutionary War Journal, 1776–1778.' *Maryland Historical Magazine*, 56 (June 1961), pp.150–173

Stuart, Charles, *New Records of the American Revolution: The Letters, Manuscripts and Documents sent by Lieut.-General Sir Charles Stuart to his Father, the Earl of Bute, 1775–79* (London: L. Kashnor, 1927)

Whinyates F.A. (ed.), *The Services of Lieut. Colonel Francis Downman, R. A. in France, North American and the West Indies, between the years 1758 and 1784* (Woolwich: Royal Artillery Institution, 1896)

Wilkin, W. H. (ed.), *Some British Soldiers in America* (London: H. Rees, 1914)

Wilkinson, James, *Memoirs of My Own Times* (Philadelphia: Printed by Abraham Small, 1816)

Willard, Margaret W. (ed.), *Letters on the American Revolution, 1774–1776* (Boston and New York: Houghton Mifflin Company, 1925)

Willcox, C. (ed.), *Major André's Journal* (Tarrytown, NY: William Abbatt, 1930)

Willcox, William B. (ed.), *The American Rebellion; Sir Henry Clinton's Narrative of His Campaigns, 1775–1782* (New Haven, CT: Yale University Press, 1954)

Williamson, John, *The Elements of Military Arrangement, comprehending the Tactick, Exercise, Maneuvers, and Discipline of the British Infantry* (London: printed for the author, 1781)

Secondary Sources

Books

Atkinson, Rick, *The British are Coming: the War for America, Lexington to Princeton, 1775–1777* (New York: Henry Holt and Company, 2019)

Bell, J.L., *The Road to Concord: How Four Stolen Cannon Ignited the Revolutionary War* (Yardley, PA: Westholme, 2016)

Braisted, Todd W., *Grand Forage 1778: The Battleground around New York City* (Yardley, PA: Westholme, 2016)

Brown, Abram English, *Beneath Old Roof Trees* (Boston: Lee and Shepard, 1896)

Cecere, Michael, *The Invasion of Virginia 1781* (Yardley, PA: Westholme, 2017)

Field, Thomas Warren, *The Battle of Long Island* (Brooklyn, NY: Long Island Historical Society, 1869)

Fuller, J.F.C., *British Light Infantry in the Eighteenth Century* (London: Hutchinson & Co., 1925)

Hagist, Don N., *Noble Volunteers: the British Soldiers who Fought the American Revolution* (Yardley, PA: Westholme, 2020)

Houlding, J. A., *Fit for Service: The Training of the British Army 1715–1795* (Oxford: Clarendon Press, 1981)

Kehoe, Vincent J.R., *The British Story of the Battle of Lexington and Concord on the Nineteeth of April, 1775* (Los Angeles: Hale & Co., 2000)

MacNiven, Robbie, *British Light Infantry in the American Revolution* (Oxford: Osprey Publishing, 2021)

Murdock, Harold, *Bunker Hill Notes and Queries* (Boston: Houghton Mifflin Company, 1927)

Paterson, James, *History of the County of Ayr: with a Genealogical Account of the Families of Ayrshire* (Edinburgh: Thomas George Stevenson, 1852)

Padelford, Philip (ed.), *Colonial Panorama, 1775: Dr. Robert Honyman's Journal for March and April* (San Marino, CA: Huntington Library, 1939)

Schnitzer, Eric H. and Don Troiani, *Don Troiani's Campaign to Saratoga – 1777: The Turning Point of the Revolutionary War in Paintings, Artifacts, and Historical Narrative* (Mechanicsburg, PA: Stackpole Books, 2019)

Smythies, R.H.R., *Historical Records of the 40th (2nd Somersetshire) Regiment, Now 1st Battalion The Prince of Wales Volunteers (South Lancashire Regiment) From its Formation in 1717 to 1893* (Devonport: A. W. Swiss, 1894)

Sterling, Anthony, *The Story of the Highland Brigade in the Crimea* (London: Remington & Company, 1895)

Strachan, Hew, *British Military Uniforms 1768–1796* (London: Arms and Armour Press, 1975)

Venter, Bruce M., *The Battle of Hubbardston: the Rearguard Action that Saved America* (Charleston, SC: History Press, 2015)

Articles and Theses

Baule, Steven M., and Don N. Hagist, 'The Regimental Punishment Book of the Boston Detachments of the Royal Irish Regiment and 65th Regiment, 1774–1775', *Journal of Army Historical Research*, Vol.88, No.353 (2010), pp.5–18

Bolton, Reginald Pelham, 'The Military Hut-Camp of the War of the Revolution on the Dyckman Farm', *The New-York Historical Society Quarterly Bulletin*, Vol.2, No.3 (October, 1918), pp.95–97

Gordon, William, 'Letter written by an American Clergyman', *Journal of American History*, Vol. 4, No. 1 (1910), pp.66–71

Hagist, Don N. and Erik Goldstein, 'Short Land Muskets for the British Light Infantry in America', *Man at Arms* (December 2009), pp.18–25

Hagist, Don N., 'Forty German Recruits: The Service of the Von Scheither Recruits in the 22nd Regiment of Foot, 1776–1783', *Journal of the Johannes Schwalm Historical Association*, Vol.6, No.1 (1997), pp.63–66

Index

From Reason to Revolution – Warfare 1721-1815

http://www.helion.co.uk/series/from-reason-to-revolution-1721-1815.php

The 'From Reason to Revolution' series covers the period of military history 1721–1815, an era in which fortress-based strategy and linear battles gave way to the nation-in-arms and the beginnings of total war.

This era saw the evolution and growth of light troops of all arms, and of increasingly flexible command systems to cope with the growing armies fielded by nations able to mobilise far greater proportions of their manpower than ever before. Many of these developments were fired by the great political upheavals of the era, with revolutions in America and France bringing about social change which in turn fed back into the military sphere as whole nations readied themselves for war. Only in the closing years of the period, as the reactionary powers began to regain the upper hand, did a military synthesis of the best of the old and the new become possible.

The series will examine the military and naval history of the period in a greater degree of detail than has hitherto been attempted, and has a very wide brief, with the intention of covering all aspects from the battles, campaigns, logistics, and tactics, to the personalities, armies, uniforms, and equipment.

Submissions

The publishers would be pleased to receive submissions for this series. Please contact series editor Andrew Bamford via email (andrewbamford@helion.co.uk), or in writing to Helion & Company Limited, Unit 8 Amherst Business Centre, Budbrooke Road, Warwick, CV34 5WE

Titles

No 1 *Lobositz to Leuthen. Horace St Paul and the Campaigns of the Austrian Army in the Seven Years War 1756-57* Translated with additional materials by Neil Cogswell (ISBN 978-1-911096-67-2)

No 2 *Glories to Useless Heroism. The Seven Years War in North America from the French journals of Comte Maurés de Malartic, 1755-1760* William Raffle (ISBN 978-1-1911512 19-6) (paperback)

No 3 *Reminiscences 1808-1815 Under Wellington. The Peninsular and Waterloo Memoirs of William Hay* William Hay, with notes and commentary by Andrew Bamford (ISBN 978-1-1911512-32-5)

No 4 *Far Distant Ships. The Royal Navy and the Blockade of Brest 1793-1815* Quintin Barry (ISBN 978-1-1911512-14-1)

No 5 *Godoy's Army. Spanish Regiments and Uniforms from the Estado Militar of 1800* Charles Esdaile and Alan Perry (ISBN 978-1-911512-65-3) (paperback)

No 6 *On Gladsmuir Shall the Battle Be! The Battle of Prestonpans 1745* Arran Johnston (ISBN 978-1-911512-83-7)

No 7 *The French Army of the Orient 1798-1801. Napoleon's Beloved 'Egyptians'* Yves Martin (ISBN 978-1-911512-71-4)*

No 8 *The Autobiography, or Narrative of a Soldier. The Peninsular War Memoirs of William Brown of the 45th Foot* William Brown, with notes and commentary by Steve Brown (ISBN 978-1-911512-94-3) (paperback)

No 9 *Recollections from the Ranks. Three Russian Soldiers' Autobiographies from the Napoleonic Wars* Translated and annotated by Darrin Boland (ISBN 978-1-912174-18-8) (paperback)

No 10 *By Fire and Bayonet. Grey's West Indies Campaign of 1794* Steve Brown (ISBN 978-1-911512-60-8)

No 11 *Olmütz to Torgau. Horace St Paul and the Campaigns of the Austrian Army in the Seven Years War 1758-60* Translated with additional materials by Neil Cogswell (ISBN 978-1-911512-72-1)

No 12 *Murat's Army. The Army of the Kingdom of Naples 1806-1815* Digby Smith (ISBN 978-1-912390-09-0) (paperback)

No 13 *The Veteran or 40 Years' Service in the British Army. The Scurrilous Recollections of Paymaster John Harley 47th Foot – 1798-1838* John Harley, with notes and commentary by Gareth Glover (ISBN 978-1-912390-25-0) (paperback)

No 14 *Narrative of the Eventful Life of Thomas Jackson. Militiaman and Coldstream Sergeant, 1803-15* Thomas Jackson, with notes and commentary by Eamonn O'Keeffe (ISBN 978-1-912390-12-0) (paperback)

No 15 *For Orange and the States! The Army of the Dutch Republic 1713-1772. Part I: Infantry* Marc Geerdinck-Schaftenaar (ISBN 978-1-911512-15-8)*

No 16 *'Men who are Determined to be Free': The American Assault on Stony Point 15 July 1779* David Bonk (ISBN 978-1-912174-84-3)*

No 17 *Next to Wellington. General Sir George Murray. The Story of a Scottish Soldier and Statesman, Wellington's Quartermaster General* John Harding-Edgar (ISBN 978-1-912390-13-7)

No 18 *Between Scylla and Charibdys: The Army of Friedrich August II of Saxony, 1733-1763. Part I: Staff and Cavalry* Marco Pagan (ISBN 978-1-912174-89-8)*

No 19 *The Secret Expedition: The Anglo-Russian Invasion of Holland 1799* Geert van Uythoven (ISBN 978-1-912390-20-5)

No 20 *'We Are Accustomed to do our Duty' German Auxiliaries with the British Army 1793-95* Paul Demet (ISBN 978-1-912174-96-6)

No 21 *With the Guards in Flanders. The Diary of Captain Roger Morris 1793-95* Peter Harington (ISBN 978-1-911628-15-6) (paperback)

No 22 *The British Army in Egypt 1801. An Underrated Army Comes of Age* Carole Divall (ISBN 978-1-911628-17-0)*

No 23 *Better is the Proud Plaid. The Clothing, Weapons, and Accoutrements of the Jacobites in 1745* Jenn Scott (ISBN ISBN 978-1-911628-16-3)*

No 24 *The Lilies and the Thistle. French Troops in the Jacobite '45* Andrew Bamford (ISBN 978-1-911628-17-0)*

No 25 *A Light Infantryman With Wellington Gareth Glover* (ed.) (ISBN 978-1-911628-10-1) (paperback)

No 26 *Swiss Regiments in the Service of France 1798-1815. Uniforms, Organisation, Campaigns* Stephen Ede-Borrett (ISBN 978-1-911628-12-5)*

No 27 *For Orange and the States! The Army of the Dutch Republic 1713-1772. Part II: Cavalry and Specialist Troops* Marc Geerdinck-Schaftenaar (ISBN 978-1-911628-13-2)*

No 28 *Fashioning Regulation, Regulating Fashion. Uniforms and Dress of the British Army 1800-1815 Volume I* Ben Townsend (ISBN 978-1-911628-09-5)

No 29 *Riflemen. The History of the 5th Battalion 60th (Royal American) Regiment, 1797-1818* Robert Griffith (ISBN 978-1-911628-46-0)

No 30 *The Key to Lisbon: The Third French Invasion of Portugal, 1810-11* (Kenton White)

No 31 *Command and Leadership: Proceedings of the 2018 Helion & Company 'From Reason to Revolution' Conference* (Andrew Bamford (ed.))

No 32 *Waterloo After the Glory: Hospital Sketches and Reports on the Wounded After the Battle* (Michael Crumplin and Gareth Glover)

No 33 *Fluxes, Fevers, and Fighting Men: War and Disease in Ancien Regime Europe 1648-1789* (Pádraig Lenihan)

No 34 *'They Were Good Soldiers': African-Americans Serving in the Continental Army, 1775-1783* (John U. Rees)

No 35 *A Redcoat in America: The Diaries of Lieutenant William Bamford, 1757-1765 and 1776* (John B. Hattendorf (ed.))

- No 36 *Between Scylla and Charybdis: The Army of Friedrich August II of Saxony, 1733-1763: Part II: Infantry and Artillery* (Marco Pagan)
- No 37 *Québec Under Siege: French Eye-Witness Accounts from the Campaign of 1759* (Charles A. Mayhood (ed.))
- No 38 *King George's Hangman: Henry Hawley and the Battle of Falkirk 1746* (Jonathan D. Oates)
- No 39 *Zweybrücken in Command: The Reichsarmee in the Campaign of 1758* (Neil Cogswell)
- No 40 *So Bloody a Day: The 16th Light Dragoons in the Waterloo Campaign* (David J. Blackmore)
- No 41 *Northern Tars in Southern Waters: The Russian Fleet in the Mediterranean 1806-1810* (Vladimir Bogdanovich Bronevskiy / Darrin Boland)
- No 42 *Royal Navy Officers of the Seven Years War: A Biographical Dictionary of Commissioned Officers 1748-1763* (Cy Harrison)
- No 43 *All at Sea: Naval Support for the British Army During the American Revolutionary War* (John Dillon)
- No 44 *Glory is Fleeting: New Scholarship on the Napoleonic Wars* (Andrew Bamford (ed.))
- No 45 *Fashioning Regulation, Regulating Fashion: Uniforms and Dress of the British Army 1800-1815 Vol. II* (Ben Townsend)
- No 46 *Revenge in the Name of Honour: The Royal Navy's Quest for Vengeance in the Single Ship Actions of the War of 1812* (Nicholas James Kaizer)
- No 47 *They Fought With Extraordinary Bravery: The III German (Saxon) Army Corps in the Southern Netherlands 1814* (Geert van Uythoven)
- No 48 *The Danish Army of the Napoleonic Wars 1801-1814, Organisation, Uniforms & Equipment: Volume 1: High Command, Line and Light Infantry* (David Wilson)
- No 49 *Neither Up Nor Down: The British Army and the Flanders Campaign 1793-1895* (Phillip Ball)
- No 50 *Guerra Fantástica: The Portuguese Army and the Seven Years War* (António Barrento)
- No 51 *From Across the Sea: North Americans in Nelson's Navy* (Sean M. Heuvel and John A. Rodgaard)
- No 52 *Rebellious Scots to Crush: The Military Response to the Jacobite '45* (Andrew Bamford (ed.))
- No 53 *The Army of George II 1727-1760: The Soldiers who Forged an Empire* (Peter Brown)
- No 54 *Wellington at Bay: The Battle of Villamuriel, 25 October 1812* (Garry David Wills)
- No 55 *Life in the Red Coat: The British Soldier 1721-1815* (Andrew Bamford (ed.))
- No 56 *Wellington's Favourite Engineer. John Burgoyne: Operations, Engineering, and the Making of a Field Marshal* (Mark S. Thompson)
- No 57 *Scharnhorst: The Formative Years, 1755-1801* (Charles Edward White)
- No 58 *At the Point of the Bayonet: The Peninsular War Battles of Arroyomolinos and Almaraz 1811-1812* (Robert Griffith)
- No 59 *Sieges of the '45: Siege Warfare during the Jacobite Rebellion of 1745-1746* (Jonathan D. Oates)
- No 60 *Austrian Cavalry of the Revolutionary and Napoleonic Wars, 1792–1815* (Enrico Acerbi, András K. Molnár)
- No 61 *The Danish Army of the Napoleonic Wars 1801-1814, Organisation, Uniforms & Equipment: Volume 2: Cavalry and Artillery* (David Wilson)
- No 62 *Napoleon's Stolen Army: How the Royal Navy Rescued a Spanish Army in the Baltic* (John Marsden)
- No 63 *Crisis at the Chesapeake: The Royal Navy and the Struggle for America 1775-1783* (Quintin Barry)
- No 64 *Bullocks, Grain, and Good Madeira: The Maratha and Jat Campaigns 1803-1806 and the emergence of an Indian Army* (Joshua Provan)

No 65 *Sir James McGrigor: The Adventurous Life of Wellington's Chief Medical Officer* (Tom Scotland)

No 66 *Fashioning Regulation, Regulating Fashion: Uniforms and Dress of the British Army 1800-1815 Volume I* (Ben Townsend) (paperback edition)

No 67 *Fashioning Regulation, Regulating Fashion: Uniforms and Dress of the British Army 1800-1815 Volume II* (Ben Townsend) (paperback edition)

No 68 *The Secret Expedition: The Anglo-Russian Invasion of Holland 1799* (Geert van Uythoven) (paperback edition)

No 69 *The Sea is My Element: The Eventful Life of Admiral Sir Pulteney Malcolm 1768-1838* (Paul Martinovich)

No 70 *The Sword and the Spirit: Proceedings of the first 'War & Peace in the Age of Napoleon' Conference* (Zack White (ed.))

No 71 *Lobositz to Leuthen: Horace St Paul and the Campaigns of the Austrian Army in the Seven Years War 1756-57* (Neil Cogswell) (paperback edition)

No 72 *For God and King. A History of the Damas Legion 1793-1798: A Case Study of the Military Emigration during the French Revolution* (Hughes de Bazouges and Alistair Nichols)

No 73 *'Their Infantry and Guns Will Astonish You': The Army of Hindustan and European Mercenaries in Maratha service 1780-1803* (Andy Copestake)

No 74 *Like A Brazen Wall: The Battle of Minden, 1759, and its Place in the Seven Years War* (Ewan Carmichael)

No 75 *Wellington and the Lines of Torres Vedras: The Defence of Lisbon during the Peninsular War* (Mark Thompson)

No 76 *French Light Infantry 1784-1815: From the Chasseurs of Louis XVI to Napoleon's Grande Armée* (Terry Crowdy)

No 77 *Riflemen: The History of the 5th Battalion 60th (Royal American) Regiment, 1797-1818* (Robert Griffith) (paperback edition)

No 78 *Hastenbeck 1757: The French Army and the Opening Campaign of the Seven Years War* (Olivier Lapray)

No 79 *Napoleonic French Military Uniforms: As Depicted by Horace and Carle Vernet and Eugène Lami* (Guy Dempsey (trans. and ed.))

No 80 *These Distinguished Corps: British Grenadier and Light Infantry Battalions in the American Revolution* (Don N. Hagist)

No 81 *Rebellion, Invasion, and Occupation: The British Army in Ireland, 1793 -1815* (Wayne Stack)

No 82 *You Have to Die in Piedmont! The Battle of Assietta, 19 July 1747. The War of the Austrian Succession in the Alps* (Giovanni Cerino Badone)

No 83 *A Very Fine Regiment: the 47th Foot in the American War of Independence, 1773–1783* (Paul Knight)

No 84 *By Fire and Bayonet: Grey's West Indies Campaign of 1794* (Steve Brown) (paperback edition)